THE MERTON ANNUAL

Studies in Culture, Spirituality, and Social Concerns

Volume 22	2009

Edited by

David Belcastro   Gray Matthews

THE MERTON ANNUAL
Studies in Culture, Spirituality, and Social Concerns

THE MERTON ANNUAL publishes articles about Thomas Merton and about related matters of major concern to his life and work. Its purpose is to enhance Merton's reputation as a writer and monk, to continue to develop his message for our times, and to provide a regular outlet for substantial Merton-related scholarship. THE MERTON ANNUAL includes as regular features reviews, review-essays, a bibliographic survey, interviews, and first appearances of unpublished, or obscurely published Merton materials, photographs, and art. Essays about related literary and spiritual matters will also be considered. Manuscripts and books for review may be sent to the editors.

EDITORS

David J. Belcastro
Dept. of Religion and Philosophy
Capital University
Bexley, Ohio 43209
dbelcast@capital.edu

Gray Matthews
Dept. of Communication
University of Memphis
Memphis, TN 38152
matthews@memphis.edu

Grateful acknowledgement is expressed to New Directions, The Merton Legacy Trust and the Thomas Merton Center at Bellarmine University for permission to print four poems by Merton and the calligraphy by Merton for the cover artwork. We wish to thank Paul Wilkes for permission to publish his interview with Lawrence Ferlinghetti.

PUBLISHED BY:
Fons Vitae
49 Mockingbird Valley Drive
Louisville KY 40207
502.897.3641
Fonsvitaeky@aol.com
http://www.fonsvitae.com

SPONSORED BY:
International Thomas Merton Society
Thomas Merton Center
Bellarmine University
2001 Newburg Road
Louisville KY 40205
502.452.8187 or 8177
merton@bellarmine.edu
http://www.merton.org/ITMS/

Further details about membership and subscribing to *The Merton Seasonal* and *The Merton Annual* are available at http://www.merton.org/ITMS/membership.htm or by contacting the Thomas Merton Center at the above address.

Library of Congress Control Number: 2009927313

ISBN 9781891785559

Printed in Canada

The Merton Annual

| Volume 22 | 2009 |

Reviews

Introduction: Angular Clouds of Unknowing

David Joseph Belcastro

The calligraphy selected for the cover of this volume of *The Merton Annual* sets the stage for the presentation of a collection of essays that focuses on Merton's poetry. The first five essays, by Michael Higgins, Lynn Szabo, Ross Labrie, Patrick O'Connell and Bonnie Thurston, were presented at the conference, *In the Dark before Dawn: Thomas Merton Poet*, sponsored by the Thomas Merton Center at Bellarmine University in October of 2007. The next four essays, by Jeffrey Bilbro, Malgorzata Poks, Deborah Kehoe and Susan McCaslin, were submitted following the conference and indicate the growing interest in Merton's poetry by scholars who represent diverse perspectives and thereby present complementary lines of inquiry into Merton's poetics.

In *Angelic Mistakes: The Art of Thomas Merton*, Roger Lipsey titles the cover's image "Beyond Philosophy" and prints beneath the title and across from the image two passages from Merton, the first from *Conjectures of a Guilty Bystander* and the second from *Learning to Love*:

> He who is called to be a monk is precisely the one who, when he finally realizes that he is engaged in the pure folly of meeting an impossible demand, instead of renouncing the whole thing proceeds to devote himself even more completely to the task. Aware that, precisely because he cannot meet it, it will be met for him. And at this point he goes beyond philosophy.

> *November 13, 1966.* Today, for a certain type of person, to "listen" is to be in a position where hearing is impossible – or deceptive. It is the wrong kind of listening: listening for a limited message, an objective sound, a sensible meaning. Actually one decides one's life by responding to a word that is *not* well defined, easily explicable, safely accounted for. One decides to love in the face of an unaccountable void, and from the void comes an unaccountable truth. By this truth one's existence is sustained in peace – until the truth is too firmly grasped and too clearly accounted for. Then one is relying on words – i.e., on his own understanding and his own ingenuity in interpret-

ing existence and its "signs." Then one is lost – has to be found once again in the patient Void.[1]

Lipsey's composition of image, title and quotations draws our attention to the depth of Merton's exploration of the interior dimensions of silence and solitude that extend far beyond the boundaries of words, concepts and images. Yet, as we well know, it is from this unfathomable depth that Merton's poetic and prophetic voice of "angular clouds of unknowing" emerges to invoke within the reader an awareness of possibilities for peace and justice in our world. Keep this and the calligraphy in mind as you enjoy the essays that follow, for each essay in its own unique way reveals some aspect of the vision that Merton labored during his lifetime to share with his world.

The authors of the essays presented in this volume have explored, discovered, and articulated insights gained from their study of Merton's poetry – insights that will enhance our understanding and appreciation of Merton as a poet whose message needs to be heard today as he opens for our world at the outset of the twenty-first century a road less traveled yet far more promising than any of the ones on the horizon.

We begin with Michael Higgins' "The Priestly Imagination: Thomas Merton and the Poetics of Critique" (11-23). Higgins finds in Merton a poet who is both prophet and priest celebrating "the world . . . with eyes of love" (11). Combining the graces of John the Baptist, John of the Cross, and John the Beloved, Merton's poetry, Higgins eloquently explains, "incarnates the word, vaporizes the specter of abstraction, celebrates enfleshment as the antidote to reason's captivity, and grounds worship in the elements of matter, the true sacrament of the Creator's sustaining love" (23). Continuing along similar lines of inquiry, Lynn Szabo's "'In the Dark before Dawn': Thomas Merton's Mystical Poetics" (24-40) provides us with an opportunity to see in Merton's priestly work the "unrequited desire" of a poet seeking "communication with God" (32). Tracing this longing of the human heart into the absence and stillness of sound, Szabo graciously helps us to see how Merton's poetry is an "attempt to express the inexpressible and transcend the confines of language itself – to enter the realm of the mystical" (27). Ross Labrie's essay, "Wholeness in Thomas Merton's Poetry" (41-60) shares much in common with what you will find in the two previously noted essays by Higgins and Szabo. All three scholars are interested in the way Merton's poetry reveals how he "sees" the world and thereby invites us to "see" in the same way. Labrie, however, takes us in a slightly different direction and offers another perspective from which to understand Merton's poetry. He draws our attention to Merton's prophetic search for wholeness that would allow humankind to see the radiance of Being that is the result of God's continued presence in the world; a presence that is of significance for the affairs of that world. Merton believed that the problems confronting humanity were the consequence of its tendency to see the world in a fragmented rather than holistic way. Labrie proceeds from here to show that the importance of this more integrated way of seeing to which Merton's poetry draws us "lies in its transformation of individual and collective patterns of desire and accomplishment into an expanded theatre of existence" wherein human beings may imitate the unifying love of their Creator, "the effect of which is to lift the mind and soul of both poet and reader off the plane of the material into a universe in which even the slightest thought and action are shown to have an immeasurable resonance" (58).

The opening three essays inevitably bring us to a familiar place in Merton studies. As noted by Higgins and underscored by Szabo and Labrie, Merton's vocation and work cannot be fully understood from one vantage point alone. Here was a man whose life unfolded in richly diverse ways as a priest, poet, and prophet; not as separate and distinct roles but roles interconnected in complex patterns of graces and tasks. In order to capture his image on canvas one would have to turn to the Cubists for directions, and they, I imagine, could very well find the task impossible. Even so, this is clearly the challenge before anyone who chooses to study Merton's poetry, for here the integration of priest, poet, and prophet is to be found most obscurely present.

Consequently, as in his journals and essays, so also in his poetry, we should expect to find changes in voice and message that mirror his distinctive formation as a cloistered monk in conversation with the world. So we now turn to Patrick O'Connell's "Islands in the Stream: Thomas Merton's Poetry of the Early 1950s" (61-105) that focuses our attention on the transitional years of the early 1950s which provide a bridge between the "traditional Merton of the 1940s and the adventurous Merton of the 1960s" (96). With exceptional skill, O'Connell offers us a fine study of Merton's fifth published book of verse, entitled *The Strange Islands*. Here we are shown once again how the contemplative vision of the monk surfaces to enlighten the world, pointing beyond the customary manner of seeing to seeing with the "One Light" that draws us in, incorporates us into itself, "in an awareness, an illumination, beyond all distinction between subject and object" (96). Ever so gradually, in this finely crafted essay, we observe the unfolding of Merton's contemplative life into the life of the world he had earlier rejected but now turns to in love.

The next three essays show how Merton's poetry engages the world. Bonnie Thurston's "'A Ray of That Truth Which Enlightens All': Thomas Merton, Poetic Language and Inter-religious Dialogue" (106-19) extends the ability to see transcendently to the present challenge of living in a religiously diverse world. Thurston explains that for Merton, dialogue with persons from other religious traditions was best approached via religious experience. If the dialogue is to be effective and authentic, it must essentially be poetic language since poetic language is the language of religious experience. Furthermore, and perhaps most importantly, it is poetic language that helps us to see in the other the presence of God and to make us receptive to the God who greets us in the other. With this in mind, conversation, not conversion, is the order of the day. As such it opens the possibility of persons from different traditions embracing one another as friends in a way that intellectual propositions cannot. With the focus on personal experiences, communication at a deep and meaningful level can be achieved in ways that dogmatic comparisons rule out.

Jeffrey Bilbro's "From Violence to Silence: The Rhetorical Means of Thomas Merton's Antipoetry" (120-49) turns our attention to a later period of Merton's poetry where Merton moves from inter-religious dialogue to dialogue with the world. Here Merton realized that he needed to discover an alternative rhetoric that would enable him to speak for peace and human rights with integrity. To achieve such a humane rhetoric, Merton turned to a form of antipoetry with the intention of disrupting the self-justifying language of the military-industrial complex and "to open space for a Zen-like silence that might reconnect his readers to a deeper ground of being, a ground from which real dialogue might begin" (120-21). Malgorzata Poks' "*The Geography of Lograire* as Merton's *Gestus* – Prolegomena" (150-69) addresses the questions raised by Bilbro. Merton, understanding his responsibility as a poet to follow the living Word of the moment, dismantles the language that provides the foundation on which unjust and violent policies are articulated and enacted. Poks' excellent study of *The Geography of Lograire* offers us an opportunity to observe how Merton skillfully presents a revisionist history of the world that "reveals the limitations and contradictions of power discourses and reclaims repressed perspectives" (166).

Deborah Kehoe, in "Thomas Merton's Ecopoetry: Bearing Witness to the Unity of Creation" (170-88) focuses on Merton's nature poems that Kehoe believes are "so prophetic in their 'greenness' that they justify the new and timely label of *ecopoetry*" (171). As such these poems represent "many of his most stirring challenges to a fragmented world" (170) and provide further insight into Merton's progress along a contemplative path that enriched his deepening insight into the interplay between God and nature. Susan McCaslin's "Pivoting toward Peace: The Engaged Poetics of Thomas Merton and Denise Levertov" (189-203) raises and addresses questions that extend the lines of inquiry explored by Thurston, Bilbro, Poks and Kehoe. In what ways is poetry transformative? How and to what extent can it pivot us toward peace? Working with the writings of Levertov and Merton, McCaslin shows how both poets grappled with these questions in their art and lives. Having left a legacy of poetry that includes overtly political poems as well as more subtly lyrical and meditative ones that enact peace by offering glimpses of a world in which self and other are so deeply intertwined, Levertov and Merton bring the reader to the awareness that war makes no sense.

In addition to these nine essays, you will find four unpublished poems by Merton (210-19) with a fine introduction by Lynn Szabo, "Shadows and Pathways" (204-209), an interview by Paul Wilkes with Lawrence Ferlinghetti (220-26), and a bibliographic essay by Gray Matthews, co-editor of *The Merton Annual*. Matthews' essay, "The Mystic's Hope: Thomas Merton's Contemplative Message to a Distracted World" (227-60), while surveying a selection of works published in 2008, adds an important note of concern at the end of this collection of essays on Merton. Here we are confronted by a troublesome question: how are we to understand the future of Merton's contemplative message in this world of seemingly endless distractions and commotion? As such, it is both a review of selected works and an essay in its own right that underscores the importance of Merton for readers today who are confronted with the challenge of living a contemplative life in a world that has all but lost any sense of what lies beneath the mere surface of things. In such a world, is it likely that Merton's poetry, or any poetry at all, will be read – and if read, understood? Even so, this should not and does not stop the poet-priest-prophet from speaking. As with Berenger in Eugene Ionesco's *Rhinoceros* or John the Savage in Aldous Huxley's *Brave New World*, Merton remains in his poetry a voice crying out in the wilderness, and this volume of *The Merton Annual* celebrates his voice that witnesses as poet-priest-prophet to the Word that is full of grace and truth.

Endnotes

1. Roger Lipsey, *Angelic Mistakes: The Art of Thomas Merton* (Boston & London: New Seeds, 2006) 110; quoting Thomas Merton, *Conjectures of a Guilty Bystander* (Garden City, NY: Doubleday, 1966) 266, and Thomas Merton, *Learning to Love: Exploring Solitude and Freedom. Journals, vol. 6: 1966-1967*, ed. Christine M. Bochen (San Francisco: HarperCollins, 1997) 160-61.

The Priestly Imagination: Thomas Merton and the Poetics of Critique

Michael W. Higgins

According to David M. Denny, the Jesuit theologian Karl Rahner "claims that the world is not fully itself until it is seen with the eyes of love and celebrated in art."[1] The poet and the priest are one in their celebration of the "mundane" and never more especially so than when the poet *is* the priest.

Think first of Thomas Merton, who thought of William Blake, master craftsman, poetic visionary, and mystical lover of Creation: "I think suddenly of Blake, filling paper with words, so that the words flew about the room for the angels to read, and after that, what if the paper was lost or destroyed? That is the only reason for wanting to write, Blake's reason."[2] The Precursor of the Incarnate Word, John the Baptist, represents for Merton the primordial hermit, history's model anchorite, "the first Cistercian and the greatest Trappist" ("St. John Baptist,"[3] l. 102); but he is also the first of three Johns. He is the Herald of the Word ("Name Him and vanish, like a proclamation" [l. 39]), and he seeks in solitude the strength to speak the word:

> I went into the desert to receive
> The keys of my deliverance
> From image and from concept and from desire. (ll. 83-85)

The paradox of John's life and mission, receiving in silence the grace to announce in the desert the "clean rock-water" that "dies in rings" ("Ode to the Present Century" [*CP* 121-22], l. 33) clearly marks the pattern of Merton's own vocation. John the Baptist is Advent's noble herald, the prophet, and the man of hope. He is the "Desert-dweller" ("St. John Baptist," l. 98), the Lamb's most eloquent spokesman and he knows "the solitudes that lie / Beyond anxiety and doubt" (ll. 98-99). Like St. Paul the Hermit in "Two Desert Fathers" (*CP* 166-68), "You died to the world of concept / Upon the cross of your humility" (ll. 53-54).

In "The Quickening of St. John the Baptist" (*CP* 199-202), Merton explores the *conception* of a contemplative vocation. The life of a contemplative, suggests Merton, is similar to the bearing of young life in the womb. Elizabeth carries the unborn John:

> You need no eloquence, wild bairn,
> Exulting in your hermitage.
> Your ecstasy is your apostolate,
> For whom to kick is *contemplata tradere*. (ll. 37-40)

For Merton the "small anchorite" (l. 27) singing in his cell is the prototype of the Christian contemplative, both "exiles in the far end of solitude, living as listeners" (l. 52). For the unborn John and the reborn Merton, "Night is our diocese and silence is our ministry" (l. 48), and they are "Cooled in the flame of God's dark fire" (l. 64). The Baptist's relationship to the Word imparts new meaning to the language of a poet who sees his life as a living celebration of the Baptist's vocation. The instrument of a poet's vision is language. The talent of the poet is to be tested by the word, and yet how shall he speak of the Word when silence is his grace and joy? "Now can we have Your Word and in Him rest" ("St. John's Night" [*CP* 171-72], l. 26).

There is another John: the one they called the Beloved: the poet-apostle, the rich visionary of Patmos, the one who speaks with deep love of "the Word that came into the world" (cf. Jn. 1:9). There is yet another John: the Spaniard who is of the Cross. This poet-mystic, whose rare gifts of lyrical genius and solemn contemplation transformed his rigorous sufferings into one living ceaseless paean to the God of men, quickened Merton's imagination and served as a crucial factor in his resolution to be a poet.

The three Johns represent the indivisible and comprehensive dimensions of Merton as a *whole man*. They each represented for him the ideals of the Christian poet-priest.

	Merton	
John the Baptist	John of the Cross	John the Beloved
herald	mystic	lover
	The Lyricist	
prophet	poet	priest
	The Ordained	
hope	faith	charity
	The Complete Man	

As Margo Swiss observes: "'The Word . . . made flesh' (John 1.14),

– Christ is (we may say) the perfect poet of the perfect poem. Poets who express a Christian *ethos* are therefore performing their version of a Liturgy of the Word" (Swiss 17).

Merton's poetics of critique is twofold: ecclesial/monastic and societal. To understand the former it is essential to grasp the spirit of the place, to taste the physical geography. As the Catholic poet-philosopher Tim Lilburn reminds us:

> I remembered one of the apothegmata
> Merton had collected: if you don't manage
> to take in the genius of the place, let it
> say its piece through you, the place will
> throw you out. And I saw that these hills,
> these poplar islands, could just shrug me off,
> no problem. With some desperation, I drove
> myself to find a way into the good graces
> of this particular bit of land.[4]

For Lilburn the hills of Saskatchewan are his sacred, defining space, and for Merton, of course, it was Gethsemani, the Abbey and the land.

Merton's ecclesial/monastic critique is best appreciated by examining select poems from *Early Poems (1940-1942)* (1971), *A Man in the Divided Sea* (1946), *Figures for an Apocalypse* (1947) and *The Tears of the Blind Lions* (1949).

Perhaps, the most eloquent statement of what the abbey meant for Merton (in the mid-1940s) can be found in the poem "Clairvaux" (*CP* 126-30). Clairvaux, one of the earliest and most celebrated of Cistercian foundations, lives again in spirit in the Abbey of Gethsemani. No longer in the Aube Valley of France but now nestled in the woodlands of Kentucky, "whose back is to the hills whose backs are to the world" (l. 6), the "model of all solitudes" (l. 3), Clairvaux/Gethsemani is inward-looking and "ever resting" (l. 7); she is an enclosure "full of sun" (l. 8), a garden bathed "in fleets of light" (l. 18), a cloister rich "in sure and perfect arbors of stability" (l. 40), and a veritable reflection of Heaven, "Where He may rest unseen by the grey, grasping, / Jealous, double-dealing world" (ll. 26-27). In the poem Merton identifies Christ as a Vintner who "Will trample in His press" (l. 43) the monks "in their quietude" (l. 37). He is also the Keystone upon whom the brothers, as the stones of the arches, lean, "Forgetting gravity in flight" (l. 56). But most important of all He is the Sun, whose rays penetrate the souls of the monks "All interlacing . . . as close as vines" (l. 35). In the garden of each monk's soul, in his interior Clairvaux, the light of perception, the light of vision, the light of grace can be seen

> Pouring in sun through rib and leaf and flower of foliate window
> Gardening the ground with shadow-light, with day and night
> In every lovely interplay. (ll. 49-51)

The intricate tracery of a stained glass window bears the imprint of the master artist, the supreme craftsman who outlines with delicate skill the clearest image of "the Maker's mind and plan" (l. 67). The "foliate window," the prism of art, can only be finely stained in the silence of "our holy cloister," in the heart of our recollected self, and must be receptive to the sensitive impressions of the Eternal Artist.

Enclosed by the "penniless hills / Hidden in the poor, laborious fields" ("Three Postcards from the Monastery" [*CP* 153-55], ll. 33-34), the monks have seen ravaged the pure dream of Nature; they have seen Eden invaded with "tons of silver" (l. 32), America's promise sold for a "Pittsburgh, in a maze of lights" (l. 48):

> We have refused the reward,
> We have abandoned the man-hunt.
> But when the contest is over
> We shall inherit the world. (ll. 40-43)

Though refused, the allure of the world is great and the security of the monastic Eden unsure. In "The Song of the Traveller" (*CP* 172-73), the speaker, a palmer or pilgrim, warns that once we have reached the "holy heights where the low world will die" (l. 12), we must not look back upon what we have rejected lest we become as "Mistress Lot" (l. 28). The monastic enclosure is not immune to the music of the world's treachery and, once bewitched by the "thin clarions" (l. 23) of worldly triumph, "all our flowery mountain will be tattered with a cost of weeds" (l. 24).

The "Pilgrim's Song" (*CP* 189-90) is a monastic canticle that celebrates what is "foolishness to the Greeks" (cf. 1 Cor. 1:23-24) and what must appear as an outrageous contradiction of secular priorities:

> We'll lose you by our stratagem
> In the amazing dusk: by the safe way that you ignore: –
> We are in love with your antagonist. (ll. 19-21)

At the heart of the monastic rejection of the world is a total acceptance of a way of life that is seen as a positive affirmation of the
values of the "appalling Cross" (l. 22).

The monk is a "grain that dies and triumphs in the secret
ground" ("Spring: Monastery Farm" [CP 169-70], l. 12), a russet
worm which hastens "as best he can / To die here in this patch of
sun" ("Natural History" [CP 182-84], ll. 22-23), and a midshipman
aboard the "lonely Abbey" (l. 11) battleship awaiting "the angel
with the trumpet of the Judgement" ("Winter Afternoon" [CP
185-86], l. 22). Enwrapped in a spiritual cocoon of Gethsemani's
weaving, the monk waits for the promised metamorphosis, ever
conscious that the world is yet with him should he deny the world.
In the light of this conviction the monastic ethos could well appear
to approve a proudly elitist, near-Manichaean spirituality. Such,
however, would be an inauthentic expression of the true monastic
spirit; but it must be admitted as a danger and one to which, at this
time in his monastic career, Merton is particularly vulnerable.

"From the Legend of St. Clement" (CP 203-204) is a meditation on a subject, generally a lesson from the Martyrology, that the
monks would be accustomed to hear during their meals. Because
of the scarcity of historical evidence associated with the life and
martyrdom of St. Clement, a not unusual situation in the early life
of the Christian Church, Merton freely mixes the legendary with
the authentic. A Bishop of Rome, Clement was sentenced to the
marble quarries of the Crimea during the reign of Trajan where he
and other Christians were eventually martyred:

> Deep in the wall of the wounded mountain
> (Where seas no longer frown)
> The songs of the martyrs come up like cities or buildings.
> Their chains shine with hymns
> And their hands cut down the giant blocks of stone. (ll. 6-10)

Every martyrdom becomes a poem, a psalm, and the opening lines
– "I have seen the sun / Spilling its copper petals on the Black Sea"
(ll. 1-2) – are highly reminiscent of the forbidding note sounded in
"From the Second Chapter of a Verse History of the World" (CP
13-19) when the unknowing victims sailed for Minos' den: "The
roaring poet sun shall play the hot sea like a lyre, / And twang the
copper coastal ridge like any vocal wire" (ll. 104-105). The mountain becomes a "prophetic cathedral" (l. 15) whose windows are
emblazoned with the acts of the martyrs who die "By the base of the

prisoners' cliff" (l. 3). Deprived of water, the followers of Clement seek succor from the bishop; and, like Moses with the Israelites in the desert, Clement gave them their water, though unlike Moses he was not put to the test. It was a lamb that led him to the spot where water could be obtained:

> The Lamb shall soon stand
> White as a shout against the sky:
> His feet shall soon strike rainbows from the rock. (ll. 20-22)

The rainbow, the sign of Yahweh's covenant with Noah after the Deluge, becomes the sign of the new covenant rendered perfect in the blood of the Lamb. The prisoners of the "marble hill" (l. 19) have drowned only to recover life. They have been baptized by blood and their lives shall "swing with fruit in other worlds, in other centuries" (l. 31). The Biblical use of water as the symbol of chaos and death and, paradoxically, also as the symbol of regeneration and vivification is ably employed when Merton contrasts the "copper petals on the Black Sea" (l. 2) with the "buried streams" (l. 23) released from the cliffs by Clement's faith. The new prisoners of the "marble hill," the monks of Gethsemani, replenish themselves with the faith of the martyrs, the waters of baptism, which "shatter the land at my feet with seas forever young" (l. 43).

There are, however, times of private and collective desiccation when the soul thirsts for the water of life and remains unslaked. "On a Day in August" (*CP* 204-206) pictures a torrid Gethsemani day when "a brown wing hovers for carrion" (l. 6) while the monks, prey to spiritual torpor, merely wait

> In the air of our dead grove
> Dreaming some wind may come and kiss ourselves in the red eyes
> With a pennyworth of mercy for our pepper shoulders.
> And so we take into our hands the ruins
> Of the words our minds have rent. (ll. 10-14)

The monks wait like the hay in the fields while "locusts fry their music in the sycamores" (l. 4) and their dream is "drowned in the din of the crickets' disconnected prayer" (l. 23). The monks "In the air of [their] dead grove" find themselves like the parched souls of *The Waste Land* for whom

> Sweat is dry and feet are in the sand
> If there were only water amongst the rock

Dead mountain mouth of carious teeth that cannot spit
Here one can neither stand nor lie nor sit
There is not even silence in the mountains.[5]

Enervated by the spiritual lassitude that has overtaken the monas-
tery the monks watch "the grasses and the unemployed goldenrod
/ Go revel through our farm, and dance around the field" (ll. 24-25).
They remain inert, passive and helpless in their "dead grove":

> In this decayed hole among the mountains
> In the faint moonlight, the grass is singing
> Over the tumbled graves, about the chapel
> There is the empty chapel, only the wind's home.
> It has no windows, and the door swings,
> Dry bones can harm no one. (Eliot 49)

For Merton, the spiritual dryness of the Gethsemani monks
precedes and occasions their realization of authentic prayer's ef-
ficacy:

> And when the first fat drops
> Spatter upon the tin top of our church like silver dollars
> And thoughts come bathing back to mind with a new life,
> Prayer will become our new discovery
>
> When God and His bad earth once more make friends. (ll. 42-46)

Such a realization is best achieved when accompanied by an
apocalyptic sentiment:

> Summon the punishing lightning:
> Spring those sudden gorgeous trees against the dark
> Curtain of apocalypse you'll hang to earth, from heaven:
> Let five white branches scourge the land with fire! (ll. 38-41)

Though those are the days of judgment and the monk functions as
both eschatological sign and sentinel "upon the world's frontier"
("The Quickening of St. John the Baptist" l. 55), they are also the
Advent days, the days of expectation and yearning.

In the seasonal poem "St. Malachy" (*CP* 209-11) Merton returns
to autumn. St. Malachy, a twelfth-century Irish Cistercian bishop,
has traditionally had his feast day on November 2 "in the days to
remember the dead" (l. 1). The saint whose "coat is filled with
drops of rain, and [who] is bearded / With all the seas of Poseidon"
(ll. 5-6) comes to the monastery where "He weeps against the gothic

window, and the empty cloister / Mourns like an ocean shell" (ll. 8-9). The bells of the monastery tower which "considers his waters" (l. 12) summon the monks to prayer and, in the language of St. Gregory the Great, "Oceans of Scripture sang upon bony Eire" (l. 24). The remains of a former season, the spoils of a richer time, are offered on the altar of propitiation:

> Then the last salvage of flowers
> (Fostered under glass after the gardens foundered)
> Held up their little lamps on Malachy's altar
> To peer into his wooden eyes before the Mass began. (ll. 25-28)

The autumn is Malachy's emblem, the sign of his complete submersion in the ocean of God's grace. Gethsemani, which he has visited, is like an anchored ship: "Rain sighed down the sides of the stone church. / Storms sailed by all day in battle fleets" (ll. 29-30). Earlier, in "Winter Afternoon," Merton had spoken of Gethsemani as a war vessel tossed about by the angry seas of "the Kentucky forest":

> . . . our lonely Abbey like an anchored battleship:
> While the Kentucky forest
> Pouring upon our prows her rumorous seas
> Wakes our wordless prayers with the soft din of an Atlantic.
> (ll. 11-14)

The monks desire to "see the sun" when the "speechless visitor" (l. 21) leaves and in his wake

> copper flames fall, tongues of fire fall
> The leaves in hundreds fall upon his passing
> While night sends down her dreadnought darkness (ll. 25-27).

Malachy, "the Melchisedec of our year's end" (l. 29), leaves the monks "And rain comes rattling down upon our forest / Like the doors of a country jail" (ll. 31-32). Incarcerated in their Advent prison, shipwrecked in their Kentucky ocean, the monks can continue to long for the sun or they can learn the lesson of Malachy and seek Christ "in those soundless fathoms where You dwell" ("Theory of Prayer" [*CP* 179-81], l. 56). In "Theory of Prayer," as in "St. Malachy," Merton knew the "ocean of peace" (l. 42), the "ocean of quiet" (l. 45) that surges within us; yet "How many hate their own safe death, / Their cell, their submarine!" (ll. 51-52). Malachy, autumn, teaches us how to die in the season of preparation, to drown in the "soundless fathoms."

The special function of the Christian poet as Advent visionary is described in the poem "In the Rain and the Sun" (*CP* 214-15), which admixes the sentiments of "On a Day in August" with those of "St. Malachy." In the first stanza Gethsemani, the "dead grove," is again "without rain" (l. 2) and the "Tall drops" (l. 4) of the "noonday dusk" (l. 3) pelt "the concrete with their jewelry" (l. 4). It is still Eliot's "decayed hole among the mountains," a place "Belonging to the old world's bones" (l. 5). The poet listens to what the thunder says, surveying the horizon as the monks scurry from the fields to the monastery for protection:

> Owning this view, in the air of a hermit's weather,
> . . . I plumb the shadows full of thunder.
> My prayers supervise the atmosphere
> Till storms call all hounds home. (ll. 6, 9-11)

The poet observes "the countries sleeping in their beds" (l. 16) as "Four or five mountains" (l. 13) of water drench the land:

> Wild seas amuse the world with water:
> No end to all the surfs that charm our shores
> Fattening the sands with their old foam and their old roar. (ll. 18-20)

The poet watches as the earth divides into the "Lands of the watermen" (l. 17), and the "Dogs and lions" caught in "the boom of waves' advantage" seek the poet's "tame home," "my Cistercian jungle." At this point in the poem the abbey becomes the familiar image of the ship, although this time not a battleship but Noah's ark with the poet as Noah. "Noah" (which Semitic-language scholars believe might mean "rest" in Hebrew), as the poet-monk of Gethsemani, offers to appease a just God with his verses, hoping thereby that "God and His bad earth once more [may] make friends" ("On a Day in August"). Like St. Clement, the poet-as-Noah seeks to "strike rainbows from the rock" ("From the Legend of St. Clement") and form a new covenant by means of his verses:

> Thus in the boom of waves' advantage
> Dogs and lions come to my tame home
> Won by the bells of my Cistercian jungle.
> O love the livid fringes
> In which their robes are drenched!

> Songs of the lions and whales!

> With my pen between my fingers
> Making the waterworld sing!
> Sweet Christ, discover diamonds
> And sapphires in my verse
> While I burn the sap of my pine house
> For praise of the ocean sun. (ll. 21-32)

The covenant will again be compromised, the "Dogs have gone back to their ghosts / And the many lions, home" (ll. 40-41), but the poet's verses shall preserve the dream of Edenic innocence so briefly captured during the Deluge aboard the bark of Gethsemani:

> words fling wide the windows of their houses –
> Adam and Eve walk down my coast
> Praising the tears of the treasurer sun (ll. 42-44).

The poet's verses, the rainbow, "the tears of the treasurer sun," are a reminder that although the innocence of Eden was once lost it is not irretrievable, living in the poet's vision and the monk's faith.

The monastery is both "the decayed hole among the mountains" and the ark-like "tame home" that offers rest to a world beset with the waves of tumult. It is the harbor in the storm and the "dead grove."

When it comes to the societal critique it is best to draw on *Cables to the Ace or Familiar Liturgies of Misunderstanding* (CP 393-454), Merton's 1968 anti-poetic epic consisting of a prologue, eighty-eight cantos / cables, and an epilogue.

Just before the book's publication Merton spoke of it in less than flattering terms in a letter to a fellow poet: "Maybe you will feel it does not communicate: it is imprecise, noisy, crude, full of vulgarity and parody, making faces, criticizing and so on."[6] He feared that it would be misunderstood, that he was less than capable of realizing the next step in the unfolding of his myth-dream: the reparation of the Fall. There is no doubt that *Cables* is a daring undertaking. It is a kaleidoscope of sixty pages of poetic experimentation and raises the "problem of word" to a new level of intensity.

> Since language has become a medium in which we are totally immersed, there is no longer any need to say anything. The saying says itself all around us. No one need attend. Listening is obsolete. So is silence. Each one travels alone in a small

blue capsule of indignation. (Some of the better informed have declared war on Language.) (#3 [*CP* 397])

There is an air of desperation about this poem precisely because it is written with a sense of urgency. It is electric in form and imagery: "electric jungle" (#14 [*CP* 404]), "their imitable wire" (#15 [*CP* 404]), "expert lights" (#15 [*CP* 405]), all contributing to the mad congestion of "the blue electric palaces of polar night" (#34 [*CP* 418]). The poem's irony is oppressive, communication and mobility are everywhere but no one hears and language has become static in the world of "the monogag" and "the telefake" (#34 [*CP* 418]). The world of immediate intimacy is a world of "Dull energies in the dust of collapsing walls" (#44 [*CP* 424-25]). It is not the garden of paradise but the wasteland of apocalypse. We have been deceived by language and the "Great Meaning," loving the inevitable, each having "his appointed vector / In the mathematical takeoff" (#52 [*CP* 431]).

   In *Cables* form is content; it does not contain or transmit a message, it simply *is* a message. The title of the poem itself suggests the identification of the means of transmission with the content transmitted, for a cable is both the electrical apparatus by which the message is channeled and the message or cablegram itself. The medium is the message. For neither Marshall McLuhan nor Merton, however, are electric communication and its creation, the "global village," any panacea:

> Some may say that the electric world
> Is a suspicious village
> Or better a jungle where all the howls
> Are banal
> NO! The electric jungle is a village
> Where howling is not suspicious:
> Without it we would be afraid
> That fear was usual. (#14 [*CP* 403-404])

Cables underscores humankind's desperate need for redemptive unity precisely because it highlights the dissensions that pervade human society, dissensions that are often the result of an egocentrism nourished by the media and the technocratic overloads. The medium is indeed the message, the form of the poem is the statement.

   Cables is a mosaic of messages of reassurance, of good fortune, which, once decoded, reveals the compelling credibility of skillful dissembling. In the Prologue Merton makes explicit his implicit contempt of the advertiser, the master scribbler of our consumerist society: "My attitudes are common and my ironies are no less usual than the bright pages of your favorite magazine. The soaps, the smells, the liquors, the insurance, the third, dull, gin-soaked cheer: what more do you want, Rabble?" (*CP* 395). By detailing the lies that have been our common diet, the poem obliges the reader to accept the implications of this ironic feedback. The cables are "familiar liturgies of misunderstanding" and it is the reader's moral and intellectual duty to reject the tyranny of lies by ceasing to misunderstand. This is best done by appreciating the intention of antipoetry, a *genre* that Merton defines as "a deliberate ironic feedback of cliche":[7]

> Marcuse has shown how mass culture tends to be an anticulture – to stifle creative work by the sheer volume of what is "produced" or reproduced. In which case, poetry, for example, must start with an awareness of this contradiction and *use* it – as antipoetry – which freely draws on the material of superabundant nonsense at its disposal. One no longer has to parody, it is enough to quote – and feed back quotations into the mass consumption of pseudoculture. (*AJ* 118)

Failure to accept the implications of this ironic feedback could result in a sentence of mass death, a possibility Merton considers in the Epilogue, where the uncommon juxtaposition of apocalyptic sentiment with an outrageously parodied advertising jargon shows not only an adept handling of "super-abundant nonsense" but an intensity of purpose by no means subdued in the poet's mature years.

The "elite" are the architects of our universal ruin, the technocrats and engineers who design the instruments of our doom. But their most effective weapon is language for language is power and the advertisers/politicians/engineers combine their respective energies to ensure that language does their bidding:

> Let choirs of educated men compose
> Their shaken elements and present academies of electronic renown
> With better languages. Knowing health
> And marital status first of all they must provide
> Automatic spelling devices or moneymaking

Conundrums to program
The next ice-age from end-to-end
In mournful proverbs

Let such choirs intone
More deep insulted shades
That mime the arts of diction
Four-footed metaphors must then parade
Firm resolution or superb command
Of the wrong innuendo (#16 [*CP* 405]).

The apocalypse is the consummate "brilliant intuition of an engineer" (#85 [*CP* 453]). Abstraction has firmly ensnared humankind, and the Cartesian *cogito* secures our continued isolation.

Look! The Engineer! He thinks he has caught something! He wrestles with it in mid-air! (#51 [*CP* 430])

The priest-poet incarnates the word, vaporizes the specter of abstraction, celebrates enfleshment as the antidote to reason's captivity, and grounds worship in the elements of matter, the true sacrament of the Creator's sustaining love.

Endnotes

1. Margo Swiss, ed., *Poetry as Liturgy: An Anthology by Canadian Poets* (Toronto: The St. Thomas Poetry Series, 2007) 20; subsequent references will be cited as "Swiss" parenthetically in the text.

2. Thomas Merton, *My Argument with the Gestapo* (Garden City, NY: Doubleday, 1969) 259.

3. Thomas Merton, *The Collected Poems of Thomas Merton* (New York: New Directions, 1977) 122-26; subsequent references will be cited as "*CP*" parenthetically in the text.

4. Tim Lilburn, ed., *Thinking and Singing: Poetry and the Practice of Philosophy* (Toronto: Cormorant Books, 2002) 173.

5. T. S. Eliot, *The Complete Poems and Plays: 1909-1950* (New York: Harcourt, Brace & World, 1962) 47; subsequent references will be cited as "Eliot" parenthetically in the text.

6. Thomas Merton, *The Courage for Truth: Letters to Writers*, ed. Christine M. Bochen (New York: Farrar, Straus, Giroux, 1993) 248-49 (9/5/66 letter to Cid Corman).

7. Thomas Merton, *The Asian Journal*, ed. Naomi Burton Stone, Brother Patrick Hart and James Laughlin (New York: New Directions, 1973) 286; subsequent references will be cited as "*AJ*" parenthetically in the text.

"In the Dark before Dawn":
Thomas Merton's Mystical Poetics

Lynn Szabo

Resonant with Thomas Merton's love of the predawn hours after the Night Vigils monastic office in which he found the silent darkness to be the ground of his creative energies, fed by contemplation and the rising sun, his "Elegy for a Trappist"[1] quietly illustrates the prophetic and poetic voices by which Merton characterizes human existence and its cavalier willingness to overlook what is of hidden significance before our unseeing eyes. In the mid-1960s, Fr. Stephen Pitra, a fellow-monk of whom Merton was fond because of his innocence and earnestness, had collapsed in the early morning, hidden in the foliage of his much-loved garden, near the gates of Gethsemani Abbey. Merton eulogized his simplicity in a fine poem, capturing Merton's own monastic values and the fertility that derived from the darkness before dawn in which Merton's apophatic, mystical poetics were birthed:

> In the dark before dawn
> On the day of your burial
> A big truck with lights
> Moved like a battle cruiser
> Toward the gate
> Past your abandoned and silent garden . . . .
>
> As if Leviathan
> Hot on the scent of some other blood
> Had passed you by
> And never saw you hiding in the flowers. (ll. 20-25, 32-35)

In his corresponding eulogy for Fr. Stephen's burial mass, Merton explains the context of the poem and his wish to honor this monk and his anonymity in the community, even in death.[2]

In the silence of "the dark before dawn," Merton finds the absence and stillness of sound to be the locus of an often unrequited desire for communication with God which becomes the possibility of experiencing, unhindered, the Divine in *logos* / *poesis* / language. In another more remarkable portrayal of this *apophasis*, he writes, in a description from May, 1965 of his life in the hermitage:

I am out of bed at two-fifteen in the morning, when the night is darkest and most silent. . . . I find myself in the primordial lostness of night, solitude, forest, peace, a mind awake in the dark . . . . The psalms grow up silently by themselves without effort like plants . . . . The plants hold themselves up on stems which have a single consistency, that of mercy, or rather great mercy. *Magna misericordia.* In the formlessness of night and silence a word then pronounces itself: Mercy.[3]

Many of the themes and contexts of Merton's poetry are synchronously emblematic of his life and his art, synthesizing its dichotomies and perplexities: artifice and the genuine; the apparent and the real; truth and falseness; silent monasticism and relentless writerly impulses; asceticism and creativity; contemplation and action; anonymity and renown; silence and words; secularism and mysticism. In such contrarieties, his poetry sounds its songs of integrity, wisdom, and hope in the face of the confounding story of twentieth-century America. Concomitantly, Merton's poetry moves us because its words function like notation in music: they are tropological, analogical, allegorical and mythopoeic, inviting his readers into his portraiture of the "beautiful terror" which is the human condition.

In his poetry, it is less clear that Merton gravitated away from his consciousness of the world and then returned to it (a pattern which some critics find in the development of his prose); rather, he continually wrote poems which wove patterns and underpinnings that combined the epiphanous spiritual revelations of his monastic vocation with the ordinariness of human life as he knew it within and beyond the monastery walls. That the poems of his early monastic experience often center on its sometimes obscure theological or liturgical contexts is not as significant as their representation of his determination to synthesize in a mystical poetics his spirituality and his lived experience.

At its finest, Merton's poetry depicts itself in a symbology engendered by the ontological and psychological parallels to his experience, beyond the realm of empiricism and metaphysics and birthing a sophisticated and penetrating wisdom arising from the analogous worlds of the poet and the mystic. He explained in his essay "Symbolism: Communication or Communion?" that "The true symbol does not merely point to some hidden object. It contains in itself a structure which . . . makes us aware of the inner meaning of life and of reality itself. . . . A true symbol takes us to the center of the circle, not to another point on the circumference."[4] His genius was to create an artistic vision replete with discourse, rhetoric, and syntactical strategies that led him away from conventional paradigms and finally, to an antipoetry (what Frederick Smock has called "burst[ing] the bonds of liturgy"[5]) that sought to engage and rout the powerful tensions which erupt when the debasement of language distorts and disrupts its possibilities for meaning.

A persuasive illustration of these convictions may be found in a comparison of his early poem "Tower of Babel" (*CP* 21-22; *IDBD* 145-46) and the later morality play (included in the 1957 volume *The Strange Islands*[6]) of similar title. In both constructs, Merton allegorizes the Biblical myth as a critique of modernism. His voice proposes a parody of the coming deconstructionist who posits that language has no determinant meaning or significance. The speaker in the early poem satirically decries that "Insofar as man is more important than God" (l. 18), the machine "Should always destroy the maker of the machine" (l. 16) – a principle that "Words also reflect . . . / Though they are meant to conceal it / From the ones who are too young to know" (ll. 19-21). In the speaker's understanding of this paradigm, language will conspire against its users to destroy that which it speaks. In this paradigm, any attempt at narrative becomes a towering Babel in which history inevitably goes forward "by the misuse of words" (l. 4); as a corollary of this "principle":

> . . . words have no essential meaning.
> They are means of locomotion
> From backward to forward
> Along an infinite horizontal plane,
> Created by the history which they themselves destroy
> They are the makers of our only reality
> The backward-forward working of the web
> The movement into the web. (ll. 22-29)

In the later drama, Merton repeats the thematic motif of the early poem in the dramatic words of the professor who plays the role of lead witness to the "functions of language":

> History is a dialogue
> Between forward and backward
> Going inevitably forward by the abuse of thought (*CP* 255).

Although more than a decade passes between the appearances of these two writings, Merton's early prescience about the "linguistic turn" (the fracture of the sign and the signifier at the foundation of much literary and cultural theory) is uncanny in its foresights. He was, as often earlier and later, ahead of his time in diagnosing the irony and cynicism about language which foregrounded postmodern debates about literature and language. Later, a similar reservoir of concerns compels his writing of *Cables to the Ace*[7] in which he adopts an antipoetics which parodies the sloganeering and propagandizing of language that he observes in American secular and popular culture in the sixties.

Impressive renderings of Merton's singular artistic vision resonate throughout his poetry and are limited neither to their forms nor to an evolving chronological progression. From his earliest interests in writing poetry, Merton's voice demonstrates his contemplative's capacity for reflection and synthesis, focusing on vast and broad-ranging complexities and on experiences far beyond his own. In the pattern of a Dantesque spiral of revelations, he continuously navigates the geography of his inner and exterior worlds with a poetic voice, compelling because of the magnetism and charisma of its temperament and resonances. His contemplative's cartography offers a third way, beyond reason and/or imagination, what has been called a "dark clarity" in which "Meaning is not something we impose, . . . but a mystery which we can discover" (quoted in Smock 58) – what is known, theologically, as apophatic wisdom. Smock posits that Merton's poetics "sought a literary equivalent to ecstatic spiritual mysticism. . . . an intensity of language to match an intensity of [human] feeling" (Smock 78-79). This I call his mystical poetics, fueled by his contemplation.

In a 1938 review of John Crowe Ransom's *The World's Body*, Merton wrote that poetry "is a kind of knowledge . . . that cannot be gained by any other means, for the poet is concerned with the aspects of experience that can never be well described – but only reproduced or imitated."[8] For him, metaphor, the medium of all poetry, represents an infinite desire to acknowledge invisible and unknown realities, the attempt to express the inexpressible and transcend the confines of language itself – to enter the realm of the mystical.

One of the many fine representations of this form of knowledge is evoked by his poem, "The Blessed Virgin Mary Compared to a Window" (*CP* 46-48; *IDBD* 27-28). In an extended trope, the simplicity of the church window becomes the metaphor of the Virgin's great will to love. Light which pours through the window's transparent glass is the harbinger of the arrival of the Holy Spirit. The poet captures the erotic union of the Annunciation through words which he gives her to describe her delight: "For light, my lover, steals my life in secret" (l. 10) and "dawn [is] my death" (l. 7). In her luminescent capture by the Light of the Spirit itself, she is reborn as the woman who "live[s] to give [her] newborn Morning to [the] quiet rooms" (l. 19). The poet dramatizes this powerful event, analogizing it as the monks' cells which would be "vaults of night, and death, and terror" (l. 21), but are now "Fill[ed] with the clarity of living Heaven" (l. 22); Mary's simplicity and strength of faith shine through her transparent obedience and sinlessness as does light through the church window. The trope is completed as the speaker internalizes Mary's depth of loving devotion not only to Christ her unborn Son but to her "other son" (l. 30), the poet/monk himself. In the intensity of light streaming through the transparent glass of the window, Merton is connected to Christ, his Brother, his Light – "the Lamb of [the] Apocalypse" (l. 42). The poem is rich with music, light and silence – the contexts of monasticism by which Merton absorbed his early theology and engaged the experiences of his own spirituality. The quiet alliterations of the liturgy and the dark silences into which he had entered overwhelm him with ecstatic joy and profound ardor. (Indeed, his love for the Virgin Mary has now become a fascination for psychologists and therapists who locate in it his recovery of the mother love that he lost at the age of six when his own mother died of cancer.)

Much later in his lovely prose-poem, *Day of a Stranger* (published in one of its numerous forms in *Papeles*, July, 1966, as *Dia de un Extrano*), Merton provides a curious South American editor with the lyric description of a "typical day" for him as a hermit monk. In a variety of tones suffused with his changing moods and insights, he transparently describes his way of life in his hermitage, St. Mary of Carmel. The piece represents Merton's voice as an accomplished writer and offers the reader a veritable catalogue of his mystical poetics, hidden in the seemingly innocuous nature of some of its narrative. Here, in some of his most evocative and poetic language, Merton offers us a microcosm of his poet/mystic's experience as solitary "stranger" who lives in the woods in a world "where words cease to resound, where all meanings are absorbed in the *consonantia* of heat, fragrant pine, quiet wind, bird

song and one central tonic note that is unheard and unuttered. . . .
In the silence of the afternoon all is present and all is inscrutable
in one central tonic note to which every other sound ascends or
descends, to which every other meaning aspires, in order to find
its true fulfilment" (*DS* 61). Elsewhere, Merton proclaims that
"No writing on the solitary, meditative dimensions of life can say
anything that has not already been said better by the wind in the
pine trees."[9] Yet, he acknowledges its vulnerability to the many
other sounds that threaten to interfere with and eclipse it. He hears
the armed SAC plane flying low over him, with its "scientific egg
in its breast" (*DS* 31) – a symbol of all that not only diminishes the
stillness of his forest home, but also carries the forces that would
extinguish the entire human story; in deft relief, he moves his listeners to the equilibrium of the natural world around him where
"precise pairs of birds" live in his immediate surroundings: with
him, they "form an ecological balance" whose "harmony gives the
idea of 'place' a new configuration" (*DS* 33).

In this beautiful evocation of the hermit's life, the ordered pri-
vacy of his solitude is set against the backdrop of the nuclear age,
providing the counterpoint to a silhouette that takes its effect from
the shadow which creates it. The result is a profound metonym for
modern human life, living out its destiny in alienation. Merton,
as this particular "stranger," avoids succumbing to alienation and
despair by listening to the sacred language of the universe – the
silence of God spoken by the wind in the pine trees.

In such a paradigm, human speech may be nothing more or less
than the wind (*pneuma*: the breath) because language is ultimately
inappropriate in describing the spiritual realities that Merton ap-
prehends in the breath of God's Spirit in the woods. His poetics are
grounded in the mysterious revelation from which he comprehends
silent communion as superior to verbal communication because its
signifiers are inferior to the "otherness" of mystical experience.

This language of the sacred reflects his bias in favor of the
simplicity, solitude, and silence of the rural life. The settings for
so much of his poetry are the Kentucky knobs and their fecund
life which reflects the integrity of all things: "a hidden wholeness"
(*CP* 363), one of whose complexities is its intimation of an "ontol-
ogy of nothingness – a silence – in which there is infinite regress
of the truths permanently hidden behind words."[10] Merton often
identifies himself with the life of the Kentucky hill-dwellers whose
homes and farms lie in the knobs bordering the monastery's

property. The poems that he writes about this aspect of his life provide a virtual farmer's almanac of life in these woods. His love for the forests, hills, streams, and the flora and fauna of the hills permeates his poetry. The influence of Thoreau's *Walden* and the transcendentalists is apparent in his poetry, his journals and myriad essays, particularly in his writings about the rural life around him. He wrote in a letter to Henry Miller, August 7, 1962: "Thoreau of course I admire tremendously. He is one of the only reasons why I felt justified in becoming an American citizen. . . . It is to me a great thing that you say I am like the transcendentalists. I will try to be worthy of that."[11]

"O Sweet Irrational Worship" (*CP* 344-45; *IDBD* 96-97) is an exquisite example of Merton's generous and transparent spiritual sensibilities brought to life in his mystic's response to the natural world. In the moments of this poem, Merton's "foolish worship" (l. 31) arises from his observations of a simple bobwhite (American quail) and the afternoon sun, perhaps outside the hermitage to which he was regularly going in order to write and contemplate by the early sixties when the poem was written. The title itself alerts the reader to the poet's joy in a worship that is "irrational" in quality. The poem arises in the manner of a Zen *koan*:

> By ceasing to question the sun
> I have become light . . . .
>
> When I had a spirit,
> . . . I was on fire. (ll. 3-4, 13-14)

He recognizes that, like the writers of the Hebrew Psalms, he was alive as spirit even before God "spoke [his] name" in "naming . . . silence" (ll. 17-18). In his identification with the natural world around him, the poet is drawn into the ecstasy of his own incarnation as a being, both human and divine:

> I am earth, earth
> My heart's love
> Bursts with hay and flowers.
> I am a lake of blue air
> In which my own appointed place
> Field and valley
> Stand reflected. (ll. 20-26)

He repeats the refrain, exulting in the delight of the revelation that he is in union with creation and God, its Maker:

> I am earth, earth
>
> Out of my grass heart
> Rises the bobwhite.
>
> Out of my nameless weeds
> His foolish worship.   (ll. 27-31)

In this lyrical hymn of worship and self-transcendence, his being becomes one with the created world's praise of God. In it,
the anagogical and anecdotal combine to present intense poetic
powers. This Zen lyric resonates with Merton's imbibing of the
Psalms over the two decades that he has now been a monk of
Gethsemani. One hears the echoes of Psalm 139: "My substance
was not hid from thee, when I was made in secret . . . and . . . in
thy book all my members were written, which in continuance were
fashioned, when as yet there was none of them" (vv.15-16); in the
lovely afternoon sun of his Kentucky valley, "A tall, spare pine /
Stands like the initial of [his] first / Name when [he] had one" (ll.
10-12). Again, one hears the music and joy of the Hebrew Psalm
in the words of the poet whose identity has always existed but is
now recognized in the air and light of this moment of exultation.
One hears also the intense gathering in of time reminiscent of Dylan
Thomas's renowned lyric, "Fern Hill": "[Time] was lovely . . . /
it was air / And playing, lovely and watery."[12] In the transparent
innocence of this encounter with the natural world, both poetic
voices discover their unity with nature and eternity. For Merton,
"All these lighted things / Grow from [his] heart" (ll. 8-9) – the
source of his mystical perceptivity.

The Zen qualities of the poem return the poet to the simplicity
of its beginnings – wind and a bobwhite and the afternoon sun.
This simple scene has elaborated itself into transcendence for the
poet who has entered its contemplative moment. The outcome is a
profound experience of "sweet, irrational worship" and a recognition of his unity with all things, natural and divine. Its spareness,
its lovely metaphors which paint the mystic's worship into the
sights and sounds of the body's perceptions; the namelessness of
Being; the refusal to dichotomize the sacred/profane, transcen-
dent/immanent; the transparent reception of the experience – all
of these aspects of the poem approach a Zen-like intuition that,
for Merton, becomes an experience of ecstatic worship produced

by the Holy Spirit.

For Merton, *poesis* is the unifying and incarnational force in the universe, spoken at the Creation by the Spirit of God. The cosmos, heavenly and earthly, is fundamentally unified in nature and intention. In this paradigm, the discourse of the cosmos is a complex poetics of the Other Who is incarnate in His creation; the natural world "burns" with the presence of God although His presence cannot be confined to the cosmos or to categories of the human imagination because it transcends all human knowledge and experience.

Silence and solitude create the conditions of a "beautiful terror" that is the paradoxical force at the center of such a poetics of the mystical or incarnational. From them emanate the hiddenness, complexity, and mystery that are the categories of many of his poems. In the predawn hours of study, writing and meditation (after Night Vigils and before Lauds) in which he worked prolifically throughout the twenty-seven years of his life as a monk, Merton's poetic sensibilities continued to be informed by his insatiable desire to seek union with God. The silence of those hours, their encompassing darkness followed by the arrival of dawn's gentle light, and the accompanying music of the natural world in which he lived, combined in the variegated tones and subjects of his corpus of poetic writings. In silence, Merton finds the absence and stillness of sound which are the locus of an often unrequited desire for communication with God but which become the possibility of experiencing, unhindered, the Divine in poetry. Merton embraces the idea that God is best sought and encountered in silence. He knows and voices it as a place into which God speaks a silent language of his own.

Such silence becomes central to the essential conditions/ disciplines which look toward defining Merton's aesthetics of mysticism that ground the confounding beauty of the mystic's apprehension of the sublime, transcendent God, whose presence leaves in its wake the "burnt men" whose encounters with solitude mark them forever – Isaiah, Moses, Elijah – Merton himself, as he so movingly portrayed in his compelling epilogue to *The Seven Storey Mountain*.[13]

The primordial condition requisite to Merton's aesthetics of the mystical is solitude. It, of all of Merton's contexts, is the ground of his engagement with language, literature, art and contemplation. Paradoxically, the more he sought it, the more it eluded him, resulting in the claim by those who knew him and have studied his writings that he talked about it much more than he lived it. In one of his many self-flagellating journal entries, written, ironically, after he had been granted his hermitage and had lived his vocation for more than twenty years, he writes:

I see more and more that solitude is not something to play with. It is deadly serious. And much as I have wanted it, I have not been serious enough. It is not enough to "like solitude," or love it even. . . . Solitude is a stern mother who brooks no nonsense. The question arises: am I so full of nonsense that she will cast me out? I pray not, and think it is going to take much prayer.[14]

Merton is well aware of the relationship between solitude and the desert from which he longed to draw the wisdom of the fathers. He knows full well the profound connections that solitude has with the wisdom of God which is revealed in abandoning oneself fully to Him. It is that place where one goes to get into the middle of everything: hiddenness, complexity, divine mystery – the aesthetic conditions of mystical encounter. But he also knows how tempting it is to evade it in favor of human engagement and relationship.

The second condition of Merton's mystical poetics is silence itself. (John Cage, in his axial study, *Silence*,[15] determined that, ultimately, there is no such thing as pure silence even in an utterly sound-proofed chamber. If nothing more, there are the sounds of the body's rhythms of pulse and breath and the music of the spheres.) Deriving from his monastic experience of solitude, the silent condition of Merton's aesthetic has as its requisite the attending, listening silence from which is born the authentic, inner self into which God speaks His Divine presence. This silence reveals itself in contemplation and its attendant prayers. Merton's little volume *Contemplative Prayer* explains that contemplative prayer "is a special way of following Christ"; its "dimensions . . . are those of [our] ordinary anguish, . . . self-searching, . . . moments of nausea at [our] own vanity, falsity and capacity for betrayal."[16] Such prayer flourishes in the absence of comfort and in pure faith and is called for every time that we face the existential dread of our own spiritual decay. For Merton, this prayer was embedded in psalmody, liturgy, *lectio divina*, and their literary fruit, poetry. In this paradigm for the silent language of God, Merton combines the *dharma*, *satori*, etc. of Eastern thought and the Sufi's *point vierge* which Merton had learned about when he read an issue of *Les Mardis de Dar-es-Salaam*, provided to him by Louis Massignon, one of the twentieth century's expert scholars of Islam.

"Love Winter When the Plant Says Nothing" (*CP* 353; *IDBD* 99) is a magnificent expression of this aspect of Merton's metaphors for the silent language of God in creation. Merton elaborates this, with particular reference to this poem, in a talk he gave to novices at Loretto Academy in the sixties while identifying the vow of obedience as a language of love hidden from them but not from God's incarnating life.[17] Jonathan Montaldo, in a series of reflections on this fecund poem,[18] elaborates this concept as central to Merton's nature mysticism. The snow-covered stones are exhorted to "Hide the house of [their] growth!" (l. 4). The transparency of the Zen moment of realization is foregrounded by the secret language of the little trees which is comprised of:

> Vegetal words,
> Unlettered water,
> Daily zero. (ll. 6-8)

Here, Merton recaptures the metonym "Daily zero" as the interpretive code of the silent language of the "little forests, meekly / Touch[ing] the snow with low branches" (ll. 1-2). The curled tree is exhorted to "Pray undistracted" (l. 9), to turn its fire inward to its "weak fort" – a "burly infant spot, / A house of nothing" (ll. 14-16). This "mad place" (l. 17) of silence is realized as the seed of the plants' lives where "growth" (l. 18) is unapparent in fiery bloom. The oxymoronic force of the poem is created by the cold and wintry "little forest" with its "low branches" which is transfigured by their silence in a "golden zero / Unsetting sun" (ll. 19-20) – an inferno of life! Peace blesses this silent place and the lifeless scene becomes the dramatic stage where one "Love[s] winter when the plant says nothing" (l. 21). The silent language of the dormant trees is the language of the transcendent energies of the super/supranatural in the natural world – far beyond human imaginative capacities to create in word or deed, or even love.

"Night-Flowering Cactus" (*CP* 351-52; *IDBD* 98-99) is, for me, the most beautiful of Merton's poems metaphorizing the fruit of contemplative prayer and his aesthetics of the mystical. The power of the icon that this flower becomes, resonates not only as its virginity is completed by the echo of the "all-knowing bird of night [which] flies out" (l. 25) of the "cavern" (l. 20), but also in the "wrought passion" (l. 13) which bursts forth from the flower's blossoming, unseen and unknown in the darkness which is the ground of its Wisdom. The union of these mysteries is ecstatic in its resonances, eliciting our deepest yearnings for union with the Divine presenced in these mysteries.

Several years ago while on one of the retreats I have regularly made at the Abbey of Gethsemani and with the Sisters of Loretto, I had the opportunity to discuss Merton's mysticism with three significant participants in its fruits: Sr. Mary Luke Tobin, Br. Patrick Hart and Br. Paul Quenon. I asked Sr. Mary Luke if Merton had ever discussed his own spiritual practice with her. She answered: "No. I took that to be private and would never have had the temerity to bring it up. He took the lead in conversations and he would have rejected notoriety about his personal prayer life. He did not want to be a self-proclaimed mystic. I think he was genuinely careful about sharing his inner life outside his writings." Asked about Merton's mysticism she said:

> I can tell you a story that I've never told anyone before about Merton's understanding of the natural and the Divine. He had come over to Loretto to say Mass for us and decided to do so beside the lake. It was the first time he was saying Mass here without his vestments on and according to the new rules (after Vatican II). I was to prepare things ahead of time but I forgot to take the water along which is meant to be added to the wine at a certain point in the sacrament. One of the sisters, realizing this, reached up at the moment when the water was needed and shook the dew from the tree overhead. Father Merton was not in any way nonplussed. He continued as though it were the natural course for events to take. For me that was a picture of Merton's mysticism – the natural and the Divine in one sacred moment.[19]

Brother Patrick was more direct in his answer to my query: "Was Merton a mystic?" "Yes," he answered. "He gained mystical intuitions from the natural / supernatural which gave him insight into reality, the Ground of Being." We continued by discussing possible connections between Merton's poetry and his spirituality.[20]

Br. Paul Quenon elaborated these connections by explaining that Merton's mysticism flowed out of the poetry, psychologically. His poetry is at the core of his writing. He had to establish his imagination at the core of some intuition, but then he had to spell it out in terms of an essay. His poems were based in his experience; the essays were about that experience. What's amazing is that for someone who lived the simple life, he writes in such a lush style. It's like there was some kind of a compensation mechanism involved. He was so rich, so voluble interiorly.

About Merton's mysticism, Quenon said that it

was not about locutions or levitations or anything like that. At least not primarily. I mean there might have some aspect of that, like the "jumping over time" that a person can have. But his writings about mysticism have an authenticity because his understanding of it comes not just from describing what he read in books but from his own experience. John of the Cross and St. Bernard gave him a vocabulary for it but you can tell from his language that it's alive.[21]

When we concluded by talking about the eighteen poems written for M. (the student nurse of Merton's affections in the mid-sixties), we considered the idea that "they were the summit of his spirituality, the moment of integration of his mysticism and his sexuality. His interest in M. is the transposition of his mystical experience onto his human experience. It was a fulfillment for him. For instance, when he's lying in his bed and he awakens and realizes that she is awakening somewhere else, it's the experience of their co-indwelling at a distance – similar to God and human beings in mystical union."

A close reading of "With the World in My Bloodstream" (*CP* 615-18; *IDBD* 188-90), one of the *Eighteen Poems* written for M., recognizes the metaphor of geography for the experience of romantic love which the human can know but not account for nor explicate. Merton imposes the landscapes of the hospital onto the inner landscape of his love for his nurse. The extremities of both topographies are present in the collusion of sight/sound imagery which is depicted in the "musical machinery / All around overhead" (ll. 3-4), the "world's machinery . . . in . . . the hot musical building" (ll. 15-17). He remembers his childhood which "remains / One of the city's living cells" (ll. 19-20); "All the freights in the night / Swing [his] dark technical bed / All around overhead /

And wake the questions in [his] blood" (ll. 25-28).

His awareness includes the experience of his own body "Bleeding in a numbered bed / Though all [his] veins run / With Christ and with the stars' plasm" (ll. 32-34). The cosmic drama of which his own experience is a part then heightens with the realization of his anguished sexuality and visceral longing for its expression now confined by his vow of celibacy:

> I grow hungry . . .
> For the unmarried fancy
> And the wild gift I made in those days
> For all the compromising answers
> All the gambles and blue rhythms
> Of individual despair . . . .
>
> Dancing in the empty room
> All around overhead
> While the frail body of Christ
> Sweats in a technical bed
> I am Christ's lost cell
> His childhood and desert age
> His descent into hell. (ll. 54, 57-61, 87-93)

The vulnerability and passion mapped here is a geography without center or polarity; only "the spark without identity / Circles the empty ceiling" (ll. 96-97). This spark is the emptiness within him which is "lost . . . in Eckhart's Castle" (l. 83) – the architecture of mystical contemplation. In the unfolding metaphor, the impact of his pain, the love he already feels for M., and his mystic spirituality converge in the poet's identification of the utter desolation of Christ's descent into hell. His words do not have the capacity to reduce his experience to substance; rather, the metaphors he chooses represent an infinite desire to acknowledge the invisible and unknown realities of his existence. Into their silent inexpressibility speak Merton's explorations in the geography which is the "beautiful terror" of his solitary life as a celibate monk.

Ultimately, silence and solitude create the conditions that are the force at the center of Merton's poetics. From them emanate the hiddenness, complexity, and mystery that are its categories. Silence becomes the fertile ground of his prolific writings and at the heart of his vexation about the seeming contradictions of the contemplative and writerly lives, there is an inner core of transcendent values

– silence, peace, and transformational experience. At the deepest level, Merton experienced the mystic's profound realization that silence is a language of its own with as much influence and power as words. The poet is silenced in the face of the ontological experiences which take place without naming or labeling, as they do in his mystical poems of the natural world, of innocence, of transcendence. Often with wit and humor, and always with intelligence, he portrays his refusal to be defeated by the notion that *logos* has been irreparably fractured, form from meaning.[22]

Finally, Merton's appropriation of that silence invests him with powers, mystical and imaginative, which allow him to metaphorize the unspeakable, creating a poetics of immanence and transcendence from his experience of the human and the divine. In such moments, the poet, as iconoclast, calls forth secrets from the un/conscious and forces the soul from its anonymity into personality. Words, then, emerge from silence, and lead into the silence which is God's speech. As such, poetry borders on three other modes of statement – light, music, and silence – which George Steiner has called the "proof of the transcendent presence in the fabric of the world."[23] Merton's poetry "dances in the water of life" in which sound and silence create their own music and art – the fruit of a mystical poetics engaging the Spirit of God in his life as a "stranger" and a monk of Gethsemani.

Endnotes

1. Thomas Merton, *The Collected Poems of Thomas Merton* (New York: New Directions, 1977) 631-32 (subsequent references will be cited as "*CP*" parenthetically in the text); Thomas Merton, *In the Dark before Dawn: New Selected Poems*, ed. Lynn R. Szabo (New York: New Directions, 2005) 43-44 (subsequent references will be cited as "*IDBD*" parenthetically in the text); first published in *Commonweal* 85 (December 9, 1966) 294.

2. In a recording of his funeral mass eulogy for Fr. Stephen, Merton reminds his listeners that Fr. Stephen beckons everyone "to look and see what's in front of [their] noses" – the anonymous, enigmatic, and unknowable, characterized in Fr. Stephen and his passing (archives of the Thomas Merton Center, Bellarmine University, Louisville, KY).

3. Thomas Merton, *Day of a Stranger* (Salt Lake City: Gibbs M. Smith, 1981) 43; subsequent references will be cited as "*DS*" parenthetically in the text.

4. Thomas Merton, *Love and Living*, ed. Naomi Burton Stone and Brother Patrick Hart (New York: Farrar, Straus, Giroux, 1979) 54-55.

5. Frederick Smock, *Pax Intrantibus: A Meditation on the Poetry of Thomas Merton* (Frankfort, KY: Broadstone Books, 2007) 77; subsequent references will be cited as "Smock" parenthetically in the text.

6. Thomas Merton, *The Strange Islands* (New York: New Directions, 1957) 43-78; *CP* 247-73.

7. Thomas Merton, *Cables to the Ace* (New York: New Directions, 1968).

8. Thomas Merton, *The Literary Essays of Thomas Merton*, ed. Patrick Hart, OCSO (New York: New Directions, 1981) 463; subsequent references will be cited as *"LE"* parenthetically in the text.

9. Thomas Merton, *"Honorable Reader": Reflections on My Work*, ed. Robert E. Daggy (New York: Crossroad, 1989) 111.

10. Edward Said, *Beginnings: Intention and Method* (New York: Columbia University Press, 1985) 280-81.

11. Thomas Merton, *The Courage for Truth: Letters to Writers*, ed. Christine M. Bochen (New York: Farrar, Straus, Giroux, 1993) 277.

12. Dylan Thomas, *The Poems of Dylan Thomas* (New York: New Directions, 1971) 195.

13. Thomas Merton, *The Seven Storey Mountain* (New York: Harcourt, Brace, 1948) 422-23.

14. Thomas Merton, *Dancing in the Water of Life: Seeking Peace in the Hermitage. Journals, vol. 5: 1963-1965*, ed. Robert E. Daggy (San Francisco: HarperCollins, 1997) 211 [2/26/65].

15. John Cage, *Silence: Lectures and Writings* (Cambridge, MA: MIT Press, 1966).

16. Thomas Merton, *Contemplative Prayer* (New York: Herder & Herder, 1969) 25.

17. Unpublished (archives of the Sisters of Loretto, Loretto, KY).

18. Jonathan Montaldo, "Loving Winter When the Plant Says Nothing: Thomas Merton's Spirituality in His Private Journals," in Patrick F. O'Connell, ed., *The Vision of Thomas Merton* (Notre Dame, IN: Ave Maria Press, 2003) 99-117.

19. Interview conducted July 2, 2002 at Sisters of Loretto Convent, Loretto, KY. (The story has been recounted in various forms to others.)

20. Interview conducted July 11, 2002 at the Abbey of Our Lady of Gethsemani, Trappist, KY.

21. Interview conducted July 11, 2002 at the Abbey of Our Lady of Gethsemani, Trappist, KY.

22. He wrote three seminal essays in which he manifests his poetics in the face of modern controversies, literary, religious, and political: "Poetry, Symbolism, and Typology" (*LE* 327-37, first published in Thomas Merton, *Bread in the Wilderness* [New York: New Directions, 1953] 51-64); "Poetry and Contemplation: A Reappraisal" (*LE* 338-54, first published in *The*

Commonweal, 69 [October 24, 1958] 87-92); and the famous "Message to Poets," written for a gathering of Latin American poets in Mexico City in 1964 (*LE* 371-74, first published in Thomas Merton, *Raids on the Unspeakable* [New York: New Directions, 1966] 155-61).

23. George Steiner, *Language and Silence: Essays on Language, Literature and the Inhuman* (New Haven, CT: Yale University Press, 1998) 367.

Wholeness in Thomas Merton's Poetry

Ross Labrie

Wholeness was an important concept for Thomas Merton both in terms of his poetics and his poetry. Merton perceived the world as most flawed in being fragmented so that the separate pieces of being – individuals, for example – pulled narcissistically towards their own centers and away from harmony and unity with others and with God. Moreover, Merton was personally sensitive to the problem of fragmentation and the need for wholeness. As a number of scholars have observed, this was because of the competing demands of monastic contemplation and Merton's felt calling as a writer.[1] Furthermore, as Michael Higgins has suggested, Merton's life was "fraught with contradictions, polarities, and wild paradoxes" that would never be reconciled but rather held in a state of tension throughout his life.[2] The problem, as Merton experienced it in the 1940s and 1950s, was that the demands of monastic contemplation and writing poetry conflicted because the writing short-circuited the process of contemplation by cannibalizing the fruits of the contemplative experience. This resulted, as Merton maintained in two important articles, in the sacrifice of a higher good – the felt presence of God in the soul – to a lesser good – the creation of a poem.[3] The tenaciousness of the problem is evident in Merton's admission in 1962 that while it was possible to doubt aspects of his monastic vocation – a doubt that he would "have to live with" – it was not possible to doubt that he was a writer.[4] While Merton readers will not likely question the depth of his monastic vocation, the polarization of his dual callings at times could be frustrating for him.

In terms of his poetics Merton described the poet Edwin Muir in 1966 as a writer who through his poetry reached the "intimate, that is ontological, sources of life" (*LE* 30). The artist's imagination was "ontological" in that it perceived the world as imbued with the wisdom of its Creator. It was also ontological in being capable of perceiving alternate worlds by which one might evaluate this world, a view of art that is apparent in William Blake, who had a considerable influence on Merton.[5] Blake's vision of the marriage of heaven and hell, for example, overcame the incompleteness and

41

dualism that for Blake marked the conventional Christianity of his day. Moreover, by searching out analogies that reveal hidden resemblances and unexpected meanings, the poet united, Merton argued, that which all but the deepest philosophical insights into experience would regard as fragmentary: "There is in all visible things an invisible fecundity," he wrote in his beautiful prose poem, *Hagia Sophia*,[6] and a "hidden wholeness" (*CP* 363). In the case of *Hagia Sophia* wholeness is found by the poet in the representation of God as both male and female.

Through the analogies embedded in metaphor and symbol the poet, Merton maintained, connected parts of being where reason might not perceive the connectedness. Citing Paul Tillich, George Kilcourse has noted the role of the religious poet as an ontologist in creating metaphorical language that can "mediate" ultimate realities (Kilcourse 51). In this respect, in an essay entitled "Theology of Creativity," Merton suggested that the poet intuitively sought to recreate the world in the "image and likeness of God" (*LE* 368). Such a re-creation of the world, made possible through the poet's imagining of alternate worlds, meant that the poet's vision was essentially paradisal as Merton explained in an essay on the poetry of Louis Zukofsky.[7] By a paradisal vision Merton meant that one saw the world and being itself as a whole including its creational origin in God. With such a wholeness of perception, Merton argued, the poet could, among other things, assign to evil its very limited place in the scheme of things. Otherwise, he argued, there was the risk that evil could dominate our view of the world.

Wholeness often presents itself in Merton's poetry as an inter-subjective consciousness of the sharing of being. In the exquisite poem, "Night-Flowering Cactus" (*CP* 351-52), for example, which appeared in *Emblems of a Season of Fury* in 1963, Merton speaks through and, as it were, *for* the flower in a delicate projection of a shared participation in being:

He who sees my purity
Dares not speak of it.
When I open once for all my impeccable bell
No one questions my silence:
The all-knowing bird of night flies out of my mouth. (ll. 21-25)

The intimacy of speaker and flower accommodates a perception of their shared creatureliness as is indicated in the image of the divine bird of night. Moreover, the "bird of night," a thinly veiled reference to God, indicates Merton's awareness of a full range of response to the divine presence in that God is present both intimately and mysteriously in the darkness of the transcendental and also immanently in creatures. Indeed, God is present in "ten thousand things," as Merton put it in *Hagia Sophia*, as "one fulness and one Wisdom" (*CP* 281).

A similar sort of awareness of the Creator immanent in things occurs in the poem "In Silence" (*CP* 280-81), which was published in *The Strange Islands* in 1957:

> O be still, while
> You are still alive,
> And all things live around you
> Speaking (I do not hear)
> To your own being,
> Speaking by the Unknown
> That is in you and in themselves. (ll. 22-28)

In the final stanza of the poem the stones burn, a fresh and paradoxical metaphor that conveys the speaker's strong perception of the living presence of God within them and hence of the ontological wholeness that underlies the speaker's vision of them.

In "In Silence" Merton appears to come close to pantheism since he depicts the stones that absorb his gaze as trying to "speak" the name of the human observer (l. 4). Although Merton conceded that some readers might see him as a pantheist, he was not a pantheist, as he explained in the opening pages of *Raids on the Unspeakable*. He asks the reader in that case, for example, not to mistake his figure of the Atlas mountains for a "world soul" or a "cosmic Adam."[8] As is evident in the above passage about the "Unknown" in nature it is quite clear, however, that in his projection of inter-subjective consciousness Merton distinguished between a God who is immanent in nature and the Christian God to whom he alludes who is both immanent and transcendent. One can notice this immanence and transcendence in "Song for Nobody" (*CP* 337-38), which appeared in *Emblems of a Season of Fury* in 1963. In that poem, which is about a sunflower, there is present in the flower's dark eye "Someone" who is "awake" (l. 11). Merton's vision of the cosmos does not involve an overlapping of God, humans, and other created beings but rather a picture of unity. This is indicated in the speaker's saying in the poem "O Sweet Irrational Worship" (*CP* 344-45) that by ceasing to "question the sun" the speaker has become "light" (ll. 3-4). For a gnostic such a complete identification of being and consciousness might be expected but in the same introductory essay in *Raids on the Unspeakable* in which Merton distances himself from pantheism he also distances himself from Gnosticism (*RU* 2). Thus, Merton's picturing of the wholeness of being is subject to some qualification. In particular, one can say that throughout his life he leaned towards existentialism. In a review of a book about William Blake in 1968, for example, he declared that the idea of God as *"process"* or as *"becoming"* was less significant than the idea of God as *"act."*[9] Thus, wholeness for Merton included its multiplicity and richness of being as well as its origin in God.

In this respect, in his well-known poem "Elegy for the Monastery Barn" (*CP* 288-89), published in *The Strange Islands* in 1957, Merton gives unexpected, ontological depth to what might otherwise be interpreted as a light and even whimsical poem:

> Fifty invisible cattle, the past years
> Assume their solemn places one by one.
> This is the little minute of their destiny.
> Here is their meaning found. Here is their end.
>
> Laved in the flame as in a Sacrament
> The brilliant walls are holy
> In their first-last hour of joy. (ll. 28-35)

The freshness of the poem stems from the gap between the mundane cattle barn and the momentous, eschatological drama that gradually comes to surround it. The poem illustrates Merton's belief that, even when there is no formal reference to God, transcendence can be part of the viewer's vision of being, even in an ostensibly unremarkable matter.[10] What counts is the observer's ability to see transcendently, that is, to see the radiance of being because of the continued presence of God in it.

Paradoxically, some might say, in his search for wholeness Merton immersed himself in silence and asceticism. Indeed, in his poetry the monastic world is often characterized by images of denial and negation – especially those of night and of the desert. As his journals and poems make evident, night is the time when Merton was awake while the rest of the world slept. Night was an occasion for contemplation, as can be seen in the early poem, "The Holy Child's Song" (*CP* 55-56):

When midnight occupied the porches of the Poet's reason
Sweeter than any bird
He heard the Holy Child. (ll. 1-3)

The nocturnal setting allows the mind to be set free from the dominance of the eye and reason, faculties that ordinarily prevail during the day. So freed, the mind is able to receive God directly and intuitively using capacities that lie dormant, as it were, in daytime. Similarly, in "The Trappist Abbey: Matins" (*CP* 45-46), another early poem, the speaker calls to his soul to "Wake in the cloisters of the lonely night" (l. 21). By the same token it is in the darkness of the night, Merton suggests in yet another early poem, "After the Night Office – Gethsemani Abbey" (*CP* 108-109) that the souls of the awakened monks "have their noon" (l. 13). As the poem makes clear, darkness permits the full range of the senses and the non-reasoning parts of the mind to emerge: "We touch the rays we cannot see, / We feel the light that seems to sing" (ll. 23-24).

The senses of touch and hearing are recruited in the darkness to provide access to the unknown depths of the soul. In Merton's posthumously published poem "The Night of Destiny" (*CP* 634-35), the speaker observes:

> Only in the Void
> Are all ways one:
>
> Only in the night
> Are all the lost
> Found. (ll. 26-30)

Here as elsewhere in Merton's writings one finds the suggestion that in the emptiness is fullness. The paradox is sustained by the riches of perception and feeling that accompany the shedding, even temporarily, of the comforts and enticements of the material world that isolate the mind and emotions from a sympathetic contact with its deeper capacities and with the rest of being.

Merton did not reject the eye, which is a prominent focus in many of his other poems, but rather he was intent on showing that our perceptions are not restricted to what the eye encounters. Rather like Helen Keller, who, without sight and hearing, showed readers how the other senses might be recruited in order to register perception and meaning and so refresh and enlarge our ways of knowing and understanding, Merton's nocturnal awareness takes in that which, heavily reliant on the eye in general, we tend to overlook. Merton's practice as a poet shows someone who was fully aware that the lyric poem, though among the smallest of the art forms, was also in a sense among the largest. This was because poetry, as opposed to prose, engaged all of the reader's senses in an attempt to provide a holistic experience of reality. In this respect he was in accord with the poet Allen Tate, who, in asserting the cognitive value of poetry, described it as a source of knowledge about a "whole object."[11]

The image of the desert flanks the nocturnal in Merton's poetry as a source of richness that paradoxically issues from emptiness. On one level the desert is the regime of asceticism that enables the soul to be freed from distractions and unwelcome desires, a sacrificial arena in which the soul offers itself to God. This is evident in the poem, "The Candlemas Procession" (*CP* 92-93), which was published in *A Man in the Divided Sea* in 1946:

> Nor burn we now with brown and smoky flames, but bright
> Until our sacrifice is done,
> (By which not we, but You are known) (ll. 18-20).

The imagery recalls T. S. Eliot's burning images in *The Waste Land*, which are allied there as well with the motif of purification. As these lines suggest, though, the burning is not an end in itself but rather a preparation of the self so that it might more easily turn toward God. Such is the import of the poem, "Two Desert Fathers" (*CP* 165-69), from *Figures for an Apocalypse* (1947), in which the true purpose of living in the desert is revealed in the example of St. Paul the Hermit:

> Because God, God
> The One I hunt and never capture,
> Opened His door, and lo, His loneliness invaded you. (ll. 43-45)

The ultimate purpose of asceticism, of living in the desert, as with the ancient fathers who lived in the deserts of Syria and Egypt, was to allow the desert hermit to meet face to face with God, something that Merton longed to do in his monastic "desert" in Kentucky.

However, it is important to realize that for Merton the desert was not just a place of denial in which by default as it were God was invited to appear. Rather, the desert was a place of love and in this sense symbolic of a greater wholeness than ideas about asceticism conventionally suggest. In his journal *Conjectures of a Guilty Bystander* Merton suggests that human beings begin by loving life, then themselves, then others. In this way they come closer to their own fulfillment or wholeness and in addition help others to attain this wholeness.[12] All of this leads to some central conclusions about the night and desert images in Merton's poetry. First of all, the desert for Merton became finally the only place, he said, where the soul could find any kind of "stability and peace" (*NSC* 275). Secondly, the desert in Merton, rather like Robert Frost's well-known image of bare November days, is the empty place that through its emptiness invites filling. In Merton's poems, for example, the images of autumn and winter, so unpromising for the eye, stir reflections at the bottom of the soul connected to his spiritual journey. Both the night and the desert in Merton's poetry silhouette the parts of the self that are different from the ego-self with its peremptory authority and its tendency to divide the self from the rest of being through self-consciousness, a constant threat to contemplation in Merton's writings.

Furthermore, both the night and the desert give rise to a freedom that is otherwise difficult to obtain, in that through their asceticism, in particular through the bypassing of the ego-self's anxieties and desires, the underlying true self emerges. This can be seen in the poem "Elias – Variations on a Theme" (*CP* 239-45) where the speaker observes that the "free" person has been "Built / Upon his own inscrutable pattern / Clear, unmistakable, not invented by himself alone / Or for himself, but for the universe also" (ll. 153-56). The poem suggests that religious contemplation will create an independent self that is sufficiently detached from its own fears and desires as to attach itself to others and to the rest of being. The reason that contemplation, fed by the atmosphere of night and desert, gives rise to such independence is that the self, distanced from the allurements and distractions of the material world, is thereby cleared of illusion, immune from the "fantasies of our own mind" and the egoistic "brutalities of our own will" (*CGB* 142).

Merton's preoccupation with wholeness encompassed the mind itself. Although he was wary about the habit of the reasoning mind to silence other parts of the mind, Merton's is clearly a reasonable voice. He was a reasonable person who nonetheless harbored a distrust of reason, not because of its inherent weaknesses but rather because of the tendency of some to see reason as the only part of the mind that one need respect. In *The Ascent to Truth* (1951) for example, he argued that in terms of religious contemplation reason was not admitted to the depth in which the will was engaged by "an obscure experience of immediate union with God."[13] Apart from the importance of the will, Merton consistently emphasized the crucial role of intuition in facilitating religious contemplation. He thought of intuition as an immediate apprehension of reality. The process started with an intuition which is then augmented methodically and empirically until the intuition was verified or not, as it were, by the gathering of subsequent evidence. What gave weight to Merton's understanding of intuition was his attaching of it to a fundamental discernment of the ultimate reality present in being. All human beings, he stressed repeatedly, have a fundamental intuition of being and of the relationship of their own being to their Creator and thereby to other created beings. This "metaphysical" understanding of being, as Merton thought of it, involved the apprehension of a truth that was "intuitively" present in "every man who lives" (*AT* 204). For Merton this latent, metaphysical, intuitive understanding was intensely available to poets especially, as can be seen in the following lines from his poetic sequence *Cables to the Ace* (1968):[14]

> I think poetry must
> I think it must
> Stay open all night
> In beautiful cellars. (#53 [*CP* 431])

Here the intuitive insights of the contemplative are one with those of the poet. What makes these intuitions possible, as has been suggested, is the nocturnal darkness. In its facilitating of intuitive leaps, darkness prevented the sort of divisive self-consciousness that Merton associated with the eye and with reason and with the tendency of each to distinguish the observer from the observed, thereby perpetuating the dividedness of experience and being.

While many Christian writers in Merton's time looked askance at the work of Freud, Merton was hospitable towards Freud for calling attention to the subconscious. At the very least, Merton argued, one could be grateful to Freud for opening up the fuller landscape of the mind and in that way exposing to criticism what Merton called the "ethic of good intentions." By shining a light on the hidden brutality and selfishness that may lurk in the subconscious, Merton maintained, the individual had the opportunity to bring his or her "*whole* house in order" (*CGB* 98). In this way psychoanalysis, Merton concluded, could perform a valuable service for

Christianity. While Merton obviously did not share Freud's view of sexuality as the most important explanatory principle underlying subconscious-driven behavior, nevertheless he concurred with Freud that dreams, for example, could be seen as a conversation between one part of the mind and another. Moreover, like Jung, Merton saw dreams as opening a world in which all human beings lived and that was therefore a source of unity among them. In his evocative prose poem *Hagia Sophia* he wrote:

> I am like all mankind awakening from all the dreams that ever were dreamed in all the nights of the world. It is like the One Christ awakening in all the separate selves that ever were separate and isolated and alone in all the lands of the earth. It is like all minds coming back together into awareness from all distractions, cross-purposes and confusions, into unity of love. (*CP* 363-64)

Perhaps the most surprising part of this reflection is the immanence of Christ within dream and within the subconscious. While Merton, as has already been suggested, was not unaware of the evil that could be present in the subconscious, he also saw the subconscious and the unconscious as deeper layers of the self where a kind of creaturely wisdom spoke of the majesty and love of God for creatures and for the goodness that was latent within them.

Merton's sense of the fertile range and depth of the mind is evident in the poetic sequence *The Geography of Lograire* (1969):[15]

WHY I HAVE A WET FOOTPRINT ON TOP OF MY MIND

> To begin a walk
> To make an air
> Of knowing where to go
> To print
> Speechless pavements
> With secrets in my
> Forgotten feet. . . .
>
> To have passed there
> Walked without a word
> To have felt
> All my old grounds
> Forgotten world
> All along

> Dream places
> Words in my feet
> Explain the air of all
> Feel it under (me)
> Stand
> Stand in the unspoken
> A cool street
> An air of legs
> An air of visions (ll. 1-7, 16-30 [*CP* 497-98]).

In this intensely personal poem with its startling opening image one sees something of Merton's anatomy of the mind when it is considered as a *whole*. The image of the wet footprint shows the mind grounded in physical and instinctual memory and that the mind's activities at various levels are pictured as inter-penetrable areas of response and understanding. In this view of the mind there is a seamless relationship between the conscious and sub-conscious giving rise to the paradox of the subconscious retaining of past experience even when the conscious mind has forgotten it. In the excerpt above, the continuum between dream, words and feet suggests a distributed sharing of memory and of meaning by the different parts of the mind, including a significant role given to parts easily overlooked by consciousness and by reason. In addition to the rational and deliberative aspects of consciousness, the speaker in the poem emphasizes the semantic importance of the subconscious both in shaping conscious thought without our realizing it and keeping the *fullness* of our memories intact should we care to look for them elsewhere than in consciousness and reason. For the poet who is the narrator of this prologue from *The Geography of Lograire* such semantic multiplicity in the kinds of words heard from various parts of the mind and self is precisely what poets are equipped to translate and to integrate with other layers of experience and awareness.

For Merton, as for Jung, the unconscious with its rich store of archetypes was connected with the underlying meaning of life.[16] In contrast, Merton characterized the fears, drives, and anxieties of the Freudian subconscious as connected to the exterior self.[17] Nevertheless, as has been suggested, the Freudian subconscious was a part of the whole, a part of which one should become aware so as to integrate it with the rest of the self. In Merton's anatomy of the mind the unconscious extended in all directions beyond the conscious mind (*NSC* 137-38). Part of this sea of unconsciousness included the Freudian subconscious, which is flooded by the animal instincts and drives that at times powerfully impinge on the conscious mind and the ego. In Merton's view the subconscious and the instinctual mind must be accepted as a mysterious and intended part of creation although he insists that it must be brought into harmony with one's higher faculties. By higher faculties he did not just mean reason but rather a kind of imprinting of the Creator's mind and providential wisdom, which Merton located in the higher reaches of the soul, well beyond the conscious and the rational. Religious faith brought the individual into contact with this divine consciousness, as it were, both within the mind and through a kind of intuitive extrapolation beyond it to the whole of being. With his eye ever on wholeness Merton argued that the role of faith was to integrate all of the unconscious, at both its highest and lowest reaches, with the rest of one's mind and life (*NSC* 138). In the case of the Freudian subconscious this would involve a pulling of the subconscious in the direction of both reason and of our highest spiritual consciousness. Faith, as he put it, "subjects our reason to the hidden spiritual forces that are *above* it" (*NSC* 138).

The poet, as the artist generally, Merton believed, drew on the subconscious and the unconscious in making poems and in particular in making and using symbols. In so doing the poet intuitively sought to unite human beings, nature and God in what Merton called a "living and sacred synthesis."[18] All things were symbolic, Merton observed, by their very nature, i.e., they pointed to something, to a Creator and to a loving Sustainer of all life in and beyond themselves.[19] The poet's symbols, therefore, are, in Merton's view, intuitive, ontological pictures of the whole, of both proximate and ultimate reality. Such is the meaning of poems like "Song for Our Lady of Cobre" (*CP* 29-30):

> The white girls open their arms like clouds,
> The black girls close their eyes like wings:
> Angels bow down like bells,
> Angels look up like toys,
>
> Because the heavenly stars
> Stand in a ring:
> And all the pieces of the mosaic, earth,
> Get up and fly away like birds. (ll. 6-13)

The poem was composed extemporaneously during a trip to Cuba in 1940 during the time when, as a young man, Merton felt the power of his religious conversion. Parallel in their distinctive beauty, a parallelism that is mirrored in the syntactical parallelism of the lines, the girls become *one* in their symbolic significance in that both groups are pictured as celestial beings – clouds in the case of the white girls, birds in the case of the black girls. As celestial beings they are capable of lifting the earth, that is, lifting other human beings up from the plane of the material and the literal into a spiritualized cosmos.

As has been intimated, for Merton the poetic symbol, when used with its full ontological weight, expressed the contextualization or wholeness of all things as the offspring of a supernal creative intelligence and providence. As Merton put it in his essay "Poetry, Symbolism, and Typology" (1953), the reason for the use of symbol instead of direct statement had to do with the challenge of getting language to express more that it could be expected to do conventionally. For Merton symbolism proceeded from the barrenness of language, and thus involved not direct statement but the artful arrangement of picture and sound to convey the fullness of experience in all of its complexity and paradox and irony (*LE* 327). The arrangement of symbolic pictures would allow for the full range of sensations, emotions and meanings associated with a particular object to be transferred to another object, thereby illuminating that object in a fresh and meaningful way. Moreover, in choosing symbols that connected the poem's foreground drama with its ontological roots the poet would be able to appeal to the deeper reaches of the self. In this way, working through the senses, symbols evoke meanings that elude, but that need not be in conflict with, rational discourse. Merton demonstrated his acute awareness of the ontological dimensions of symbolism in an essay entitled "Symbolism: Communication or Communion?" (1966). There he was struck by the ontological depth of primitive art in which hunter/artists portrayed their feelings of oneness with the animals they hunted and with whom they shared an existence as creatures (*LL* 70-72).

One of the most arresting ontological symbols in Merton's poetry is contained in "Elegy for a Trappist" (*CP* 631-32) from 1966. The poem eulogized Father Stephen, who was something of an eccentric at the Abbey of Gethsemani in that he was obsessed with flowers and with gardening. Having been forced by his abbot for many years to restrain his passion for gardening so that he might live the balanced life of a Cistercian, Father Stephen was later permitted to give as much time to gardening as he wished, and he did so. Merton notes that the flowers that Father Stephen grew were typically given to visitors or placed decoratively around the monastery so that all might enjoy their beauty. Into this innocuous setting Merton introduces the symbol of the Leviathan. The symbol emerges from some otherwise prosaic detail in the poem as Merton describes the coming and going onto the monastery grounds of a large and noisy truck just before dawn on the day of Father Stephen's burial:

> The brief glare
> Lit up the grottos, pyramids and presences
> One by one
> Then the gate swung red
> And clattered shut in the giant lights
> And everything was gone
>
> As if Leviathan
> Hot on the scent of some other blood
> Had passed you by
> And never saw you hiding in the flowers. (ll. 26-35)

The poem's complex tone depends upon the imbalance of the innocent and ostensibly inconsequential figure of Father Stephen alongside the epic and evil figure of the biblical Leviathan. The speaker implies that Father Stephen's eccentricity will likely cause him to be bypassed as a possible subject of veneration by church officialdom. Ironically, the Leviathan concurs with this view and gives Father Stephen a pass as someone too inconsequential for even evil to bother with. All of these shades of meaning occur in the poem without any direct commentary. Moreover, the different and even contrary views of Father Stephen – the humor, pathos, and yet deep respect and affection with which he is treated in the poem – are suspended in a complexity that is the hallmark of lyric poetry in its attempt to capture the whole of experience. The effect of this complexity is that, Merton's poem excepted, one comes to see the world as barer and poorer than it otherwise might have been had Father Stephen's significance as one who was wholly immersed in God been more generally recognized.

In Merton's view the distinction between symbolic and literal communication had everything to do with *language*, and not only with the choice of words but crucially with their arrangement, so that the paraphrasing of a poem would always be problematic. In the aforementioned essay, "Poetry, Symbolism, and Typology," he wrote:

> [The poet] seeks above all to put words together in such a way that they exercise a mysterious and vital reactivity among themselves, and so release their secret content of associations to produce in the reader an experience that enriches the depths of his spirit in a manner quite unique. A good poem induces an experience that could not be produced by any other combination of words. (*LE* 327)

The poet, then, is as much architect as wordsmith, placing words next to each other so as to create a field of associations and fresh analogies that imply rather than articulate meaning. In this way poetic language can transcend the limiting, semantic parameters of straightforward prose. Although Merton judged the focus on language to be the important difference between prose and poetry, he had strong reservations about language. The businessman, the politician, and the propagandist, he argued in "Message to Poets," were addicted to the power of language while the poets explored the mystery of experience as what he paradoxically termed "ministers of silence" (*RU* 160). Language had been given to human beings by the Creator, Merton suggested, not to obtain power over others but rather to point to the ontological silence where language fell short. In fact, as he noted in *Thoughts in Solitude* (1958), the communication of God's reality could be subverted through a "conceptual unreality" produced by a "no-man's land of language."[20] In spite of this, God could remain present to an individual after language had receded. In that eventuality God's "brightness," Merton indicated, would remain intact "on the shores of our own being" (*TS* 86).

In *The Ascent to Truth* (1951) he insisted that no verbal expressiveness could adequately express the reality of God (*AT* 92). This awareness of the limits of language in conveying ultimate reality was one of the aspects of Zen that attracted Merton. In *Thoughts in Solitude* he attempted to reconcile the tension between language and silence by suggesting that silence should precede a final utterance, a final glimpse of life's significance (*TS* 91). Language, however, was needed in order to bring human beings to the threshold of silence where large realities exist (*TS* 114). In fact, in *No Man Is an Island* (1955), he proposed a paradigm of experience that included alternating waves of language and silence.[21] As Lynn Szabo has observed, this was in fact Merton's strategy as a poet, evoking words from the silence of contemplative experience and then following the return of those words into the silence.[22] As he indicated in a recorded talk at the Abbey of Gethsemani in the 1960s, Merton thought of himself as creating pools of silence in his poetry through the manipulation of rhythm and through the use of shorter lines to increase the space given to silence.[23]

For Merton *music* straddled the border between language and silence as in the poetry of Louis Zukofsky (*LE* 129). This allowed poetry to express a fuller or more whole reality than would otherwise be the case, since the ineffable evocativeness of music, Merton believed, opened up the large, unspoken realities at the heart of being. Merton was accustomed to treating poetry as a musical form, as is evident in his reading of Rilke, whose poems he sang aloud, "making up *Lieder*."[24] In his essay "In Silentio" Merton spoke of the music that one could hear in the silence of the wisdom implanted in human beings by their Creator and of the music of one's own unconscious being.[25] The reader is able to hear music in poetry, even in silent reading, through an inner ear, as it were. This creates a mental landscape in which, as opposed to conceptual speech, one is drawn beyond the literal into a fuller response to being that involves the whole reader, whose senses, subconscious memories, thoughts, and emotions are all engaged at once.

Furthermore, in one of the taped conferences to his fellow monks in the 1960s Merton suggested that the poem as song inevitably, as all music essentially did, engendered a loving state of mind that easily opened out into a blissful consciousness of being ("Poetry of Paradise"). Such is the theme of the poem, "A Psalm" (*CP* 220-21), which was published in *The Tears of the Blind Lions* (1949):

> But sound is never half so fair
> As when that music turns to air
> And the universe dies of excellence. (ll. 15-17)

As is suggested here, the music of poetry, conveyed through its rhyming echelons of sound, allows the reader to migrate past the boundaries of conventional experience into a spiritualized cosmos. Having crossed this threshold, one enters a space in which all minds are united, as is made evident in the posthumously published poem "Rilke's Epitaph" (*CP* 620):

> *Music (O pure*
> *Contradiction)*
> *Everybody's*
> *Vision.* (ll. 15-18)

Here one sees the role of music in reconciling the poles of rational discourse through an intuitive perception of oneness that unites both argument (*"Vision"*) and arguer (*"Everybody's"*).

Nevertheless, although he recognized the power of music in widening the circle of poetic meaning, Merton was also acutely aware of the tension between language and silence, as can be seen in Canto #80 of *Cables to the Ace* (1968):

> Slowly slowly
> Comes Christ through the ruins
> Seeking the lost disciple
> A timid one
> Too literate
> To believe words (#80 [*CP* 449]).

The poem deftly conveys a wariness about the ability of language to bring one close to ultimate reality, producing a stalemate that the figure of Christ overcomes in the poem by moving in person towards the marooned soul. In some of his poems Merton lowers the audibility of his poems to a level close to silence and stillness in order to accommodate the role of both language and silence in the continuum of poetic meaning. This can be seen in "The Reader" (*CP* 202-203) from 1949. The scene in the poem is enveloped in silence prior to Merton's reading to his fellow monks during a meal that was otherwise eaten in silence:

> Light fills my proper globe
> (I have won light to read by
> With a little, tinkling chain)
>
> And the monks come down the cloister
> With robes as voluble as water.
> I do not see them but I hear their waves.
>
> It is winter, and my hands prepare
> To turn the pages of the saints:

And to the trees Thy moon has frozen on the windows
My tongue shall sing Thy Scripture.

Then the monks pause upon the step
(With me here in this lectern
And Thee there on Thy crucifix)
And gather little pearls of water on their fingers' ends
Smaller than this my psalm. (ll. 7-21)

The sibilance of the poem, sustained by the soft "s" sounds, is offset only very slightly by the orderly procession of the incoming monks. The imagery reinforces the silence as in the "pearls of water" on the monks' hands, which have been lightly dipped in holy water as the monks entered the refectory. The drops of water are smaller, the speaker confides, than the prayer he is about to read. The psalm is "small" not in its spiritual import but rather in its only very slight intrusion into the silence. The winter setting intensifies the silence and the iciness linked with the figure of the crucified Christ deepens the scene's significance as a symbol of asceticism and sacrifice. The water imagery, however, with its fertile associations, offsets this deathly imagery, implying that this is a death that leads to rebirth. In the midst of this pattern of imagery, sounds, and meaning there is the felt tenderness of the speaker towards the figure of Christ hanging on the cross in the refectory. This brings about an assimilation of the immediate scene involving the monks into the eschatological spiritual drama that has drawn Christians together since the time of Christ. While "The Reader" is one of Merton's most accomplished poems, its form is so transparently a mirror of its content that its language and poetic structure, though of a high order, do not call attention to themselves. "The Reader" expresses with considerable poetic skill the balance between language and silence sought by Merton. It is also an example of poetic wholeness through which concrete particulars of image, sound and rhythm evoke their ontological context in one intuitive grasp of experience and reality.

While not all of Merton's poems are so technically subtle and indirect in causing this ontological background to emerge, virtually all of Merton's poems seek to make this background apparent. As has been intimated throughout this essay, the link between wholeness and ontological awareness issues from the mind's ability, in religious contemplation especially, to transcend its own self-consciousness in order to have an "immediate experience" of

Being.[26] The mind's connection with the rest of being is not only metaphysical but also inevitably social since it brings one into contact with the "other" with whom one is already creationally united anyway, Merton observed, "in God" (*ZBA* 24). The value of wholeness in Merton's poetry lies in its transformation of individual and collective patterns of desire and accomplishment into an expanded theater of existence. In this larger theater, human beings in Merton's poetry attempt to imitate the perceived, unifying love of their creator, the effect of which is to lift the mind and soul of both poet and reader off the plane of the material into a universe in which even the slightest thought and action are shown to have an immeasurable resonance.

Endnotes

1. The tension between contemplation and writing has been well documented by a number of Merton scholars, including an illuminating analysis of the issue by Patrick O'Connell: "Poetry and Contemplation: The Evolution of Thomas Merton's Aesthetic," *The Merton Journal* (UK) 8.1 (Easter 2001) 2-11. Other useful sources include Bonnie Thurston, "Poetry and Contemplation: Notes on the Development of Thomas Merton's Theology of Art," *Studia Mystica* 2.4 (Winter 1979) 21-40; George A. Kilcourse, *Ace of Freedoms: Thomas Merton's Christ* (Notre Dame, IN: University of Notre Dame Press, 1993) *passim* (subsequent references will be cited as "Kilcourse" parenthetically in the text); and Victor Kramer, "Merton's Published Journals: The Paradox of Writing as a Step Toward Contemplation," in Patrick Hart, ed., *The Message of Thomas Merton* (Kalamazoo, MI: Cistercian Publications, 1981) 23-41.

2. Michael W. Higgins, *Heretic Blood: The Spiritual Geography of Thomas Merton* (Toronto: Stoddart, 1998) 9.

3. See Thomas Merton, "Poetry and the Contemplative Life," in *Figures for an Apocalypse* (New York: New Directions, 1947) 95-111 and "Poetry and Contemplation: A Reappraisal," in *The Literary Essays of Thomas Merton*, ed. Patrick Hart, OCSO (New York: New Directions, 1981) 338-54 (subsequent references will be cited as "*LE*" parenthetically in the text).

4. Thomas Merton, "First and Last Thoughts: An Author's Preface," in *A Thomas Merton Reader*, ed. Thomas P. McDonnell, rev. ed. (Garden City, NY: Doubleday Image, 1974) 17.

5. See Thomas Merton, *The Seven Storey Mountain* (New York: Harcourt, Brace, 1948) 85-88, 189-91, 202-203.

6. Thomas Merton, *Hagia Sophia* (Lexington, KY: Stamperia del Santuccio, 1962); Thomas Merton, *The Collected Poems of Thomas Merton* (New York: New Directions, 1977) 363-71 (subsequent references will be cited

as "*CP*" parenthetically in the text).

7. Thomas Merton, "Louis Zukofsky – the Paradise Ear" (*LE* 128-33).

8. Thomas Merton, *Raids on the Unspeakable* (New York: New Directions, 1966) 2; subsequent references will be cited as "*RU*" parenthetically in the text.

9. Thomas Merton, "Blake and the New Theology" (*LE* 9).

10. See Thomas Merton, *New Seeds of Contemplation* (New York: New Directions, 1961) 24; subsequent references will be cited as "*NSC*" parenthetically in the text.

11. Allen Tate, ""Literature as Knowledge," in *Collected Essays* (Denver: Swallow, 1959) 48.

12. Thomas Merton, *Conjectures of a Guilty Bystander* (Garden City, NY: Doubleday, 1966) 106; subsequent references will be cited as "*CGB*" parenthetically in the text.

13. Thomas Merton, *The Ascent to Truth* (New York: Harcourt, Brace, 1951) 194; subsequent references will be cited as "*AT*" parenthetically in the text.

14. Thomas Merton, *Cables to the Ace* (New York: New Directions, 1968); *CP* 395-454.

15. Thomas Merton, *The Geography of Lograire* (New York: New Directions, 1969); *CP* 457-609.

16. Thomas Merton, "Poetry and Scripture" [audiocassette #AA2905] (Kansas City, MO: Credence Communications, n.d.).

17. Thomas Merton, *The Inner Experience: Notes on Contemplation*, ed. William H. Shannon (San Francisco: HarperCollins, 2003) 25.

18. Thomas Merton, *Love and Living*, ed. Naomi Burton Stone and Brother Patrick Hart (New York: Farrar, Straus, Giroux, 1979) 60; subsequent references will be cited as "*LL*" parenthetically in the text.

19. Cited in Mark Van Doren, "Introduction," *The Selected Poems of Thomas Merton*, enlarged ed. (New York: New Directions, 1967) xiii.

20. Thomas Merton, *Thoughts in Solitude* (New York: Farrar, Straus and Cudahy, 1958) 85; subsequent references will be cited as "*TS*" parenthetically in the text.

21. Thomas Merton, *No Man Is an Island* (New York: Harcourt, Brace, 1955) 261.

22. Lynn R. Szabo, "The Sound of Sheer Silence: A Study in the Poetics of Thomas Merton," *The Merton Annual* 13 (2000) 221.

23. Thomas Merton, "Lyric Poetry" [audiocassette #AA2460] (Kansas City, MO: Credence Communications, n.d.).

24. Thomas Merton, *Dancing in the Water of Life: Seeking Peace in the Hermitage. Journals, vol. 5: 1963-1965*, ed. Robert E. Daggy (San Francisco: HarperCollins, 1997) 305.

25. Thomas Merton, *Silence in Heaven* (New York: Studio Publications/ Thomas B. Crowell, 1956) 24.

26. Thomas Merton, *Zen and the Birds of Appetite* (New York: New Directions, 1968) 24; subsequent references will be cited as "*ZBA*" parenthetically in the text.

Islands in the Stream:
Thomas Merton's Poetry of the Early 1950s

Patrick F. O'Connell

The Strange Islands,[1] Thomas Merton's fifth published book of verse, which made its first appearance on March 27, 1957, played a very significant role in his development as a poet. As a number of commentators on the book have pointed out, it is a "transitional" volume[2] – the only collection of Merton's poetry to appear in the 1950s, and one that gives a first glimpse of the direction that his verse would take in the final decade of his life, when he would once again turn to poetry as a major dimension of his creative life and a significant expression of his spiritual life. Merton had published four books of poetry in rapid succession between 1944 and 1949 – he wasn't quite as prolific as this schedule suggests, since the first two volumes, *Thirty Poems*[3] and *A Man in the Divided Sea*,[4] included work that dated back as far as 1939, a year after his baptism and two years before he entered the Abbey of Gethsemani, but nonetheless his productivity was quite impressive. Then, for a number of reasons, this fecundity seems to have dried up. Even before *The Tears of the Blind Lions*,[5] his fourth volume, appeared in 1949, he was talking about no longer writing poetry,[6] and as Michael Mott notes, this decision was reinforced after T. S. Eliot, who had been given copies of Merton's books of verse by James Laughlin of New Directions, concluded that Merton's work was "hit or miss," that he "wrote too much and revised too little" (Mott 242) – legitimate criticisms but hardly the last word on Merton's poetry, though for a while Merton may have taken it that way.

There were of course other reasons that contributed to this poetic eclipse, among them no doubt his increasing responsibilities in the monastery, where he began teaching young monks in 1949 and was named master of students, in overall charge of their formation, in 1951; his own uncertainty that poetry and contemplation were compatible, evident in his 1947 essay "Poetry and the Contemplative Life";[7] and also the change in focus that resulted from his unexpected success as a prose writer, beginning with his best-selling autobiography *The Seven Storey Mountain*[8] in 1948 and continuing with the appearance of *Seeds of Contemplation*[9] the next year. But there is a sense also that by the late 1940s Merton had written himself out in the characteristic vein of his early verse, and needed to allow his poetic imagination to lie fallow for a while. That fallow period ended with *The Strange Islands*, a considerable part of which was written in a style strikingly different from his earlier verse and reflected his own spiritual and intellectual development during the intervening years.

It should be noted, however, that Merton never *completely* stopped writing poetry.[10] In the early '50s poems appeared sporadically, and some even made it into print. What they generally have in common is their "occasional" character – they were prompted by some particular event that seemed to need to be expressed in verse. It was more a case of the occasion finding the poem than of the poem, or the poet, seeking out the occasion. And they *were* relatively few and far between – apparently not more than a couple of poems per year in the years between 1950 and 1955. What really encouraged Merton to begin to focus on verse composition again was the request in 1953 from the composer Paul Hindemith, or more precisely from his devout Catholic wife, to provide a text which Hindemith could set to music. Merton worked through three separate versions of the long piece over the next two years, and while it was never scored by Hindemith, the result, the modern morality play *The Tower of Babel*, became the heart of Merton's new volume of poetry.[11]

Merton's "retirement" from poetry, then, was never absolute, and the time period separating the new book from its predecessors was actually significantly shorter than the publication dates would indicate. As early as February 16, 1955, Merton wrote to his publisher James Laughlin that "I think I have another small volume of poetry shaping up,"[12] and on July 27 the text of what was initially called *Tower of Babel and Other Poems*, consisting of the play and ten shorter poems, was sent to a typist in New York to be prepared for publication.[13] Because of the number of other Merton works already scheduled for 1955 and 1956, the appearance of the collection was delayed until early 1957; in the interim the title was changed to avoid confusion with the limited edition of the play which also appeared in 1957,[14] the new title being taken from a line of the "Spiritual Canticle" of St. John of the Cross.[15] In the meanwhile, the prospect of a new volume seems to have stimulated Merton's poetic creativity, so that by the time the book was ready to go to press the number of short pieces had more than doubled, to 21. Many of these new poems were in the spare, stripped-down style that George Woodcock has called the poetry of the desert,[16] which Merton had already begun to experiment with by 1954,[17] and which he would continue to use in many of the best poems in his next volume, *Emblems of a Season of Fury* from 1963.[18] With *The Strange Islands* Merton once again found his voice as a poet, and the final dozen years of his life proved to be as prolific for his poetry as his first years in the monastery had been.

The poems of the early 1950s, sporadic and occasional as they were, did keep the poetic spark alive in Merton so that it could be blown into a steadier flame once he had determined to assemble another collection of his verse. A careful examination of a half dozen of these poems,[19] which fall chronologically into three groups of related pairs, can provide some helpful insights into Merton's literary and spiritual preoccupations during these years: in the first pair the recently ordained priest-poet uses the order of the Mass to structure two poems that move in quite different directions; the second pair finds Merton bidding farewell to topics and themes that had been important to the initial phase of his career as a poet, while the final pair shows him beginning to engage new areas of concern, both social and spiritual. Each of these poems is a significant achievement and each in its own way exemplifies the character of *The Strange Islands* as a transitional volume, for Merton's poetics and even for his life in general.

* * * * * * *

The earliest of the new poems included in *The Strange Islands*[20] is "A Prelude: For the Feast of St. Agnes" (*SI* 91-92; *CP* 283), originally composed as a journal entry for January 20, 1950,[21] the eve of the feast day of the child martyr, executed at the age of thirteen during the Diocletian persecution at the beginning of the fourth century.[22] Agnes was a favorite saint of Merton's, having been the subject of his earlier poem "St. Agnes: A Responsory," written in 1943 and included in *Thirty Poems*, his first published collection.[23] Both pieces are liturgical in inspiration, but whereas the first is a meditation on an antiphon for her feast day, here the focus is on the presence of St. Agnes in the text of the Mass, which Merton, ordained on May 26, 1949, had been celebrating for less than eight months at the time of writing the poem. The "Prelude" thus gives witness to both continuity and change in the poet's devotional life.

The opening lines describe the saint, in a stylized depiction that apparently owes something to early artistic representations as well as to her office, and invite her participation in the speaker's Mass:

> O small St. Agnes, dressed in gold
> With fire and rainbows round about your face:
> Sing with the martyrs in my Mass's Canon![24] (ll. 1-3)

The color of her dress, sign of her glorified state, reflects the "frequent occurrence of representations of the child martyr in 'gold glasses'" (Butler 135) in early Christian art, while the vivid frame surrounding her face probably owes something to the second antiphon of her office, in which she proclaims, "*Christus circumdedit me vernantibus atque coruscantibus gemmis pretiosis*"[25] ("Christ has encompassed me with shimmering, spring-like precious jewels"). The substitution of "fire and rainbows" for the gems makes Agnes a kind of archetypal figure, as the rainbow, emblem of the covenant in Genesis 9:13, is juxtaposed with fire, itself an eschatological sign, so that she is surrounded by images of ultimate destiny, of judgement and of salvation. The invitation to join the martyrs in song is a reference to the inclusion of Agnes' name in the Roman canon, along with that of other "apostles and martyrs," from John the Baptist and Stephen through a group of seven women martyrs, of whom Agnes is the fourth. While there is no mention of singing in the invocation of these martyrs in the Mass, they are listed just before the so-called minor elevation that concludes the canon, in which the priest offers the consecrated elements to the Father in the words: "*Per ipsum, et cum ipso, et in ipso, est tibi Deo Patri omnipotenti, in unitate Spiritus Sancti, omnis honor et gloria*"[26] ("Through Him, and with Him, and in Him, all honor and glory is yours, God, Almighty Father, in the unity of the Holy Spirit"), which were indeed sung in the Latin High Mass, and which are quite similar to words of praise sung in the Book of Revelation, part of a passage that will be alluded to repeatedly throughout the poem: "Amen. Blessing and glory, wisdom and thanksgiving, honor, power and might be to our God forever and ever. Amen" (7:12). In asking Agnes, with the other martyrs, to join their voices to his, the poet is implicitly suggesting that in doing so they are continuing to participate in their own heavenly liturgy, that the Mass therefore transcends the distinction between heaven and earth.

This recognition of the Mass as the point of intersection between time and eternity is further developed in the lines that follow:

> Come home, come home, old centuries
> Whose soundless islands ring me from within,
> Whose saints walk down a winter morning's iris,
> Wait upon this altar stone
> (Some of them holding palms
> But others hyacinths!).[27] (ll. 4-9)

Here the repeated summons to the "old centuries" to return "home" is a call for the past to be made present; this of course is the function of the Eucharist with regard to the saving events of the Last Supper and of Calvary, but here the focus is on the early history of the Church, to which Agnes and the other martyrs belonged. The liturgy is the context in which the events of earlier eras of Church history are properly situated and appreciated, and appropriated – made one's own. The Mass has the power to recall the past from the distance and inaccessibility of "soundless islands" to a vocal participation in the saving mystery celebrated at the altar. The altar stone, which of course contains martyrs' relics, is recognized as a point of intersection of temporal and eternal, past and present, far and near. The saints of old are imaged as descending to join the celebration on the "iris," the rainbow of line 2, now serving as a bridge between heaven and earth, some with hyacinths, dark red flowers of the iris family that are associated with martyrdom, an adaptation of the pagan myth of Hyacinth, from whose blood the flowers sprang up. Those carrying palms are the saints who "stood before the throne and before the Lamb, wearing white robes and holding palm branches in their hands" in Revelations 7:9, and who participate in the song of praise that begins "Salvation comes from our God, who is seated on the throne, and from the Lamb" (7:10), and continues with the verses already quoted. St. Agnes herself is traditionally depicted holding a palm branch, no doubt in reference to this passage, which also links her to the Lamb of God ("*Agnus Dei*" in Latin), whose name so closely resembles her own, a connection never explicitly made in the poem but subtly evoked throughout.

The lines that follow again address Agnes directly:

> I speak your name with wine upon my lips
> Drowned in the singing of the quiet catacomb.
> My feet upon forget-me-nots
> I sink this little frigate in the Blood of silence
> And put my pall upon the cup

Working the mystery of peace, whose mercies must
Run down and find us, Saint, by Saint John's stairs.[28] (ll. 10-16)

The poet's declaration here is not literally true in the context of the canon of the Mass. It functions rather as a kind of anticipatory fore-shadowing of communion in the blood of Christ still to come (cf. 1 Cor. 10:16), and so as a symbolic expression of the "communion" of saints. As a martyr, Agnes has answered affirmatively Christ's question to James and John: "Can you drink of the cup I am to drink of?" (Mk. 10:38), so the imagery here suggests the speaker's invocation is a vicarious participation in her faithful witness. It is paired with the startling metaphor of being "Drowned" in the singing of the choir of martyrs, which recalls the second part of Jesus' question: "or be baptized with the baptism with which I am baptized." As the martyrs were plunged into the baptism of death, for and with Christ, so the speaker is immersed in their hymn of praise to "the Lamb that was slain" (Rev. 5:9-10, 12, 13; 7:10, 12), imaginatively sharing in their, and his, sacrifice commemorated in the Mass. The singing is paradoxically associated with "the quiet catacomb," since it is not perceptible to the senses, and because it originates not from the catacombs themselves, where the liturgy is no longer celebrated in secret at the site of the martyrs' graves, but surrounding the heavenly throne.

The speaker then moves on to describe the fraction rite that follows the minor elevation and the recitation of the Our Father, in which the consecrated host is broken and a fragment dropped into the chalice. The "forget-me-nots" on which the priest is said to stand are a reminder that the Eucharist is *anamnesis*, the re-presentation of the saving events of the pasch. The image of the particle of the host as a "little frigate" is an unusual one (with per-haps a submerged play on the verb *"fregi"* – "I broke" – as well as a verbal echo of "forget" in the previous line); here again Christ's words on the cup and the baptism are evoked: "sink" echoes the drowning two lines earlier, as the "Blood of silence" recalls mention of the wine in line 10, as well as of the "quiet catacomb," but now the focus has been shifted to Christ's own sacrificial death.

The replacing of the pall upon the chalice that follows the fraction rite may also recall the different pall that is spread over a coffin and so reinforce the identification of the chalice with the cup of suffering which Christ's disciples must share in following him. In any case the speaker's description of this rubric leads into an evident reference to the "*Agnus Dei*" that immediately follows, the triple invocation of the Lamb of God in a prayer for mercy (recited twice, which may explain the plural "mercies" here) and for peace: the paschal "mystery" of Christ's death brings reconciliation with God and with one another, the gracious gift of mercy that is described as descending from above "by St. John's stairs," a reference to the words of Jesus to Nathanael at the end of the first chapter of the Gospel of John, which promise a vision of "the angels of God ascending and descending on the Son of Man" (1:51), who is himself the "stairs," the new Jacob's ladder, by which the angelic messengers of mercy "run down" (implicitly paralleling the martyrs who "walk down" the iris in line 6) to "find us." It is worth noting that this reference to the Son of Man is the culmination of a series of titles in the first chapter of John that begins with John the Baptist's identification of Jesus as "the Lamb of God who takes away the sins of the world" (Jn. 1:20), the source of the triple invocation of the *Agnus Dei* prayer.

The quatrain that follows abruptly switches the focus to the speaker's own spiritual state:

> No lines, no globes,
> No compasses, no staring fires
> No candle's cup to swing upon
> My night's dark ocean.[29] (ll. 17-20)

Expressed in terms of the nautical imagery already central to earlier sections of the poem, these lines are a stark expression of the speaker's need to be found by the divine mercies, because in the obscurity of his journey he recognizes himself as powerless to find his own way – he is without navigational aids, without illumination, whether from "staring fires" (an ironic echo of the "stairs" two lines earlier) on shore, or even from a "candle's cup" (implicitly contrasting with the cup on the altar in line 14) held out over the deep. The speaker's situation is thus analogous to Christ's own utter desolation and sense of abandonment in the dark night of his passion, represented in this poem by the sinking of the host's fragment, the "little frigate," in "the Blood of silence."

The progression from visual to auditory imagery in the following quatrain reinforces this implicit parallelism, the two stanzas corresponding to these two aspects of the description in line 13 and thus indirectly to the two symbols of Christ's sacrifice in Mark 10:38; while the poet does not claim that the apophatic experience he depicts is a participation in Christ's passion, these correspondences suggest that it has at least the potential to be so:

> There the pretended horns of time grow dim.
> No tunes, no signals claim us any more.
> The cities, cry, perhaps, like peacocks.
> But the cloud has come.[30]   (ll. 21-24)

The context, in which "There" refers back to "my night's dark ocean," might suggest warning blasts of foghorns in particular, but mention in the following line of "No tunes, no signals" indicates that the horns, despite pretensions to a spurious significance, no longer have any power either for diversion or for direction. All sounds fade into obscurity, including the peacock cries of the cities, presumably to be associated with the vanity of which the birds are traditionally the emblem. While the cloud that appears in the concluding line of this stanza seems to be yet another image of obscurity, paradoxically (as the transitional "But" indicates) it is also a symbol of divine presence and guidance (cf. Ex. 13:21-22, 14:19, 40:34-38; 1 K. 8:10-12 – the latter two references associated with the tent of meeting in the desert and with the Lord's glory in Solomon's temple, respectively – particularly apt for this liturgical context). The speaker recognizes that he has not been abandoned to wander without direction and purpose, that the mercies descending on the Son of Man, the Lamb of God, have indeed found him.

With the coming of the cloud, the focus of the poem returns to the liturgical setting, leading to a final invocation of St. Agnes that echoes but significantly alters the opening lines:

> I kneel in this stone corner having blood upon my wrist
> And blood upon my breast,
> O small St. Agnes, dressed in martyrdom
> With fire and water waving in your hair.[31]   (ll. 25-28)

The Mass is now evidently completed and the speaker is engaged in a prayer of thanksgiving – but anointed with blood on wrist and breast. Like the wine on his lips earlier, this description is to be understood figuratively, of course. In the exodus context signaled by the reference to the cloud, it suggests that he has been signed with the sacrificial blood of Christ as the lintel and doorposts of the Israelites in Egypt were marked with the blood of the paschal lamb (Ex. 12:7), the last of the implicit references to the *Agnus Dei* that recur throughout this poem addressed to St. Agnes. While he does not claim identification with the martyrs, or with the martyrs' identification with Christ, this symbolic anointing does indicate that the action of the Mass, the "Working [of] the mystery of peace" (l. 15), brings one into alignment with this archetypal pattern, opens one to authentic self-surrender, a genuine dying to oneself, as exemplified and fully realized by St. Agnes, to whom the poet turns once again in his final lines. Here she is "dressed" not in gold but "in martyrdom," a more radical expression identifying her with those who "have washed their robes and made them white in the blood of the Lamb" (Rev. 7:14) (the same group previously described as standing "before the throne and before the Lamb, wearing white robes and holding palm branches in their hands" [7:9]); to be clothed "in martyrdom" is to have "put on the Lord Jesus Christ" (Rom. 12:14), for all who "were baptized into Christ," and so have shared his death, are "clothed . . . with Christ" (Gal. 3:27). The child martyr is now described not merely as framed with "fire and rainbows" but "With fire and water waving in [her] hair," a combination recalling Isaiah 43:2: "When you pass through the water, I will be with you; in the rivers you shall not drown. When you walk through fire, you shall not be burned; the flames shall not consume you." She has passed unharmed – in the most profound sense – through the perils of the new exodus journey and emerged from ultimate adversity ornamented and enhanced by what had been forces of destruction. So the poem concludes with the final invocation of St. Agnes as one who models the transformation made available to all in the Eucharist, the paschal journey through death to new life, with and in the Lamb who was slain, the Lamb who takes away the world's sins, who bestows mercies and who grants the only peace that endures.

* * * * * * *

When Merton returns to poetic composition, almost a year later, the focus is once again on the Eucharist, but the new poem is anchored not in the temporal cycle of the Church year but in the specificity of place. "Early Mass" (*SI* 89-90; *CP* 281-82) was first published in April, 1952,[32] but its subtitle, "St. Joseph Infirmary – Louisville" indicates that it must have been written during or shortly after Merton's stay at the hospital in November 1950, when he spent almost a month there after nose surgery (see *ES* 436-42).[33] The Masses he celebrated at St. Joseph's were presumably the first he said outside of the abbey – we know from his journal that he presided at Mass for a day of recollection on November 5 (see *ES* 437), and again at the community Mass on Thanksgiving Day, November 23, so the chaplain could go home for his turkey dinner (see *ES* 443). Whether either of these is the specific "early" Mass in question cannot be determined, but the reference to the place in the subtitle and to the month in the poem itself make clear that the poem is linked to this extended visit. The poem is of particular interest, however, not just as a significant incident in his still new priest-hood, but especially in its foreshadowing of a much more famous visit to Louisville more than seven years later.[34] The openness to the world that characterizes Merton's experience at Fourth and Walnut is already evident, albeit in a much less developed way, in this reflection on celebrating mass out "in the world."

The poem begins with prayer, addressed to Christ, and then modulates into an invitation to the congregation:

> There is a Bread which You and I propose.
> It is Your truth. And more: it is ourselves.
> There was a wickedness whose end is blessing.
> Come, people, to the Cross and Wedding! (ll. 1-4)

The word "propose" here seems an odd choice of vocabulary, but is being used quite precisely to mean "place before" or "make available." There is a strong sense of synergy here, of Christ and the speaker working together to offer spiritual nourishment to those present at the Mass. The bread, perhaps surprisingly, is initially identified with "Your truth," with word[35] rather than sacrament, or rather with both (as in John 6:35-50 and 51-58): in the Mass one is first fed by God's word, the truth taught by and about Christ, and then by the Eucharist itself, which expresses the truth of the Incarnation, God's presence and availability in Christ. The speaker than goes on to reflect the truth that, as St. Augustine put it,[36] those who *receive* the Body of Christ are called and empowered to *become* the Body of Christ: it is the Eucharist that creates the Church, establishing both its identity with Christ and its vocation to feed others. This power, as the subsequent lines point out, is due to the paschal foundation of the Eucharist: the wickedness of Christ's rejection and crucifixion finds its "end," both its conclu-sion and its purpose, in the "blessing" of new life: the Eucharist is the celebration of the blessings of salvation through the risen Christ, and the act of blessing the Lord for the gift of redemption. It is in this rite, which unites past and future, the sacrifice of the cross and the wedding banquet in the Kingdom of God, that the worshipping community is invited to participate.

The sense of the reciprocal relationship between Christ and his priest continues in the next section of the poem:

> His are the mysteries which I expound
> And mine the children whom His stars befriend.
> Our Christ has cleanly built His sacred town. (ll. 5-7)

The mysteries of Christ which the priest expounds in breaking open the word are the Cross and Wedding, redemption and union with God in Christ. The children, the gathered congregation, are the speaker's in so far as he exercises the role of a parent in feeding, nourishing, with the recognition that they are Christ's children first of all and his own because he is sharing in Christ's nurturing role. They are befriended by "His stars" perhaps because, as this is an "early" Mass, the stars provided light to help them find their way, but more generally because the stars provide guidance for the journey that is their entire lives. The third line here alters the pattern as the speaker identifies himself with the congregation and speaks of "Our Christ" and "His town" – which is described as being already built, as the Church, the community of the faithful: it is "cleanly" built, one of Merton's favorite words, here suggestive of the Bride without spot or wrinkle of Ephesians 5, to be identified with the New Jerusalem[37] of Revelations 21; the Mass is thus a foreshadowing of the wedding feast, the marriage of the Lamb and His Bride, a sacrament of the city of God. The heavenly city is hidden within the earthly city, but as will become apparent as the poem develops, not simply as a sign of contradiction but as an instrument of transformation.

From within the Holy City the entire cosmos can be perceived as testifying to Christ. The world itself becomes a sacrament, a witness to the goodness of Christ the Word:

> What do the windows of His city say?
> His innocence is written on your sky!
> Because we think His Latin we are part of one another,
> Together when I am away.[38] (ll. 8-11)

The universe itself proclaims the vindication of Christ dead and risen; for those with a sacramental awareness, "the heavens declare the glory of God" (Ps. 19:1); the cosmos reflects the same truth as the liturgy, which thus does not remove one or alienate one from the created world, but allows one to see creation as transfigured "in Christ." And this shared awareness, represented here by a common liturgical language, continues to unite all members of Christ's body wherever they may happen to be participating in the Mass – in the city, in a monastery, or elsewhere. One may perhaps hear an echo here of Merton's actual homily, affirming his continued presence with his new community even after he returns to Gethsemani.

The invitation of line 4 is now repeated with the summons to

> Come to the ark and stone
> Come to the Holies where His work is done,
> Dear hasty doves, transparent in His sun![39] (ll. 12-14)

The ark of the covenant, kept in the Holy of Holies, the innermost room of the Temple, and the stone that the builders rejected which has become the cornerstone (1 Peter 2:7), respectively symbolize the Wedding of the Lord and the people and the Cross that makes possible this union, and liturgically the tabernacle and altar as well, the two most sacred places in the sanctuary, "the Holies where His work is done," beginning with the thrice repeated "*Sanctus*" ("Holy, Holy, Holy") that signals the start of the canon, the most sacred part of the Mass. It is an invitation to enter into the place and time of God's work of salvation, the most solemn and important point in the liturgy. The assembly is addressed as "Dear hasty doves," a term of endearment for the Bride from the Song of Songs (1:15, 2:12, 14, 4:1, 5:2, 6:9), encouraged to fly quickly to the "Holies" like the swallows finding nests near the altar in Psalm 84; they are themselves like the windows of the previous stanza, through which the divine light of Christ is able to shine.

The speaker then prays that through the liturgy the land of promise, the land of milk and honey, or honeycombs (another image associated with the Bride in the Song of Songs [4:11, 5:1]) might be encountered and experienced right there in Louisville, even right there in the hospital:

> Gather us God in honeycombs,
> My Israel, in the Ohio valley!
> For brightness falls upon our dark.[40]
>
> Death owns a wasted kingdom.
> Bless and restore the blind, straighten the broken limb.
> These mended stones shall build Jerusalem.[41] (ll. 15-20)

The coming of daylight signals the defeat of the forces of darkness through the revelation of God's new creation, God's new community. Death no longer rules: his "kingdom" is both fruitless ("wasted") and conquered (laid waste), a declaration that recalls Paul's question, "Death where is your victory?" (1 Cor. 15:55). Echoing line 3, this proclamation of the end of wickedness is paired with a prayer for blessing, a request for healing that reflects the *"Domine, non sum dignus"* ("Lord, I am not worthy") prayer that immediately precedes communion; the pairing of the blind and the lame recalls Christ's words to the followers of John the Baptist in Matthew's Gospel, where "the blind [who] regain their sight" and "the lame [who] walk" (11:5) are signs of the inbreaking of the messianic age. The prayer of petition gives way to prophetic proclamation, as those who have been healed are seen as "mended stones," the "living stones" of 1 Peter 2:5 who are to be joined with Christ the cornerstone to create the holy nation, the New Jerusalem, the City of God already built by Christ through his own redemptive work but still to be actualized, incarnated, within the specific circumstances of one's own place and time.

This recognition leads to the third and final invitation, to approach the communion rail:

> Come to the golden fence with folded hands
> And see your Bird, kneel to your white Beloved.
> Here is your Father at my finger's end![42]   (ll. 21-23)

Not only is Christ received but the entire Trinity is encountered; in and through Christ the Holy Spirit is perceived and the Father is found. Christ is described as the "Beloved," a term that not only suggests his identity as the Bridegroom but recalls specifically the words "This is my beloved Son" spoken by the Father at his baptism (Matt. 3:17) as the Spirit ("your Bird") descended in the form of a dove. At this point the world beyond the communion rail likewise recalls the baptism scene: as at the Jordan, "The clouds are torn";[43] the audience is told to "Summon the winds of fall,"[44] an image of power traditionally associated with the Holy Spirit (cf. Jn. 3:8; Acts 2:2); the November light that breaks through the clouds is commanded: "On street and water, track and river, shine"[45] (ll. 24-25), pairings that incorporate both land and water, both the formally built and the rough and undeveloped, both the general and the specific. Then come the key lines of the entire poem, the rite of dismissal when the celebrant calls upon the congregation to

"Open the doors and own the avenue / For see: we are the makers of a risen world, . . ."[46] (ll. 26-27). They are called to take the vision of the Holy City into the city beyond the chapel, to take an active, creative role in transforming the world by living out in their daily lives the paschal mystery they have just celebrated, by witnessing to the resurrection here and now in what is paradoxically characterized as a "new / Brown universe" (ll. 27-28) – a description that is accurate for November, of course, but appropriate symbolically as well, for this newness is evident only to the eyes of faith – the cosmos is not yet green, but is being renewed nonetheless.

The poem then concludes by expressing the effect the celebration has had on the speaker himself: the liturgy of this new universe "Sweetly consumes my bones" (l. 29) – as the Body of Christ has been consumed by the communicants, so the priest has been totally absorbed by the unexpected, overwhelming sense of having experienced the world of redeemed, risen life, of finding the City of God, the Bride of the Lamb, in the midst of the earthly city. It is a revelation of the city's true identity, not owned by death but by a redeemed people filled with the life of Trinitarian love. Any sense of opposition between the monastery and the world has been transcended. The full implications of this discovery may have to wait for a later encounter, but already in 1950 there has been a remarkable, unanticipated recognition that the eschatological kingdom is hidden, and revealed, in the midst of ordinary reality.

* * * * * * *

The original title of "The Annunciation" (*SI* 93-94; *CP* 284-85), Merton's next poem, was "Christmas 1951,"[47] which dates it to about a year after "Early Mass." It will turn out to be the last of Merton's specifically Marian poems, a series that began with "Song for Our Lady of Cobre" (*TP* [3]; *CP* 29-30), written in Cuba in the spring of 1940, a year and a half before he entered the monastery. While it represents the final example of what had been a rich vein of devotional verse, in its own way it also signals Merton's shift toward greater openness to the world. The poem begins in the apocalyptic tone that had characterized much of Merton's poetry of the late 1940s (including his most recent Marian work, "To the Immaculate Virgin on a Winter Night" [*TBL* 27-28; *CP* 218-19]):

> Ashes of paper, ashes of a world
> Wandering, when fire is done:

We argue with the drops of rain! (ll. 1-3)

This brief, elliptical opening segment creates an analogy by juxtaposition between microcosm and macrocosm: the remains of burnt paper carried off by the wind suddenly become a reminder and foreshadowing of the fiery end of the world, obliterated and swept away without any apparent direction. The attitude of the speaker is evidently one of bleak disillusion with the world, and apparent disappointment that such destruction is not fully accomplished: to "argue with the drops of rain" is to express resentment that the fire has been doused before the paper (standing in for the world) has been completely consumed. Thus the initial stance appears to be one of strong "world rejection."

But the much longer and more elaborately developed section that follows reveals that such an attitude is in fact pre-Christian, that the desire for a purifying destruction is incompatible with Incarnation, which effects a renewal and transformation of the world:

> Until One comes Who walks unseen
> Even in elements we have destroyed.
> Deeper than any nerve
> He enters flesh and bone.
> Planting His truth, He puts our substance on.
> Air, earth and rain
> Rework the frame that fire has ruined.
> What was dead is waiting for His Flame.
> Sparks of His Spirit spend their seeds, and hide
> To grow like irises, born before summertime.
> These blue things bud in Israel. (ll. 4-14)

The first two lines here actually form part of the opening sentence, the tone and sense of which they radically modify. It is important to recognize that there is a double perspective at work here: despite the use throughout the poem of the narrative present, the speaker is clearly aware of the full significance of the events being described as he would not be if he were observing them in "real time." Thus his use of the conjunction "Until" indicates that even before his presence is perceptible, the arrival of the mysterious "One . . . Who walks unseen" has already invalidated the assumptions on which the argument with the rain was based, but only in retrospect is this objective transformation subjectively recognized.

Only after accepting the full implications of the Incarnation, after realizing that the One who has come walks "in elements" not only in the sense that he is present in the midst of material devastation, but more profoundly, as subsequent lines will make clear, that he is "in" these elements, in matter, as his own embodiment, could the poet speak of "elements we have destroyed." The pose of righteous rejection of the world taken in the opening lines has been undermined and discarded; there has been a revelation and acknowledgement of responsibility, a recognition that speaker and audience are not merely passive observers but active destroyers, implicated in the state, and fate, of the world. (Even the dactylic pattern of the stresses in this line puts particular emphasis on "we," reinforced by the echo of the long "e" from "Even" and "unseen," and picked up by "Deeper" in the following line.) Only in the two final sections of the poem will the speaker return to the personal implications of the Word made flesh for himself and his audience. The remaining lines of this verse paragraph explore what it means for the created world as a whole.

The Incarnation is described as "Deeper than any nerve" in that it does not operate merely at the level of sensation; the phrase "flesh and bone" recalls the words of Adam about Eve: "This one at last is bone of my bones and flesh of my flesh" (Gen. 2:23), thus expressing an identification of Christ the new Adam with humanity in as intimate a bond as that of the first Adam with Eve, a total embrace of the human condition, in all its ambiguity, associated with the first parents. The participial phrase "Planting his truth" then suggests a garden setting, a renewal of paradise, a new beginning for the world, while the clothing image of the main clause, "He puts our substance on," functions as a kind of reversal of the nakedness of the fallen first couple in Genesis 3, but what is "put on" is not merely a matter of outward appearance but the very essence of human nature. Thus there is a sense of renewal, of a new creation, that is confirmed by the listing of the elements of "earth, air and rain" which "Rework the frame that fire has ruined." This apparent opposition between fire and the three other elements is immediately countered as the destructive fire of passion and hatred give way to the vital "Flame" of the Holy Spirit, whose "Sparks" are implicitly identified with the Truth planted through the Incarnation, "seeds" hidden to germinate and blossom in due time. The process is only begun, not fully accomplished, but the first signs of new life, "born before summertime," have begun to appear, the "blue things" that "bud in Israel": the plural suggests that there is more than one sign (perhaps an implicit reference to John the Baptist?), but the color blue points to the sign par excellence, the Virgin Mary.

At this point, then, there is a sudden switch from the more general, cosmic context developed thus far to a concrete and specific focus on the girl who makes all this possible, from divine action to human response. The section that follows is not chronologically later than the previous lines, but reflects on the same event from a different angle, "from below" – a more Lucan perspective to complement the largely Johannine presentation that preceded it:

> The girl prays by the bare wall
> Between the lamp and the chair.
> (Framed with an angel in our galleries
> She has a richer painted room, sometimes a crown.
> Yet seven pillars of obscurity
> Build her to Wisdom's house, and Ark, and Tower.
> She is the Secret of another Testament
> She owns their manna in her jar.) (ll. 15-22)

The starkness of the two opening lines here, with their string of monosyllables broken only by the preposition, stress the "ordinariness" of the extraordinary person, referred to simply as "[t]he girl," rather than with familiar titles that would too quickly and too facilely anticipate the outcome of her encounter with the angel, who has not yet appeared. The lengthy parenthesis contrasts the bareness of the setting, emphasizing Mary's poverty and simplicity, with the "richer painted room" of artists' imaginations. The frame surrounding such paintings sets the scene apart from the rest of life, from the cosmic "frame" of all creation referred to earlier, as the "crown" that the Virgin is sometimes given (though a symbolically apt reference to the angel's words about the "throne of David" at the Annunciation [Lk. 1:32]) removes her both from her actual setting and from her identity with the rest of humanity. These lines condense what Merton had said more discursively two years earlier in *Seeds of Contemplation*:

> It is most fitting to talk about her as a Queen and to act as if you knew what it meant to say she has a throne above all the angels. But this should not make anyone forget that her highest privilege is her poverty and her greatest glory is that she is most

hidden, and the source of all her power is that she is as nothing in the presence of Christ, of God. It is because she is, of all the saints, the most perfectly poor and the most perfectly hidden, the one who has absolutely nothing whatever that she attempts to possess as her own, that she can most fully communicate to the rest of us the grace of the infinitely selfless God.[48]

As the reference to Proverbs 9:1 ("Wisdom has built her house, she has set up her seven columns") – significantly altered to "seven pillars of obscurity" – indicates, it is Mary's emptiness, her openness to God's word, that makes her the embodiment of wisdom. As Merton had written in *Seeds of Contemplation*, "To share her humility and hiddenness and poverty and concealment and solitude is the best way to know her: but to know her thus is to find wisdom."[49] Paradoxically, it is precisely this hiddenness that makes her "Wisdom's house, and Ark, and Tower" (titles familiar from the Litany of the Blessed Virgin): she is the first house in which incarnate Wisdom will dwell, the ark of the covenant that bears the sign of union with the God of Israel (often associated with Mary at the Visitation), the tower of David/tower of ivory from which the Messiah-King reigns. She is thus the "Secret," the most profound truth, of the Old Testament, the embodiment of the hidden meaning of all salvation history that has preceded her and is about to be uncovered. She is, in the words of the litany, the "Spiritual vessel, Vessel of honor, Singular vessel of devotion" in which the nourishment of the divine word, the "bread from heaven," is to be found (cf. the command of Moses in Exodus 16:32-34 to keep an omer of manna in an urn – described in Hebrews 9:4 as a "gold jar" – to be stored in the ark of the covenant).

The poet then resumes the description of the Annunciation scene interrupted by the parenthetical caution:

> Fifteen years old –
> The flowers printed on her dress
> Cease moving in the middle of her prayer
> When God, Who sends the messenger,
> Meets His messenger in her Heart.
> Her answer, between breath and breath,
> Wrings from her innocence our Sacrament!
> In her white body God becomes our Bread. (ll. 23-30)

The encounter with the angel here is presented as a moment of supreme inwardness, absolute stillness, when the flowers on her dress, the outward sign of the budding of new life described earlier, "[c]ease moving" with the rise and fall of her breathing at the *kairos* moment of the arrival of the messenger (the literal meaning of "*angelos*") and the "*fiat*" of her acceptance of the message. The contemplative union in the girl's heart with the God who is already present there makes possible the enfleshed union of divinity and humanity in her womb.

The rather startling leap to a focus on the sacramental presence of Christ as "our Bread" that concludes this section creates a parallelism with the closing reference to the manna in the previous verse paragraph, the nourishment of the Old Testament being fulfilled in that of the New, and suggests as well the maternal role of feeding her children – not with milk but with bread, solid food (cf. 1 Cor. 3:2, Heb. 5:12-14); but the mention of "her innocence" implies as well a contrast with the fall that foreshadows the reference to Eden in the section which follows: as Eve's answer to the tempter led to the food bringing death, so Mary's answer to the divine messenger leads to the food bringing immortality, that actually fulfills the deceptive promise made by the serpent: "you shall be as gods" (Gen. 3:5). Thus the traditional contrast between Eve and Mary is presented from a fresh perspective. In addition, the use of the verb "Wrings" with its overtones of effort and pain serves as a reminder that the process by which "God becomes our Bread" involves not just conception and birth but suffering and death, the full scope of the Incarnation hinted at but not further developed here.

The consequences of Mary's decision are presented in cosmic and mythic terms in the lines that follow:

> It is her tenderness
> Heats the dead world like David on his bed.
> Times that were too soon criminal
> And never wanted to be normal
> Evade the beast that has pursued
> You, me and Adam out of Eden's wood.
> Suddenly we find ourselves assembled
> Cured and recollected under several green trees. (ll. 31-38)

As Mary was implicitly contrasted with Eve in the previous lines, so here she compared to Abishag, the virgin whose warmth kept the aged King David alive in 1 Kings 1:1-4. The allusion may initially seem strained, and even in questionable taste, but it does convey that the consequences of her *"fiat"* extend beyond the Church (the focus of the sacramental reference of the previous section) to all creation; it is through her "tenderness" that the "Flame" of the Holy Spirit (l. 11) is communicated to the dead world – the period of "waiting" is now over and the time of cosmic renewal has begun. The comparison to David in this context recalls specifically the angel's words that the child to be born will be given "the throne of David his father" and that "of his kingdom there will be no end" (Lk. 1:32, 33), a reminder that whereas Abishag's warmth was temporary, Mary's tenderness brings forth the true "Son of David" not through sexual intercourse but by "the power of the Most High" (Lk. 1:35), and that it is through the "Son of the Most High" (Lk. 1:32), who "puts our substance on" (l. 8) that "the dead world" is revivified. If the effects of the Incarnation are presented in cosmic terms in this comparison, in the lines that follow they are considered in a mythic context that allows both poet and reader to discover that this story is their story. The entire course of history is encompassed in the description of the "too soon" fallen world, alienated from its divine source and thus rejecting its "normal" state of intimacy with God, which nevertheless is able to "[e]vade" the seemingly inevitable eschatological catastrophe initially described in the opening lines of the poem. The apocalyptic "beast," described in Revelations 13 and identical to the devil that roams about like a roaring lion in 1 Peter 5:8, has been rampant since the expulsion from paradise, in pursuit of "[y]ou, me and Adam," but has not been able to achieve a definitive triumph. Instead, "we find ourselves" – with the deeper implications of discovering our most authentic identity – if not back in paradise, at least in a grove that is a reminder of "Eden's wood," an image of a renewed earth marked by the restoration of community ("assembled"), by the healing of the wounds of sin ("cured"), and by a sense of wholeness, both social and personal ("recollected").

This description conveys an overwhelming sense of relief at the sudden change in the situation. How it has happened is explained in the final section of the poem:

> Her prudence wrestled with the Dove
> To hide us in His cloud of steel and silver:
> These are the mysteries of her Son.
> And here my heart, a purchased outlaw,
> Prays in her possession

Until her Jesus makes my heart
Smile like a flower in her blameless hand. (ll. 39-45)

Mary's "prudence," a complement to her "tenderness" in line 31,
is presented as the explanation for how "we" were able to escape
the beast. Like the parallel reference, it is embedded in a startling
and seemingly inappropriate image that is likewise a compressed
scriptural allusion: "wrestled" calls to mind the scene of Jacob
wresting with the angel in a life-changing encounter with the
divine (Gen. 32:25 ff.), yet here the "wrestling" is not just with the
angelic messenger but with the Dove, the Spirit of God. It is of
course not Mary herself but her prudence that is engaged in this
figurative struggle, which refers to her question "How can this be
since I have had no relations with a man?" (Lk. 1:34), which follows
immediately after the angel's mention of the second Old Testament
figure (after David) whose life and mission is to find fulfillment
in the events now being realized: "he will rule over the house of
Jacob forever" (Lk. 1:33). Jacob's struggle is thus recognized as
prefiguring and preparing for this moment, and Gabriel's reply,
"The Holy Spirit will come upon you and the Power of the Most
High will overshadow you" (Lk. 1:35), draws on the image of the
cloud, the traditional symbol of the divine presence that in the
poem is presented as having soteriological significance: the cloud,
with its attributes of steel (defense) and silver (preciousness), both
overshadows Mary to effect the Incarnation and also provides
concealment and protection for sinful humanity, fleeing from the
ravenous beast. Incarnation and salvation are not two distinct operations of the cloud, but two intrinsically related aspects of same
divine act, made possible by the human act of surrender to the
divine will. They are "the mysteries of her Son," the enfleshment
of the Word that brings about not only the redemption of humanity
(ll. 33-40) but the regeneration of the cosmos (ll. 31-32) that was
the initial focus of the poem's reflections (ll. 4-14). The focus shifts
here from Mary to Christ himself, and from the Annunciation to
the entire mystery of the divine plan, but all contained in and made
possible by Mary's "yes" to the angel's message.

In the four concluding lines the poet appropriates this message,
in two stages: first the heart prays, then the heart smiles. In describing his heart as "a purchased outlaw," the speaker acknowledges
himself as not simply a victim of the beast's pursuit but as one
legitimately banished (from Eden), his crime perhaps intended

to refer particularly to the destruction of the elements mentioned in the opening lines of the poem (the "Until" clause here echoing that in line 4, with "One . . . Who walks unseen" now identified as "her Jesus," the first time in the poem that either mother or son is explicitly named). The description of the heart as "purchased" is perhaps intended to recall those cultures in which those who had been outlawed by a crime of violence are reintegrated into the community by the payment of "wergild," a blood price; in any case the scriptural meaning of redemption – "bought with a price" (1 Cor. 6:20, 7:23) – is evident enough. The link of "purchased" with "possession" implies that the speaker's heart now belongs to Mary, that it was bought for her and given over to her. The result of this prayer of the heart, made possible and valid by Mary's own prayer (ll. 15, 25), is the heart can, indeed must, smile, an expression of joy and peace that is a complete reversal of the anger and disillusion that scorned the created world at the poem's outset. This is the work of "her Jesus," a work that is recognized as a gift comparable to, even as it is incomparably greater than, the simple presents children typically give their mothers. The final simile specifies the nature of this "possession": compared to a flower (not just printed on her dress now but held in her hand), the poet's heart has itself become an emblem of life and beauty, equated with the "Sparks of His Spirit" (l. 12) that symbolize the renewed spiritual vitality of the Incarnation, and has been incorporated into the process of re-creation of which the fifteen-year-old girl, whose own heart was the locus of a divine encounter like no other, has been shown to be both the preeminent image (thus the flowers on her dress) and the indispensible vehicle.

* * * * * * *

As "The Annunciation" is the last of Merton's Marian poems, so the well-known "Elegy for the Monastery Barn"[50] (*SI* 99-100; *CP* 288-89) serves as a kind of coda to the long series of poems about Gethsemani that date all the way back to "The Trappist Abbey: Matins" (*TP* [15]; *CP* 45-46) composed during or shortly after his first visit to the monastery during Holy Week 1941; written to mark the burning down of the Gethsemani cow barn in early August 1953,[51] the elegy also serves as a kind of farewell to what had been a rich and fruitful vein of his poetry, reflections on the settings, rituals and activities of monastic community life.

It opens with the figurative part of what will become an elaborate analogy:

> As though an aged person were to wear
> Too gay a dress
> And walk about the neighborhood
> Announcing the hour of her death, . . .[52] (ll. 1-4)

What is immediately evident here is the incongruity of the old lady's actions, which initially seem to be simply inappropriate, a sign of approaching senility perhaps, but modulate into something more, a vivid, even shocking yet somehow "prophetic" act. The old person is presented as a familiar figure in a specific environment, a local "character" already known to the neighbors, who now suddenly appears in an unfamiliar role, as an announcer of death, a sign of mortality that refers specifically to herself but implicitly to the human condition common to everyone.

The comparison is then applied to the abbey barn, which is likewise old, and becomes gaudily "dressed," and makes a proclamation relating to her imminent end:

> So now, one summer day's end,
> At suppertime, when wheels are still,
> The long barn suddenly puts on the traitor, beauty,
> And hails us with a dangerous cry,
> For: "Look!" she calls to the country,
> "Look how fast I dress myself in fire!"[53] (ll. 5-10)

What is striking about this description are not just the parallels with the old woman, but also the unique aspects: the terms of the comparison provide only a beginning of a response to the actual events – there is a "surplus" of meaning transcending the imagined analogy. "Too gay a dress" becomes "the traitor, beauty," a much more enigmatic description. Only at the end of the stanza are we told that the beauty in question is the self-destructive beauty of fire, that the "dress" does not merely attract attention to her approaching death but is actually its cause. The personified barn thus resembles not just the old person of the opening lines but a reckless younger woman willing to escape her usual situation, to stop being taken for granted, even at the cost of her own life. On the literal level, the fire makes the ordinarily plain barn at once attractive, compelling and dangerous; imaginatively, it becomes an image of self-contradictory human behavior, self-promotion inseparable from self-destruction.

The speaker then goes on to reflect on his own and his community's previous lack of awareness of the potential for this cataclysmic event that had already been present but unperceived:

> Had we half guessed how long her spacious shadows
> Harbored a woman's vanity
> We would be less surprised to see her now
> So loved, and so attended, and so feared.[54] (ll. 11-14)

While the transformation seems sudden and radical, the signs were there but unnoticed. Literally, the barn had long been a prime candidate to catch fire, though no one had realized it; figuratively, long ignored and suppressed desires have a tendency to break forth in an extreme way, so that the notice that is finally achieved is a profoundly ambiguous one, a mixture of attraction and repulsion, love and fear, but either way, "so attended": given attention, surrounded like a noblewoman by attendants, those summoned to carry out her commands.

The irony is that this desire for notice leads not to intimacy but to isolation. In fact there had been a kind of intimacy before, as the monks had worked within her "airless heart" and had not only filled her full of hay but "burst [their] veins" to do so – as though she were filled with their own life blood. The scene becomes a kind of parody of an abortive romance, with the prospective lovers operating at cross-purposes: they failed to understand her, but she didn't see how in their own way they did appreciate her and were close to her:

> She, in whose airless heart
> We burst our veins to fill her full of hay,
> Now stands apart.
> She will not have us near her. Terribly,
> Sweet Christ, how terribly her beauty burns us now![55]
> (ll. 15-19)

There is almost a sense of injured righteousness here on the part of the speaker: "we" are excluded, rejected, kept at a distance. This type of beauty does not deepen a relationship but makes it impossible. A magnificent isolation replaces unremarkable interaction, as though the former is considered preferable even though it is self-consuming. But the last sentence here, the prayer addressed to "Sweet Christ," suggests that something more is disturbing the speaker: he and his brothers are "terribly" burned by the barn's beauty – not literally since the fire keeps them at a distance, but nonetheless severely, not superficially. The intimation is that the real terror here is the profoundly disquieting and threatening convergence of beauty and disintegration, the sense of the contingency of all earthly beauty, of all material reality. The fantasy of the barn as an old lady or a spurned lover has simply been a way of trying to construct a scenario that would keep the more radical implications of the barn's destruction, its implications for the speaker and his companions themselves, at a distance. With the invocation of Christ the initial fantasy framework is, or must be, transcended as inadequate to the authentic meaning of the fire.

A different interpretive framework is needed, and is discovered in the second half of the poem. The change of focus is marked by a recognition that the barn offers a more profound "legacy / More delicate . . . and more rare"[56] (ll. 20-21), than the "terrible" recognition of the ambiguous nature of earthly beauty. The perception of the barn changes, from an exemplification of isolation to an icon of solitude: the speaker's attention shifts from the surface, the exterior, to the interior of the barn, which is perceived as an emblem of calm, tranquil resignation, a model of peaceful acceptance of the transitory nature of all created things:

> Who knew her solitude?
> Who heard the peace downstairs
> While flames ran whispering among the rafters?
> Who felt the silence, there,
> The long, hushed gallery
> Clean and resigned and waiting for the fire? (ll. 22-27)

Each of the three progressively longer questions posed presupposes the same answer: no one. The true meaning of the barn is apparent only now. There is an implicit critique of the perspective taken earlier in the poem. The real "announcement," the authentic proclamation, was missed. An alternative interpretation of the fire has become possible only after coming to terms with being "burned" by its terrible beauty and realizing that what is at issue is one's own reaction to impermanence, to the fleeting nature of all that exists in space and time, including oneself. The true message of the barn is not the showy attention-seeking outer appearance but the hidden, unrecognized acceptance of inevitable dissolution that is an intrinsic element of authentic solitude.

Yet this sense of contingency is not to be interpreted as rendering temporal existence meaningless – quite the opposite. The fifty years of the barn's existence are imaged as "Fifty invisible cattle"[57] (l. 29) which return to share in the barn's destiny and "Assume their solemn places one by one" (l. 30) in a procession that bears an uncanny resemblance to a community of monks entering their own choir stalls. This climactic moment is perceived as a *"kairos,"* the "little minute of their destiny"[58] (l. 31) that is not a negation of the meaning of earthly life, but a revelation, an epiphany of its significance: the years return to bear witness, to give testimony that their work has been completed: "Here is their meaning found. Here is their end" (l. 32). The fire is now perceived as a kind of baptism, a death that is an act at once of self-surrender and self-transcendence, a paschal transformation that includes the promise of rebirth, new life; it is a sign of joy because earthly destruction is the burning away of all that is not God's, of all that is not God:

> Laved in the flame as in a Sacrament
> The brilliant walls are holy
> In their first-last hour of joy.[59] (ll. 33-35)

And yet the poem does not end with this "first-last hour of joy." The final section suggests that the audience is not prepared to confront the full implications of this sacramental awareness:

> Fly from within the barn! Fly from the silence
> Of this creature sanctified by fire!
> Let no man stay inside to look upon the Lord!
> Let no man wait within and see the Holy
> One sitting in the presence of disaster
> Thinking upon this barn His gentle doom![60] (ll. 36-41)

The fire is finally perceived as a "type" of the consummation of all things, a foreshadowing of ultimate eschatological encounter with the God who is "a consuming fire" (Heb. 12:29), whom "no man can look upon and live" (Ex. 33:20). As one could not remain within the barn without getting consumed by the fire oneself, so the warning to flee to safety arises from the humble recognition that one is not yet ready to encounter the "Holy One" so directly and immediately. There is a need to make the solitude, the silence, the peace of the barn one's own before experiencing the divine presence. At this point there must be a willingness to be content with comprehending the sign rather than participating in what is signified. There is a refusal of premature closure, of unearned consolation, an awareness of being unprepared to undergo the radical purification symbolized by the fire, yet the final words of the poem testify to the recognition that the barn's fate is a manifestation not of God's harsh judgement but of "His gentle doom." If the encounter with the fire provokes fear, it also, in the terms set out earlier in the poem, calls for attentiveness, and ultimately serves as a promise of love.

* * * * * * *

"The Guns of Fort Knox"[61] (*SI* 21-22; *CP* 228-29) is an early articulation of the prophetic stance against war that will become an increasingly important part of Merton's message in the final decade of his life.[62] While the exact date of composition is not known, since it was included in the initial gathering of poems for the volume made in mid-1955, it must predate the first of Merton's mature prose writings against war by some five years at least. As is so often the case, themes and motifs that first appear in the more intuitive, symbolic context of Merton's verse are later elaborated in more developed fashion in articles and prose volumes.

The opening section of the poem describes the effect of artillery practice at Fort Knox, the military reservation located some miles away from Gethsemani but still heard and even felt there, at least imaginatively:

> Guns at the camp (I hear them suddenly)
> Guns make the little houses jump. I feel
> Explosions in my feet, through boards.
> Wars work under the floor. Wars
> Dance in the foundations. Trees
> Must also feel the guns they do not want
> Even in their core.
> As each charge bumps the shocked earth
> They shudder from the root. (ll. 1-9)

The initial focus is on sound, and the opening is almost whimsical as the little houses jump as though they are startled, caught by surprise, but before the end of the second line it is apparent that not the sound but the impact of the burst shells is responsible for the reaction. Beneath the surface of apparently peaceful life, war is at work like a sapper, undermining the seemingly secure structures. The parallel sentence is even more damning. If "Wars / Dance in the foundations," they are not merely an alien presence but somehow an intrinsic part of the building. This is a symbolic picture of a civilization built on war, riddled with self-contradiction, doomed to destroy itself by the very means it professes to use as a source of protection. Not only human artifacts but nature itself is threatened and attacked: a parallel is developed between the speaker who "feel[s] / Explosions in [his] feet" and the trees which "Must also feel the guns . . . / Even in their core" (the final word linked to "boards," "floor" and "Wars" in previous lines). The reference to "the guns they do not want" sounds rather flat and prosaic, but functions as a laconic understatement that implicitly makes the point that while natural objects have no choice in the matter, among human beings there must obviously be those who do in fact want the guns and the power they command. While people may take the shelling for granted, the earth itself is "shocked" both literally and symbolically – subject not only to violent concussions but to a profoundly disturbing surprise. Likewise the trees "shudder" as they tremble from the effect of the guns, but analogously in a reaction of horror and revulsion. The impression is given that the guns are hostile to the earth itself, a threat to the integrity of creation.

The section that follows is a surprising, indeed "shocking" apostrophe addressed to the guns themselves:

> Shock the hills, you guns! They are
> Not too firm even without dynamite.
> These Chinese clayfoot hills
> Founded in their own shale
> Shift their feet in friable stone. (ll. 10-14)

This apparent encouragement of the guns to keep up their destabilizing barrage, is soon revealed to be heavily ironic. The remark that the hills are unstable "even without dynamite" may suggest, particularly in the context of the Kentucky landscape, that the environment is already under assault from various mining operations, so that this is just one more stage in exploiting the natural resources of the area. The guns are urged to knock down the "Chinese clayfoot hills," standing in for the current enemy and like them perceived as actually being weak and unstable beneath an imposing surface. The speaker mockingly calls upon the guns to do to the hills now what they'll do to the Chinese when the time comes! Even the comment that the hills "Shift their feet" (of clay) may be intended to recall the oft-repeated scene in movie westerns where the bullying villains force the powerless decent folks to "dance" by firing at the ground in front of them, compounding the sarcasm at the absurdity of artillery pounding the fragile hills as if asserting its arrogant mastery over them.

The poem then returns to third-person description as it shifts into grim fantasy mode. Turning the hills into ruins can't prevent "the armies of the dead" from rising up once more:

> Such ruins cannot
> Keep the armies of the dead
> From starting up again.
> They'll hear these guns tonight
> Tomorrow or some other time.
> They'll wake. They'll rise
> Through the stunned rocks, form
> Regiments and do death's work once more. (ll. 15-21)

The scene is a parody, of course, of the general resurrection and final judgement, with guns instead of trumpets to wake the dead, who come forth not to meet their eternal destiny but as warriors ready to renew their violence, to "do death's work once more." The guns unleash forces beyond their control, beyond the conscious intent of their masters, if they have any. The phrase "cannot / Keep" suggests that the ostensible purpose of the guns is to suppress the forces of death, a reflection of the official justification that military exercises are necessary to secure life, liberty and property, but the poem proposes that whether by intention or not, they are actually in the service of death. The scene of one of apocalyptic horror, marked by the progression from "They'll hear" to "They'll wake. They'll rise . . ." – initially envisioned as happening "tonight" though subsequently put off into a less imminent future. Like the "shocked earth," the "stunned rocks" are dazed, bewildered, astonished by the barrage and thereby rendered impotent to block the passage of the dead into the world above, as in some grisly horror film.

To conclude the poem the speaker addresses the guns directly once again, warning that this "is not / The right resurrection" (ll. 23-24). The activity of the guns becomes a grotesque perversion of the power of God, a reversal of the Creator's work: instead of Christ's harrowing of hell the guns "punch the doors of death" (l. 25), as if trying to penetrate a besieged town by violent assault; in this case success would unleash uncontrollable forces of anarchy and destruction that have been repressed, rather than freeing the souls of the just to eternal glory. In usurping the power of God to raise the dead the guns threaten to initiate not the new life of the reign of God but the triumph of death and even of the demonic, as the final lines imply that war lets loose destructive powers that are indeed infernal:

> Let them lie
> Still. Let them sleep on,
> O Guns. Shake no more
> (But leave the locks secure)
> Hell's door. (ll. 26-30)

The "doors of death" are now identified with "Hell's door," which if unlocked would allow the forces of evil to reduce the earth itself to a hell. As the assault on the doors was described in language reminiscent of John Donne's holy sonnet "Batter my heart," in which the speaker calls on God not merely to "knocke, breathe, shine" but to "breake, blowe, burn"[63] in order to enter the usurped town of his soul, so here the diction echoes the beginning of the sestet of Donne's sonnet "At the round earth's imagin'd corners," where the speaker, who had initially called for the "numberless infinities / Of soules" to arise, now prays, "But let them sleepe, Lord."[64] Yet in both cases requests made to God in Donne's poems are made to the guns here, another indication of the idolatrous pretensions of military power. Merton's poem also recalls the situation in Thomas Hardy's "Channel Firing,"[65] spoken by the dead themselves who are awakened by "gunnery practice out at sea," and are reassured by God "That this is not the judgement-hour"; but whereas Hardy uses the bemused comments of Parson Thirdly and his fellow skeletons to make his powerful critique of militarism, the apocalyptic "Regiments" who are imagined as arising in Merton's poem are much less benign than Hardy's residents of a rural churchyard. The stakes have been raised considerably in the decades of war and rumors of war that separate the two poems, and the sense of foreboding has heightened. There is no assurance that the triple request made to the guns at the end of the poem will be heeded: the implication seems to be that unless the guns grow silent, an unlikely scenario, it is only a matter of time before the gates of hell will indeed be blasted open and the spectral armies released to "do death's work once more." In its grim warning about the full ramifications of what at this point is simply preparation for war, the poem creates an uncanny parallel with what its author will be saying in the following decade about the unintended but uncontrollable consequences that would inevitably follow from initiating a "limited" nuclear exchange, which would indeed be the equivalent of unlocking the doors to hell.

* * * * * * *

If "The Guns of Fort Knox" prefigures Merton's deepened social consciousness, the final poem in *The Strange Islands*, the aptly named "Stranger"[66] (*SI* 101-102; *CP* 289-90), expresses some of his mature contemplative insight.[67] The first sixteen lines of the poem (really the first nineteen, despite the period after line 16) are all a single sentence, a series of precisely articulated, exquisitely balanced natural details, observed by "no one":

> When no one listens
> To the quiet trees
> When no one notices
> The sun in the pool
>
> Where no one feels
> The first drop of rain
> Or sees the last star
>
> Or hails the first morning
> Of a giant world
> Where peace begins
> And rages end:
>
> One bird sits still
> Watching the work of God:
> One turning leaf,
> Two falling blossoms,
> Ten circles upon the pond.
>
> One cloud upon the hillside,
> Two shadows in the valley
> And the light strikes home.   (ll. 1-19)

These opening lines can be read in two ways: "no one" can be seen as the absence of an attentive consciousness, a lack of awareness of the simplicity of the rhythms of the natural world, the patterns of creation, as contrasted to the bird, a symbol of contemplative awareness, whose stillness is an openness to the divine presence in creation, to "*theoria physike*" or natural contemplation.[68] But "no

one" can also be read in a positive way, in that it is only by surrendering one's own analytic, discriminating mind, renouncing a
separate "self," by letting go of the distinction between observer
and observed, subject and object, that an authentic appreciation of
the creation as a theophany, a manifestation of the divine, becomes
possible; only by identifying with the patterns of the natural world,
as the bird does, by participating in them connaturally,[69] from
within, as it were, does their meaning manifest itself.

The first section pairs hearing and sight, with the verbs "listens to" and "notices" suggesting a greater attentiveness than
simply "hears" and "sees." Listening to the quiet trees requires a
particular attunement to what is not immediately obvious, while
noticing the reflection of light from the sky in the water is a perception of wholeness linking upper and lower worlds. In both cases
by paying attention one recognizes a limpid, lucid simplicity and
order that is easily overlooked. The second unit shifts from time
to place, "When" to "Where," while extending the pattern to the
sense of touch – feeling the sensation of rain on the skin, which
itself complements the sun in the pool of the previous lines. The
first drop of rain is in turn balanced by the last star, a focal point
of pre-dawn clarity which of course marks the passage from
night to day, but as light in darkness signals the simultaneous,
complementary presence of both. Awareness of beginnings and
endings requires particular sensitivity, paying attention to points of
transformation, passages from one state to another. The response
here is not to the generic but to the particular, the unique, to one
raindrop or one star among countless others; it is a response to
unrepeatable moments, a need to be fully present to the now, not
through a process of reflection or analysis but in the immediacy
of fully engaged experience.

The third segment continues the verbal pattern of the previous
three lines ("feels / / . . . Or sees . . . / Or hails . . ."; "first drop . . .
/ . . . last star / . . . first morning"), but the focus now shifts from
the sacramental to the eschatological, from living fully in the present to living in a continuous process directed toward an ultimate
fulfillment. The assumption here seems to be that the same capacity to perceive the significance of natural processes is involved in
"hail[ing]" – both greeting and celebrating – the inbreaking of the
Kingdom of God, the reign of *shalom*: recognizing the *kairos*, the
acceptable time, the day of salvation, requires the same kind of attunement as perceiving the presence of the Real hidden within the

real in each moment. The microcosm and the macrocosm (literally the "giant world"), the first drop of rain and the first morning of a redeemed cosmos, both involve seeing the world as it should be, glimpsing the creation as it came forth from the hand of God and as it will be when the nations no longer "rage" (Ps. 2:1) and the world is restored to its perfection.

It is only after this series of discrete details has been presented that the main clause of the opening sentence is reached: the alternative to a careless inattention is the one bird who "sits still"[70] and watches the work of God, not as a disengaged consciousness outside the fabric of creation but with a sapiential awareness, an intuitive, participatory recognition of the whole in every part. God's work includes all that has already been described, and also what is now enumerated: simple, seemingly inconsequential actions which are nonetheless charged with the divine presence for those who have the eyes to see and ears to hear, who can perceive the "suchness" of things, the hidden "*logoi*," the principles of order within each created thing, that participate in the Logos, the creative Word that is their source (see *ICM* 128-32). In the turning leaf, the falling blossoms, the ever-expanding circles on the pond, the sense of movement is paramount: God's work is happening right now. In the clouds moving across the hillside and the valleys the shifting patterns of shadow and light again suggest the dynamism of God's work, culminating in the illumination of "the light strikes home," the shaft of light that penetrates the shadows and suggests the flash of awareness, of comprehension that truly hits home, breaks through all illusions and misperceptions to transfigure reality.

Given this image of fulfillment, the sudden appearance of the terminology of aggression, conflict, warfare in the following lines (though prepared for by the word "strikes") seems incongruous and disconcerting:

> Now dawn commands the capture
> Of the tallest fortune,
> The surrender
> Of no less marvelous prize! (ll. 20-23)

The implication is that what is presented as natural and uncomplicated for the bird – and for "no one" – in the first half of the poem is now perceived as involving struggle, capture, surrender. The light of dawn, the light that strikes home, must overcome resistance in order to claim the tallest fortune, the marvelous prize. What is this prize, this fortune? The remainder of the poem will supply the answer, as the focus shifts from the outer world to the world within, from the Logos present in creation, in nature, to the Divine Word hidden within the human spirit, through which the human person participates, or can participate, in this cosmic harmony on the most profound level.

> Closer and clearer
> Than any wordy master,
> Thou inward Stranger
> Whom I have never seen,
>
> Deeper and cleaner
> Than the clamorous ocean,
> Seize up my silence
> Hold me in Thy Hand! (ll. 24-31)

The Stranger who is addressed by the speaker (the "I" who now explicitly appears for the first time in the poem) paradoxically is a figure of profound intimacy, "more intimate to me than I am to myself"[71] in St. Augustine's classic description, whose teaching is superior to "any wordy master," any external source of wisdom, and of equally profound mystery, beyond sight and beyond comprehension.   The prayer that the speaker offers in the second of these quatrains asks that the Stranger take possession of his silence, which has depths that go to the center of his being and so to the center of reality – the ocean is an image of immensity and depth, but it is surpassed in this regard by authentic silence, which in its greater purity is able to penetrate to the source of being beneath the "clamorous" surface of life. In asking that the Stranger "Seize up" his silence, capture it, make it his own, he echoes the command of the dawn in line 20 and so reveals that it is this silence, the reality of the authentic self deeper that words can reach, that emptiness where one is "no one," where one's identity is grounded in the nameless infinite, which is "the tallest fortune," the "marvelous prize." To be surrendered into the hand of God, to be so grasped by this Stranger, is to be immersed in the boundless divine mystery, and so to be empty of all and filled with all. In the parallel phrases "Seize up my silence" and "Hold me in Thy Hand," mystery and intimacy, struggle and self-gift, are balanced and united.

The consequence of this surrender is a radical freedom that transcends all partial categories, all dualities:

Now act is waste
And suffering undone
Laws become prodigals
Limits are torn down
For envy has no property
And passion is none.

Look, the vast Light stands still
Our cleanest Light is One! (ll. 32-39)

Neither acting nor suffering are ends in themselves, but means to the end of union with God: when the end is reached the means can be relinquished. All busyness, all efforts to save oneself by one's own efforts, are revealed as useless: one is detached from results, accomplishments, achievements. Neither what one does nor what one endures is of ultimate significance, but rather who one is in God's sight, in God's hand. At this point laws themselves have become prodigals, extravagantly, foolishly generous, not restrictive but lavish; limits are torn down because the infinite has no boundaries, and there is no longer a "self" to be bound (the first-person references have once again disappeared). Envy has no property because all sense of possessiveness, of competition has disappeared; by losing the desire for another's property, another's possession, envy loses its own "property," its distinctive quality, its essential attribute – envy ceases to be envy; and passion is no property because passion is no longer proper, no longer an attribute of one who is grounded in stillness and silence, who has reached that state of balance, calmness and equilibrium known as *apatheia*, beyond the control of the passions and therefore no longer in need of externally imposed limits and laws. The prodigal law is the law of Christ, the law of love, the abundance of the grace of God beyond the limits distinguishing what is proper to oneself, what separates one self from another.

One no longer has a self with its own properties, for in the end there is only the Light, which "stands still" (as the bird sits still in line 12), which is "cleanest" (as the speaker's silence was "cleaner" in line 28) because it is absolutely pure light, without imperfection, without shadow, with nothing interfering with its shining, and is One – not only undivided, undeflected, but all-encompassing. It is the divine, eternal, infinite Fullness of which all the natural objects and events previously noted were partial reflections – it is Unity beyond all divisions, all properties, all partial truths. Yet it is

"Our" light – for we have been drawn into it, incorporated into it, in an awareness, an illumination, beyond all distinction between subject and object. These final lines of the final poem in *The Strange Islands* thus suggest that while this volume may be a transitional work, a bridge between the traditional Merton of the 1940s and the adventurous Merton of the 1960s, it is not without moments of insight that transcend even these categories, these dualities, these "properties," when the "One Light" indeed "strikes home."

Endnotes

1. Thomas Merton, *The Strange Islands* (New York: New Directions, 1957) (subsequent references will be cited as *"SI"* parenthetically in the text); for an overview of the contents, see the entry in William H. Shannon, Christine M. Bochen and Patrick F. O'Connell, *The Thomas Merton Encyclopedia* (Maryknoll, NY: Orbis, 2002) 453-56 (subsequent references will be cited as *"Encyclopedia"* parenthetically in the text).

2. See Michael Mott, *The Seven Mountains of Thomas Merton* (Boston: Houghton Mifflin, 1984) 302 (subsequent references will be cited as "Mott" parenthetically in the text); Bonnie Thurston, "The Light Strikes Home: Notes on the Zen Influence of Merton's Poetry," in Bonnie Thurston, ed., *Merton & Buddhism: Wisdom, Emptiness & Everyday Mind* (Louisville, KY: Fons Vitae, 2007) 199 (subsequent references will be cited as "Thurston, 'Light'" parenthetically in the text); Robert Waldron, *Poetry as Prayer: Thomas Merton* (Boston: Pauline Books & Media, 2000) 137 (subsequent references will be cited as "Waldron" parenthetically in the text).

3. Thomas Merton, *Thirty Poems* (Norfolk, CT: New Directions, 1944); subsequent references will be cited as *"TP"* parenthetically in the text.

4. Thomas Merton, *A Man in the Divided Sea* (New York: New Directions, 1946).

5. Thomas Merton, *The Tears of the Blind Lions* (New York: New Directions, 1949) (subsequent references will be cited as *"TBL"* parenthetically in the text); this volume contains only seventeen poems, the smallest number of any of Merton's poetry collections.

6. See the journal entry for January 29, 1949: "For my own part, this evening I was thinking, 'Maybe I am finished as a writer.' Far from disturbing me, it made me glad. Nothing seems so foolish as to go on writing merely because people expect you to write. . . . Anyway I certainly find it extremely difficult to believe in myself as a poet" (Thomas Merton, *Entering the Silence: Becoming a Monk and Writer. Journals, vol. 2: 1941-1952*, ed. Jonathan Montaldo [San Francisco: HarperCollins, 1996] 273 [subsequent references will be cited as *"ES"* parenthetically in the text]). See also the entry for March 20, 1949, the day following his deacon-

ate ordination, with its remarkable disclosure of what was preoccupying his attention during the ceremony: "The first thing that happened was that, kneeling in the sanctuary after ordination and during Mass, I realized clearly that I ought to stop writing poetry and be definite about it too. I went to Reverend Father afterwards and he said all right. And I have recovered a great deal of interior liberty by that one thing. In the afternoon I tore up all the rough notes for a poem. They had been lying around for a few days" (*ES* 294).

7. Thomas Merton, *Figures for an Apocalypse* (New York: New Directions, 1947) 95-111 (first published in *The Commonweal* 46.12 [July 4, 1947] 280-86).

8. Thomas Merton, *The Seven Storey Mountain* (New York: Harcourt, Brace, 1948).

9. Thomas Merton, *Seeds of Contemplation* (New York: New Directions, 1949).

10. In the headnote for "Major Orders," Part Three of *The Sign of Jonas*, presumably written in the latter part of 1952, Merton summarized the rationale for his decision to cease writing verse, but added that the decision was not absolute: "I decided to stop trying to be a poet any more. I did this first of all because I realized that I had never really been a good poet anyway, and it seemed to me that by continuing to write poetry I would only be imposing an illusion on the people who thought my poetry was good. In so doing, I would run the risk of coming to believe, myself, that it was good. What I was trying to do was, I think, all right. It was a movement toward integrity. If I could not write well, I would stop wasting words, time, paper, and get rid of this useless interference in my life of prayer. Since that day, in order to relax the element of pride that may have insinuated itself in this resolve, I have written verse where I thought charity demanded or permitted it – for instance some lines for Saint Agnes, which were never really finished off into a poem, which occur later in this book, and which are simply an expression of personal devotion to her. I have written two other poems besides, both of them on occasions which called for some expression of personal affection and gratitude. To write thus is not, according to my vocabulary, an attempt to 'be a poet'" (Thomas Merton, *The Sign of Jonas* [New York: Harcourt, Brace, 1953] 127-28). (The other two poems referred to are almost certainly "Early Mass" and "The Annunciation.")

11. See *Encyclopedia* 490-91 for an overview.

12. Thomas Merton and James Laughlin, *Selected Letters*, ed. David D. Cooper (New York: Norton, 1997) 109; subsequent references will be cited as "*TMJL*" parenthetically in the text.

13. See the note included with the setting copy of *The Strange Islands* in the archives of the Thomas Merton Center, Bellarmine University,

Louisville, KY.

14. Thomas Merton, *The Tower of Babel: A Morality* (New York: New Directions, 1957).

15. The thirteenth stanza of the poem reads: "My Beloved is the mountains, / And lonely wooded valleys, / Strange islands, / And resounding rivers, / The whistling of love-stirring breezes" (*The Collected Works of St. John of the Cross*, trans. Kieran Kavanaugh, OCD and Otilio Rodriguez, OCD [Garden City, NY: Doubleday, 1964] 714).

16. George Woodcock, *Thomas Merton, Monk and Poet* (New York: Farrar, Straus, Giroux, 1978) 51, 62.

17. See the long poem "Elias – Variations on a Theme" (*SI* 36-42; Thomas Merton, *Collected Poems* [New York: New Directions, 1977] 239-45 [subsequent references will be cited as "*CP*" parenthetically in the text]), which, according to Merton, "represents what the author had going through his head in the Christmas season of 1954" (*SI* 14). For an analysis, see Patrick F. O'Connell, "The Geography of Solitude: Thomas Merton's 'Elias – Variations on a Theme,'" *The Merton Annual*, 1 (1988) 151-90.

18. Thomas Merton, *Emblems of a Season of Fury* (New York: New Directions, 1963).

19. It is clear from Merton's correspondence that two of the original group of ten poems, "How to Enter a Big City" and "Nocturne," were composed later that the others, since he mentions that they had not yet been censored when they were sent (unpublished October 31, 1955 letter to James Laughlin, Thomas Merton Center files; unpublished August 17, 1955 letter to Naomi Burton Stone, Friedsam Memorial Library files, St. Bonaventure University, Olean, NY). The poem "Sports without Blood – A Letter to Dylan Thomas" (*SI* 27-31; *CP* 232-36), was written in 1948 and originally intended for publication in *Tears of the Blind Lions*, but for some reason had been omitted from that volume (see *Strange Islands* 14). Thus these six poems, along with "Elias," are those that were composed during the period when Merton was otherwise "on hiatus" from writing poetry.

20. Excluding "Sports without Blood" as well as the poem "Like Ilium" (*CP* 723-24), which is dated 1949 but was not included in any of the volumes of verse published during Merton's lifetime.

21. There are actually two different earlier versions of the poem, in the original journal entry for this date (*ES* 400) and in revised form in *The Sign of Jonas* (270); the latter version, which was of course the earliest published and is in fact the most familiar, since many times more people have read *Sign of Jonas* than *Strange Islands*, is also found in the "Uncollected Poems" section of *Collected Poems* (789-90), even though it is clearly a draft of the same poem found in *Strange Islands*, and despite the fact that there is a note to that effect on the relevant page of the setting copy

of *Collected Poems* in the New Directions files in the Houghton Library at Harvard University.

22. See *Butler's Lives of the Saints,* edited, revised and supplemented by Herbert J. Thurston, SJ and Donald Atwater, complete edition, vol. 1 (Westminster, MD: Christian Classics, 1956; rpt. 1991) 133-37; subsequent references will be cited as "Butler" parenthetically in the text.

23. *TP* [22]; *CP* 54-55; the date is found in Merton's own hand in a copy of *A Man in the Divided Sea* (which includes *Thirty Poems* in an appendix) now at the Thomas Merton Center.

24. Both journal versions read ". . . fire in rainbows . . ."; in the original version the third line reads "Sing with the seven virgins in my Canon," changed in *Sign of Jonas* to ". . . the seven martyrs . . ." – presumably because neither Perpetua nor Felicity, the first two of the seven women mentioned in the canon, were in fact virgins; omission of the number in the final version allows the reference to include the eight men mentioned along with the seven women. *Entering the Silence* (but not *Sign of Jonas*) includes the additional line "I am your priest" followed by "My feet upon forget-me-nots," transposed to a later position in subsequent versions.

25. *Breviarium Cisterciense,* 4 vols. (Westmalle, Belgium: Typis Cisterciensibus, 1935), *Pars Hiemalis* 565.

26. Latin texts of the Mass are taken from the *Saint Joseph Daily Missal,* ed. Hugo H. Hoever, SOCist (New York: Catholic Book Publishing Co., 1959).

27. Both earlier versions read "O centuries"; "saints come down this"; "To wait upon our prayers with hyacinths." The change to "walk" in the final version avoids the repetition of "come," already used twice two lines earlier, and likewise the change to "a" avoids using "this" in two successive lines; the switch to "this altar stone" makes explicit the focus on the altar as the point of convergence, while adding the reference to palms connects the passage to the scene in Revelations 7.

28. Both earlier versions read "your lovely catacomb", which thus focuses exclusively on Agnes and lacks the paradoxical connection between "singing" and "quiet"; in both *Sign of Jonas* and here the line "My feet upon forget-me-nots" has been moved to this new location, but in the former it is part of the previous sentence; both earlier versions read "Blood of Peace", which lacks the connection of "silence" with "quiet" two lines earlier, and repeats "peace" twice within three lines; both these versions read: "Working our peace, our mystery, who must / Run down and find you, saint, . . ." which is less closely aligned with the *Agnus Dei* prayer's reference to both mercy and peace, seems to personalize "mystery," presumably to be identified with Christ, who then would be descending upon himself, and has him finding "you," St. Agnes, rather than "us," a rather odd reading that might seem to suggest the saint was

discovered to be missing from heaven and a search party (if only a party of one) was sent out to find her.

29. Both earlier versions read the two final lines here as one, and follow it with "where no signals claim us" (*Entering the Silence*), which becomes "No signs, or signals claim us" (*Sign of Jonas*); a revised version of this line becomes the second line in the following section in the final version. In the first version, only the final two lines of the poem will follow this line.

30. By moving a revised version of what had been the final line of the previous stanza in the earlier versions after the opening line here, Merton makes clear that the antecedent of "There" is "ocean" in what is now the immediately preceding line. The final line of this section is not present in *Sign of Jonas*, and the preceding one reads: "The cities cry like peacocks in their sleep." Ross Labrie suggests that the revised line here is "more blurred and indecisive," an indication that in this poem "[s]ome of the changes are retrogressive" (Ross Labrie, *The Art of Thomas Merton* [Fort Worth: Texas Christian University Press, 1979] 124 [subsequent references will be cited as "Labrie, *Art*" parenthetically in the text]), but while it is true that the new line is more prosaic, it does better convey the impression that the speaker is immersed in silence and thus unable actually to hear the cries, and so can only conjecture what they might sound like.

31. *Sign of Jonas* reads: "I speak your name with blood . . . / With blood . . ." which creates an effective parallel with line 10, but might seem to suggest that the blood is that of Agnes rather than of Christ, and is in fact extra-liturgical, since there is no occasion for actually speaking her name later in the Mass.

32. *The Commonweal* 56 (April 18, 1952) 48.

33. A note in Merton's handwriting attached to two holograph drafts of this poem now in the King Library archives at the University of Kentucky reads: "1st and 2nd drafts of poem 'Early Mass' written Nov. 1950" – the first draft is untitled; the second contains both the final title and subtitle.

34. The celebrated Fourth and Walnut "epiphany" of March 18, 1958: see Thomas Merton, *A Search for Solitude: Pursuing the Monk's True Life. Journals, vol. 3: 1952-1960*, ed. Lawrence S. Cunningham (San Francisco: HarperCollins, 1996) 181-82, and the more familiar revised description of the experience in Thomas Merton, *Conjectures of a Guilty Bystander* (Garden City, NY: Doubleday, 1966) 140-42.

35. While at the hospital, Merton was also working on *Bread in the Wilderness* (New York: New Directions, 1953), his book on the Psalms that uses the image of bread for word in the same way (see *ES* 442).

36. "So the Eucharist is our daily bread. . . . [T]he special property to be understood in it is unity, so that by being digested into his body and

turned into his members we may be what we receive" (*Sermon* 57.7.7).

37. In the earlier versions of the poem, line 7 reads: "Our Christ has cleanly built Jerusalem!"

38. The first draft reads "this city," which becomes "His city" in the second draft, and "our sky," which becomes "your sky" in the second draft; the two final lines in the first draft read: "I speak His sober Latin. You are part of Us. / We are together when I am alone" while the otherwise identical second draft substitutes "Him." for "Us."

39. The first two lines of the opening section in the first draft read: "Come, citizens, to where His work is done. / Come to the quiet Lamb. I am his angel." In this second draft the last sentence is omitted, and the rest of the passage is cancelled and replaced by: "Come to the quiet Lamb / Come to the altar where His work is done."

40. The first draft of these lines reads: "Brightness has fallen on our wilderness / Manna has grown about us in the dark. / Come to this commonwealth. Our Tents are in the sun." In the second draft "The Truth" replaces "Manna," the third line is omitted, and "Gather us God in honeycombs and own His treasures." is inserted as the second line.

41. The first draft of these lines originally read: "Death has a wasted kingdom. Though this world is dying / These dirty stones shall build a sacred town"; then "Mended" replaces "These dirty" and a new first line is inserted: "Blessings restore the blind, straighten the lame." The second draft reads: ". . . the world be ill" and "These mended stones . . ." and ". . . straighten the broken limb." – in a line that now follows "Death . . . ill."

42. The first draft reads: "Flower along the altar-rail, my little ones! / Here is your Bird, here is your white Beloved / Here is your Father at my finger's end!" In the second draft, "Run to the golden fence," replaces "Flower . . . altar-rail," "And see . . . come to . . ." replaces "Here is . . . here is . . ."

43. The two earlier drafts read: "The clouds have fled".

44. The first draft reads: "Put up the flags of fall"; the second draft is identical to the published version.

45. The first draft reads: "Sail and water".

46. The first draft reads: "Open the gates. Behold the air, the trees, the golden avenue!" [following successively cancelled "steps!" "town" "houses!"]. In both the first and second drafts, "I am" becomes "We are" ["Because we are" in the second draft], and both follow "world," with "the brothers of a new".

47. It still retains this title in the "tentative arrangement" of the book's contents put together at New Directions and dated October 2, 1956 (included in the file with the setting copy of the poems, now at the Thomas Merton Center). It had first been published in *The Commonweal*

57 (December 26, 1952) 307, as "Christmas 1951 – For the Carmelites"; as Merton notes in his Preface to *The Strange Islands*, it was one of the poems (along with "Stranger" and "Elias – Variations on a Theme") produced "in response to a 'billet' from the New York Carmel" for songs to be sung around the Christmas crib at the convent (14).

48. Thomas Merton, *Seeds of Contemplation*, rev. ed. (New York: New Directions, 1949) 89 (subsequent references will be cited as "*SC* (rev. ed.)" parenthetically in the text; note that in this revised edition, which appeared some months after the initial publication of *Seeds of Contemplation*, the Marian material included as the last part of chapter 13, "Through a Glass," in the original edition (100-103), is considerably expanded and made into a new chapter 14, "Electa ut Sol" (87-92 in the revised version, which thus has 28 chapters rather than the first edition's 27). The slightly different original version of this passage is found on page 102 of the first edition.

49. *SC* (rev. ed.) 88; the original version of this passage (101) is identical except for the phrase ". . . the only way . . . " – replaced by ". . . the best way . . ."

50. For previous discussions, see Michael W. Higgins, *Heretic Blood: The Spiritual Geography of Thomas Merton* (Toronto: Stoddart, 1998) 138-41 (subsequent references will be cited as "Higgins" parenthetically in the text); George A. Kilcourse, *Ace of Freedoms: Thomas Merton's Christ* (Notre Dame: University of Notre Dame Press, 1993) 69-70 (subsequent references will be cited as "Kilcourse" parenthetically in the text); Victor A. Kramer, *Thomas Merton: Monk and Artist* (Kalamazoo, MI: Cistercian Publications, 1987) 83-84; Labrie, *Art* 128; Ross Labrie, *Thomas Merton and the Inclusive Imagination* (Columbia: University of Missouri Press, 2001) 154-55 (subsequent references will be cited as "Labrie, *Inclusive Imagination*" parenthetically in the text); Thérèse Lentfoehr, *Words and Silence: On the Poetry of Thomas Merton* (New York: New Directions, 1979) 90-92 (subsequent references will be cited as "Lentfoehr, *Words and Silence*" parenthetically in the text); Mott 286.

51. See Merton's comments on the genesis of the poem in his Preface to *Strange Islands*: "'Elegy for the Monastery Barn' was written after the cowbarn at Gethsemani burned down, one August evening in 1953, during the evening meditation. The monks left the meditation to fight a very hot fire and the poem arrived about the same time as the fire truck from the nearest town" (14). See also his August 11, 1953 letter to Mark Van Doren in which he sends the poem (Thomas Merton, *The Road to Joy: Letters to New and Old Friends*, ed. Robert E. Daggy [New York: Farrar, Straus, Giroux, 1989] 25) as well as comments on the poem in his July 24, 1959 letter to Van Doren (*Road to Joy* 34-35) about its inclusion in Merton's *Selected Poems*, and Van Doren's own appreciative comments

(which quote from this letter) in his Introduction to that volume (Thomas Merton, *Selected Poems* [New York: New Directions, 1959; enlarged ed. 1967] xi-xii).

52. In a much revised holograph draft of the poem, now in the King Library archives at the University of Kentucky, "about the neighborhood" replaces cancelled "in unfamiliar streets" and "hour" replaces cancelled "day"; a typed second draft, also in the King Library archives, is identical to the published version in these lines.

53. The holograph draft reads: "Here at the summer day's end / When wheels are still / And it is suppertime / Suddenly the long barn claps [replacing cancelled "puts"] on the [replacing cancelled "her"] traitor, beauty / . . ."; the typed draft also reads: "Suddenly the long barn . . ."

54. The holograph draft reads "for years" instead of "how long" and includes the additional line "And her ancient beams" after "shadows"; the final line reads: "so loved and feared." The typed draft reads "in this hour" for "now" in l. 13 (the holograph seems to read "words" at this point).

55. In the holograph draft this section reads: "She in whose airless heart we entered / Bursting . . . hay / Now will no longer have us near, for terribly / . . ."

56. In the holograph draft, "legacy" replaces cancelled "present" and is followed by "For us: . . . far more rare." The typed draft reads: ". . . a different legacy".

57. The holograph draft reads: "Greater than invisible cattle".

58. The holograph draft reads: "Making this moment dense with God's eternity." and lacks the following line.

59. In the holograph draft, "Laved" replaces cancelled "Anointed".

60. The holograph draft reads: "Fly from the barn, . . . / Of this chamber . . . fire / And from this sacred judgement that [   ] / Frightens + [   ] useless hose in the yard. / / Let no man look upon the Lord / Let no man see the Holy / One seated on the silence of disaster / . . ."; "inside" is also missing in the typed draft, which also reads: ". . . be within, and see . . ."

61. For previous discussions, see Higgins 141-43; Thérèse Lentfoehr, "Social Concern in the Poetry of Thomas Merton," in Gerald Twomey, ed., *Thomas Merton, Prophet in the Belly of a Paradox* (New York: Paulist Press, 1978) 120-21.

62. A journal entry for March 16, 1949 (*ES* 293) reveals both that Merton had long been disturbed by the gunnery practice, and that his attitude toward it at the time of writing the poem represented a return to and deepening of the "feeling of uneasiness" that had been allayed, temporarily, by his sense of detachment from secular anxieties at the time of his ordination to the deaconate: "Since I began this retreat, my

attitude toward the artillery that I can hear practicing all day at Fort Knox has changed considerably. For seven years it had given me a feeling of uneasiness in the pit of my stomach. Now I realize the Church's mission in the world. It makes no difference essentially whether the world be at war or at peace because the Church is going to emerge victorious anyway. The Kingdom of Christ is being established, and the crimes and stupidity of men and devils, instead of hindering our progress, is only pushing us forward – and doing so sometimes a lot faster than our bodies would like. Yet it is no contradiction to pray for peace, as the whole Church does, for peace is the will of God and peace depends on union with His will, war being the fruit of its violation."

63. *The Complete Poetry of John Donne*, ed. John T. Shawcross (Garden City, NY: Doubleday Anchor, 1967) 344.

64. *Complete Poetry of John Donne* 340-41.

65. *The Complete Poetical Works of Thomas Hardy*, 2 vols. (New York: Oxford University Press, 1982, 1984) 2.9-10.

66. For previous discussions, see Waclaw Grzybowski, *Spirituality and Metaphor: The Poetics and Poetry of Thomas Merton* (Opole: Uniwersytet Opolski, 2006) 146-51; Kilcourse 63-64; Labrie, *Inclusive Imagination* 33-34; Lentfoehr, *Words and Silence* 56-57; Thérèse Lentfoehr, "The Zen Mystical Poetry of Thomas Merton," in Donald Grayston and Michael W. Higgins, eds., *Thomas Merton: Pilgrim in Process* (Toronto: Griffin House, 1983) 18, 22; Bonnie Thurston, "Wrestling with Angels: Some Mature Poems of Thomas Merton," in Patrick F. O'Connell, ed., *The Vision of Thomas Merton* (Notre Dame, IN: Ave Maria Press, 2003) 99-201; Thurston, "Light" 202-205; Waldron 133-51.

67. While a number of commentators, most notably Bonnie Thurston in "The Light Strikes Home," have associated this poem with Merton's growing attraction to Eastern wisdom in general and Zen in particular, what is remarkable about "Stranger" is that it was almost certainly written before Merton had much in-depth exposure to Zen teaching. The poem was composed some time before the end of July 1955, when it was sent with the rest of what was then to be called *Tower of Babel and Other Poems* to be retyped. In his February 16, 1955 letter to James Laughlin that first mentions his "small volume of poetry shaping up" (*TMJL* 109), he also asks if Laughlin had run across any books "by D. Suzuki" on Zen Buddhism, adding "I think that is how you spell him," and mentioning he is anxious to track some down (*TMJL* 108), suggesting that he as yet has had little if any acquaintance with his work, though his interest in Zen has been sparked. In a May 7, 1956 letter to Laughlin, he writes, "I have finally found the Zen books I was looking for in the Library of Congress and am borrowing them from there. Zen is fierce, but terrifically practical" (*TMJL* 114).

68. See Thomas Merton, *An Introduction to Christian Mysticism: Initiation into the Monastic Tradition 3*, ed. Patrick F. O'Connell (Kalamazoo, MI: Cistercian Publications, 2008) 121-35; subsequent references will be cited as *"ICM"* parenthetically in the text. (These notes are from the text of conferences given by Merton to newly ordained monks in 1961.)

69. See Merton's description of "connatural" knowing as a "mode of apprehension" that "reaches out to grasp the inner reality, the vital substance of its object, by a kind of affective identification of itself with it" (*Literary Essays of Thomas Merton*, ed. Patrick Hart, OCSO [New York: New Directions, 1981] 347).

70. A possible allusion to T. S. Eliot's "Teach us to sit still" ("Ash Wednesday," in T. S. Eliot, *The Complete Poems and Plays: 1909-1950* [New York: Harcourt, Brace & World, 1962] 61).

71. St. Augustine, *Confessions* 3.6.11.

"A Ray of That Truth Which Enlightens All": Thomas Merton, Poetic Language and Inter-religious Dialogue

Bonnie Thurston

At St. Peter's Basilica in Rome, on October 28, 1965, the Catholic Church in its *Declaration on the Relationship of the Church to Non-Christian Religions* (*Nostra Aetate*) affirmed that it "rejects nothing which is true and holy" in other religions, that it "looks with sincere respect upon those ways of conduct and of life, those rules and teachings which, though differing in many particulars from what she holds and sets forth, nevertheless often reflect a ray of that Truth which enlightens all."[1] Coming centuries after Justin Martyr who, following the opening chapter of St. John's Gospel, attributed truths in non-Christian religions to the Word of God who enlightens everyone who comes into the world (John 1:9), this statement provided official "recognition of other religions as entities with which the Church can and should enter into dialogue" (Abbott 662, n. 11).

By 1965 Thomas Merton had already entered that dialogue and was in conversation with major voices from other religious traditions: Rabbis Abraham Heschel and Zalman Schachter, the Muslim Abdul Aziz, Zen Buddhist D. T. Suzuki, Hindu Amiya Chakravarty, and Chinese religions scholar John C. H. Wu, to name but the most famous of Merton's dialogue partners.[2] Writing of the ways Merton is a "parable for our time," William Reiser, SJ correctly points out that the monk anticipated the phenomenon of globalization, was aware of "humanity's interconnectedness," and thought that "faith without solidarity is dead."[3] As Patrick O'Connell so eloquently put it in his entry on "Interreligious Dialogue" in *The Thomas Merton Encyclopedia*, "Interreligious dialogue is at the heart of Merton's contemplative alternative to cross-cultural misunderstanding or to a soulless global 'culture' dedicated to efficiency, pragmatism, and profits."[4]

At the outset, let me clarify my language and explain my approach to the role of poetry in inter-religious dialogue. I do not write about Merton's well-documented "ecumenism," his openness to other Christians.[5] The Greek root of the English word "ecumenism" is *oikos*, house. Ecumenism is a conversation *within* the house of Christianity. The existence of Baptists and Greek Orthodox and Roman Catholics and Presbyterians and Pentecostals and so many other kinds of Christians does prove Christianity to be, exactly as Jesus said, a house of many rooms (John 14:2). But all these are cousins within the same family or household. Inter-religious dialogue is the conversation between (or among) Christians and non-Christians. In this conversation, too, Merton excelled, as the *"Merton and . . ."* series of books from Fons Vitae Press is documenting.[6]

Any number of Merton's poems have as their explicit subject some aspect of non-Christian religions and the way poetic language, itself, advances religious dialogue. I will focus primarily on the latter, but provide a reminder of the extent of the former.[7] The category of "Merton's Inter-religious Poetry" would include the following (and this is far from a complete list) – Merton's conversation with Judaism is evident in many poems on characters from the Hebrew Bible, poems found largely (but not exclusively) in the pre-1957 volumes, in the verse play *The Tower of Babel* (itself a reflection on language), and in what we might call the "Holocaust" poems of the 1960s: for example, "Chant to be Used in Processions around a Site with Furnaces" (*CP* 345-49) or "Epitaph for a Public Servant" (*CP* 703-11). There are seven explicitly Islamic poems in *The Collected Poems* (also found in Baker & Henry 287-305), three of which are long, multi-sectioned poems: "Song for the Death of Averroes" (*CP* 325-29) "Readings from Ibn Abbad" (*CP* 745-52) (which also appears in *Raids on the Unspeakable*[8]), and "East with Ibn Battuta" (*CP* 538-44) in *The Geography of Lograire*.[9] While carried on largely in his letters and journals, the dialogue with Hinduism is reflected in the poems "Darjeeling" (*CP* 700-701), "Kandy Express" (*CP* 715-21) and "Songs of Experience; India, One" (*CP* 753-55). Many scholars of Merton's poetry have noted that the change of technique evident in his poetry from the late 1950s onward mirrors, and may be the result of, his study of Zen.[10] This Zen-like quality is seen in poems like "Song for Nobody" (*CP* 337-38), "Messenger from the Horizon" (*CP* 349-51), "Night-Flowering Cactus" (*CP* 351-52) and "Love Winter When the Plant Says Nothing" (*CP* 353). "The Ox Mountain Parable" (*CP* 970-71) in *The Collected Poems*[11] and Merton's volume *The Way of Chuang Tzu*[12] (a book of which Merton, himself, was particularly fond) amply attest to his interest in Chinese religions.

I will not explicate any of these poems. Instead, I address the more theoretical issue of the use of language in poetry and in dialogue, relying heavily on Merton's own ideas found in "Contemplation and Dialogue" in *Mystics and Zen Masters* (203-14) and "Monastic Experience and East-West Dialogue," the notes for a paper to have been given in Calcutta in October, 1968 which appears as Appendix IV in the original edition of *The Asian Journal*.[13] When it is appropriate, I will illustrate ideas by pointing to poems in the 1963 volume *Emblems of a Season of Fury*,[14] which represents Merton's re-emergence as a poet, contains poems which reflect his interest in inter-religious dialogue,[15] and employs his more mature poetic voice and techniques.

Beyond the rather superficial but ever-present task of the poet to find fresh subject matter, why would Merton make so many poetic forays into other religions? Why not just stick to prose in his inter-religious vocation? Several related answers suggest themselves. First, poetry is the language of religious experience, and Merton's entree to dialogue is direct religious experience rather than doctrine. Second, the sort of religious experience in question was contemplative. Merton thought good religious poets must be, in some sense, contemplatives. From the outset of his vocation as writer and monk, two of Merton's primary interests were the proper use of language and the nature of the contemplative life. The two come together in the poetry of dialogue, particularly Merton's engagement with the three founded religions, Buddhism, Christianity and Islam. Third, the principles of good religious dialogue as Merton outlined them also apply to the writing of good religious poetry. The remainder of this essay discusses these three ideas.

Poetry is the Language of Religious Experience

The written sources collected after their deaths indicate that the Buddha, the Christ and the Prophet used language allusively and metaphorically as much as prescriptively. They spoke in poetry not dogma; their language was metaphorical as often as it was literal. There is a long tradition in Christian theology which predates St. Augustine or St. Thomas Aquinas, who most clearly articulated it, that religious language, like biblical language, is metaphorical. We compare what we cannot fully know (God), with what we can know (God's creation). A is understood in terms of B. This metaphorical process is at the root of religious language, and it *is* the poetic process itself. As Merton asked in "A Messenger from the Horizon": "When a message has no clothes on / How can it be spoken?" (ll. 41-42). Answer: by analogy or metaphor. Metaphorical language is the "clothes" of a religious "message."

In *The Sacred and the Profane* Mircea Eliade noted that "a religious symbol conveys its message even if it is no longer *consciously* understood in every part. For a symbol speaks to the whole human being and not only to the intelligence."[16] (Italics Eliade's) Such an insight is consonant with Merton's criticism of the Christian's use of language in which "Even God has become another conceptual unreality in a no-man's land of language that no longer serves as a means of communion with reality."[17] God is not a concept, an intellectual proposition. Serious or committed religious persons are taken up entire into their religion. Their religious experience is not only (or even primarily) intellectual assent, but involves affect, volition, bodily disposition. Poetic language, metaphor, symbolism, all speak "to the whole human being." The Buddha, the Christ, the Prophet spoke metaphorically and symbolically and thus appealed to whole persons. It is metaphors and symbols that speak to our whole humanity and that raise us to the universal level. Again, Eliade: "For it is through symbols that man finds his way out of his particular situations and 'opens himself' to the general and universal. Symbols awaken individual experience and transmute it into a spiritual act, into metaphysical comprehension of the world. . . . [B]y understanding the symbol [the religious person] *succeeds in living the universal*" (Eliade 211-12) (Italics Eliade's). Again, to quote Merton in "Song: If You Seek . . ." (*CP* 340-41): the symbol is "the unexpected flash / Beyond 'yes,' beyond 'no,' / The forerunner of the Word of God" (ll. 19-20).

Merton's entree into religious dialogue was just this sort of direct experience. As Paul Pearson writes in the introduction to William Apel's book on Merton's interfaith letters, "Merton's approach to . . . dialogue was centered on the religious experience of others rather than on the doctrinal expression of their traditions" (Apel xiii). Poetic language embraces the whole person in a way intellectual propositions cannot, and personal experiences allow for communication at a level that dogmatic comparisons rule out. Poetry is the language of what in "Grace's House" (*CP* 330-31) Merton calls "this archetypal, cosmic hill, / this womb of mysteries" (ll. 45-46).

Indeed, Merton's life, itself, prepared him for inter-religious dialogue. In an important article published in Volume 15 of *The Merton Annual*, Allan McMillan points out that Merton knew "meaningful dialogue between different religions would not be well served by theological debate alone or by merely comparing religious practices."[18] McMillan documents seven lessons Merton learned at various points in his life that served him well in interfaith dialogue. I will not indicate the biographical locus of each, but here are the seven lessons that McMillan has isolated:

> (1) that dialogue is relational; not debate; (2) that persons are more important than faith expressions; (3) that contemplation and mystical prayer are a meeting ground for dialogue and are available to us and to all; (4) that we come to understand by experience, not by concept; (5) that interfaith dialogue can be an 'honest encounter' without seeking the 'ecclesial conversion' of the other; (6) that interfaith dialogue challenges us to entertain change in our own hearts and (7) that such change is not personal gain, but God-given through us to others. (McMillan 208)

"Relational," "personal," "experiential," "encounter" – these are the terms that characterize Merton's point of engagement with dialogue. He commended this approach in the paper to have been delivered in Calcutta in October, 1968: "even where there are irreconcilable differences in doctrine and formulated belief, there may still be great similarities and analogies in the realm of religious experience." "[O]n this existential level of experience and of spiritual maturity, it is possible to achieve real and significant contacts" (*AJ* 312). "Similarity" and "analogy" – such terms describe the poetic process: seeing likenesses, making comparisons. McMillan notes "many examples of how perceptive and sensitive Merton was in the act of dialogue. He showed that he could go quickly to the heart of the matter by poetically writing on several levels at the same time" (McMillan 203). "Poetically writing on several levels" again suggests the multi-valence of poetic language in the context of religious dialogue. Over and over in articles on Merton and religious dialogue scholars note both his existential approach to dialogue and that poetic or symbolic language is crucial to its articulation.

Contemplative Experience and Religious Dialogue

Just as religious experience calls for a particular kind of language (poetic), the religious experience that Merton finds crucial to dialogue is of a certain kind, contemplative. Whether one looks at the life of the Buddha, the Christ or the Prophet, one finds a contemplative stance. As Merton wrote in "Contemplation and Dialogue," "one may find in all races and in all traditions both the capacity for contemplative experience and the fact of its realization even on a very pure level. This capacity and this realization are therefore implicit in all the great religious traditions, whether Asian or European, whether Hindu, Buddhist, Moslem or Christian" (*MZM* 209). And contemplatives tend to express their insights metaphorically. Indeed, almost from the beginning, Merton understood the connection between aesthetic and contemplative experience. In fact he thought that aesthetic experience was a form of, or at least could lead to, contemplative experience.

Writing in *The Seven Storey Mountain* of his M.A. work on William Blake, Merton said, "from my very childhood, I had understood that the artistic experience, at its highest, was actually a natural analogue of mystical experience. It produced a kind of intuitive perception of reality through a sort of affective identification with the object contemplated."[19] In both the 1947 and the 1958 versions of an article on poetry and contemplation (both published in *Commonweal*[20]) Merton asserts that "No Christian poetry worthy of the name has been written by anyone who was not in some degree a contemplative" (*FA* 99; *LE* 345). In the 1958 reappraisal he continues, "the true poet is always akin to the mystic because of the 'prophetic' intuition by which he sees the spiritual reality, the inner meaning of the object he contemplates . . . . All good Christian poets are then contemplatives in the sense that they see God everywhere in . . . creation and . . . behold the created world as filled with signs and symbols of God" (*LE* 345). In an article in *The Catholic World* entitled "Christian Culture Needs Oriental Wisdom," Merton wrote: "Wisdom is not penetrated by logical analysis. The values hidden in Oriental thought actually reveal themselves only on the plane of spiritual experience, or perhaps, if you like, of aesthetic experience."[21] Merton frequently highlighted the complementarity of contemplative and aesthetic experience. Indeed, in an article on Merton and religious poetry Timothy Materer argued persuasively that Merton thought that "art will take us up a Jacob's ladder to a supra-sensual or spiritual realm. Once in that realm through the aesthetic experience, we have then moved closer to a religious experience as well."²²

My premise is that the converse is also true. Once we are in the realm of contemplative experience, in this case religious dialogue, only aesthetic language, poetic language, is the proper vehicle for communication. "[F]or us to name the things that share our own silence with us," to use Merton's beautiful phrase in *Thoughts in Solitude* (*TS* 69), our ordinary use of language is too crude. Something more subtle and allusive is required. In those important notes for the Calcutta talk Merton said, "True communication on the deepest level is more than a simple sharing of ideas, of conceptual knowledge, or formulated truth." What is necessary is "'communion' beyond the level of words, a communion in authentic experience which is shared not only on a 'preverbal' level but also on a 'postverbal' level" (*AJ* 315). Merton calls, first, for a sharing of silence, because, as Lynn Szabo so beautifully and concisely says, "silence is the language of the seemingly absent God."²³ Most of Merton's own writing, and certainly his poetry (and perhaps all poetry), is as Materer said in 1970, an attempt to "use language to suggest experiences beyond rational discourse" (Materer 577).

In his discussion of Merton's dialogue with Eastern religions, the first of William Shannon's five insights is that "Merton came to see very early the importance of experience as a locus for theological reflection."²⁴ Shannon's second point is "the understanding that words cannot adequately capture the religious experience." Merton understood "the inadequacy of language to express the experience of ultimate reality" (Shannon 216). Language may be inadequate, but it is not useless. Language is all that Merton, or anyone else for that matter, has for such expression. And the most appropriate kind of language for the work of inter-religious dialogue at the level of experience, particularly contemplative experience, is metaphorical or poetic language, because symbols like fire, light, darkness, path, journey, wandering, thirst are common to human spiritual experience regardless of religious tradition.

Let me summarize to this point: I have highlighted relationships between two themes pervasive in Merton's thought that remind us that religious language is by nature metaphorical. Because it engages the whole person, metaphorical language is especially appropriate to describe religious experience. Religious experience is Merton's point of entree to inter-religious dialogue which is carried on most deeply at the experiential and expressed at the metaphorical levels. If there is an element of truth in these statements, and Merton seemed to think there was, I am led to wonder whether the principles of good religious dialogue might apply to the writing of good poetry, or at least good religious poetry.

Principles of Religious Dialogue and the Writing of Poetry

In "Monastic Experience and East-West Dialogue," after defining what he means by "monastic," addressing the problems of language, and highlighting the importance of the "existential level of experience" (*AJ* 312) in dialogue, Merton closed his talk with five "wrong ways that are to be avoided" (*AJ* 316) in dialogue. They are as follows: (1) Such dialogue must "not become just another way of adding to the interminable empty talk . . . with which modern man tries to convince himself that he is in touch . . . with reality. This contemplative dialogue must be reserved for those who have been seriously disciplined by years of silence and by a long habit of meditation." (2) "[T]here can be no question of a facile syncretism, a mishmash of semireligious verbiage . . . that . . . takes nothing with full seriousness." (3) "[T]here must be scrupulous respect for important differences." (4) "[A]ttention must be concentrated on what is really essential to the monastic quest," which Merton believes to be "true self-transcendence and enlightenment." (5) "[Q]uestions of institutional structure, monastic rule, traditional forms of cult and observance must be seen as relatively secondary" (*AJ* 316-17). How might these caveats about dialogue point toward "correct ways" of writing the poetry of religious experience and cross-religious experience?

First, while most poets will hardly be disciplined by years of silence and meditation (for which many poets can breathe a sigh of relief!) most, including in my view Merton, could be silent more and write less. If poetry in our day is to be a force for good, it must avoid facile "empty talk" and arise from a silence that has listened profoundly to all levels of the current reality. A good deal of the enmity in our world arises from speaking too soon and too much and listening too little.

Second, such poetry must scrupulously avoid what Merton called semireligious verbiage and pieties and "a devotionalism that admits everything and therefore takes nothing with full seriousness" (*AJ* 316). Put positively, such poetry must be fresh and innovative in form and expression. Good religious poetry is first of all good poetry.

Third, what in dialogue Merton calls "scrupulous respect for important differences" in poetry might be called scrupulous attention to detail, to things as they are, to honesty in subject matter, rhetoric and technique. "This concept: going out to the thing and giving oneself to it, allowing it to communicate its essence, allowing it to say what it will, reveal what it will, rather than trying to bring it into the confines of self, altering and changing it by possession of it" was, according to John Howard Griffin, "one of Thomas Merton's profoundest orientations."[25]

Fourth, and related to Merton's third point, self-transcendence is critical to the poetic endeavor. All who have taught creative writing classes know that student poets often use poetry as an emotional outlet. Their poetry is all about themselves, which may not be a bad thing for emotional development, but (unless they are Walt Whitman) might be catastrophic for their development as poets. Especially if one is to write good religious poetry, one must begin with self-transcendence and the knowledge that, not to put too fine a point on it, it is not about us. We must avoid what in "Contemplation and Dialogue" Merton called "consecrated narcissism" (*MZM* 213). William Thompson thought that Merton's contribution to transcultural consciousness was precisely the realization that "to celebrate and confess faith in the risen Christ is to commit oneself to that passage from absorption to universality, from partiality to final transcultural integration, which the Easter faith proclaims."[26] In "A Letter to Pablo Antonio Cuadra concerning Giants," Merton made the point this way: "Since the Word was made Flesh, God is in man. God is in *all men*. All men are to be seen and treated as Christ" (*CP* 380). He continued: "It was certainly right that Christian Europe should bring Christ to the Indians of Mexico and the Andes, as well as to the Hindus and the Chinese: but where they failed was in their inability *to encounter Christ* already potentially present in the Indians, the Hindus and the Chinese" (*CP* 381).

Finally, the structures, rules and forms which Merton felt characterized monastic life also, in another mode, characterize poetry. A *regula*, a rule or trellis, gives guidance and structure and can greatly assist the process of growth. The formal elements of poetry can help the poet to shape the idea and the experience, but are secondary. The "rules" are meant to assist poets, but not when they become the central focus of the poem. In the good use of a poetic form, like the good use of a religious practice, the form does not call attention to itself.

Conclusion

In their essay "A World-Embracing Prophet: Catholic Imagination and the Transcultural Believer," Fred and Michael Herron note that "Merton displays an openness to the evocative and revelatory power of other cultures and ways of undertaking the human journey." Such openness, they believe, is ultimately "a reflection of our receptivity to the divine, present in the other."[27] Merton himself articulated exactly this point in his letter to Cuadra when he writes, "God speaks, and God is to be heard, not only on Sinai, not only in my own heart, but in the *voice of the stranger*" (CP 384). Thomas Merton's participation in inter-religious dialogue was precisely one of the ways he listened for God. As McMillan noted, "As a contemplative monk he explored contemplative traditions wherever he found them, especially those which combined poetry and art with the mystical expression" (McMillan 202). Why? Because for Merton the interface of art and contemplation was a primary locus of encounter with the Divine, with Christ.

Furthermore, Merton's entrance into dialogue with other religious persons from the point of his own experience of prayer and of the spiritual life was a primary means by which he overcame the very difficult problem of dualism in Christian spirituality. He writes in "Contemplation and Dialogue" that genuine dialogue "requires the communication and sharing . . . of religious intuitions and truths which may turn out to have something in common, beneath surface differences." It "seeks the inner and ultimate spiritual 'ground' which underlies all articulated differences" (MZM 204). Paul Knitter noted that Merton's deep, authentic experience of God was not an experience of an object, but an immediate experience of Being.[28] Merton said as much in 1958 in "Poetry and Contemplation: A Reappraisal." Writing of mystical contemplation he says, "we are no longer facing God as an 'object' of experience or as a concept which we apprehend." Merton continues, "the aesthetic intuition is also beyond objectivity – it 'sees' by identifying itself spiritually with what it contemplates" (LE 348). In Merton's life both poetry and inter-religious dialogue were ways he penetrated surface appearances for the inner reality of a life beyond subject-object dualism. This attitude pre-dated his study of Zen to which it is often attributed, and is seen reflected in the "voicelessness" of poems like "Song for Nobody" (*CP* 337) and "Love Winter When the Plant Says Nothing." (*CP* 353)

But beyond personal spiritual practice, poetry has a prophetic function that is related to interfaith expression. In his "Message to Poets" (February, 1964), Merton wrote "To prophesy is not to predict, but to seize upon reality in its moment of highest expectation and tension toward the new" (*RU* 159). A similar idea underlies both the poem "Advice to a Young Prophet" (*CP* 338-39) and "A Letter to Pablo Antonio Cuadra concerning Giants," both of which appear in *Emblems of a Season of Fury* (still heart-stoppingly and tragically contemporary). It is this "tension toward the new" which characterizes Merton's last two long and experimental poems, *Cables to the Ace*[29] and *The Geography of Lograire*, both of which reflect his immersion in the issues of interfaith dialogue. Speaking of Merton's world view as that of the artist-intellectual, Peter Kountz wrote:

> The artist then is one who lives with the knowledge of what could be and with a sadness and anger at what actually is. The artist is a person of the heart for whom even the worldview becomes, at its very core, *l'affaire d'amour*. From the heart the artist writes or paints or composes in order to create the world of the heart. The artist, acting out of faith and a consuming desire for the good, creates the "substance of things hoped for; the evidence of things not seen."[30]

In the polarized world in which we live, where difference is demonized with catastrophic results, the interface of Merton's practice of poetry and of inter-religious dialogue is of immense practical importance. It reminds us first and foremost that openness to the other is often openness to the Divine Who is radically Other. As Merton wrote to Pablo Antonio Cuadra, "It is my belief that we should not be too sure of having found Christ in ourselves until we have found him also in the part of humanity that is most remote from our own" (*CP* 382-83). "God is to be heard . . . in the *voice of the stranger*." We must find God "in our enemy, or we may lose him even in our friend" (*CP* 384). The language of this encounter will seldom be the language of religious dogma. Merton noted that "Christ is found not in loud and pompous declarations but in humble and fraternal dialogue" (*CP* 383). Nor is it the language of politics and what passes for diplomacy, but the language of poetry, allusive, metaphorical, symbolic language that takes us to the shared depths of the human psyche. Thus it reminds us that the truth of the Buddha, the Christ and the Prophet, the "truth which enlightens all," waits quietly for us as we grow toward more poetic uses of language. It reminds us that the common experiences of human life are our most important and profound points of contact with those who, on the surface of it, seem different from us. It reminds us to celebrate our commonality, therefore, perhaps, making of our lives, and our life together, a kind of poetry.

Endnotes

1. Walter M. Abbott, SJ, ed., *The Documents of Vatican II* (New York: Guild Press/America Press, 1966) 662; subsequent references will be cited as "Abbott" parenthetically in the text.

2. A helpful introduction to these conversations is William Apel's *Signs of Peace: The Interfaith Letters of Thomas Merton* (Maryknoll, NY: Orbis, 2006); subsequent references will be cited as "Apel" parenthetically in the text.

3. William Reiser, SJ, "Thomas Merton: A Parable for Our Time," *The Merton Seasonal* 29.2 (Summer 2004) 10-11.

4. Patrick O'Connell, "Interreligious Dialogue," in William H. Shannon, Christine M. Bochen and Patrick F. O'Connell, *The Thomas Merton Encyclopedia* (Maryknoll, NY: Orbis, 2002) 220.

5. See, for example, E. Glenn Hinson, "Expansive Catholicism: Merton's Ecumenical Perceptions," *Cistercian Studies* 14.3 (1979) 290-304, or William O. Paulsell, "Thomas Merton's Ecumenical Landscape," *The Merton* Seasonal 28.3 (Fall, 2003) 15-19.

6. See Rob Baker and Gray Henry, eds., *Merton & Sufism: The Untold Story* (Louisville, KY: Fons Vitae, 1999) (subsequent references will be cited as "Baker & Henry" parenthetically in the text); Beatrice Bruteau, ed., *Merton & Judaism: Holiness in Words* (Louisville, KY: Fons Vitae, 2003); Bonnie Thurston, ed., *Merton & Buddhism: Wisdom, Emptiness & Everyday Mind* (Louisville, KY: Fons Vitae, 2007). Volumes on Merton and Hinduism and Merton and Taoism are projected for the series, which also includes the "ecumenical" volume *Merton & Hesychasm: The Prayer of the Heart*, ed. Bernadette Dieker and Jonathan Montaldo (Louisville, KY: Fons Vitae, 2003).

7. Thomas Merton, *The Collected Poems of Thomas Merton* (New York: New Directions, 1977) 247-73; subsequent references will be cited as "*CP*" parenthetically in the text; also found in Baker & Henry 287-305.

8. Thomas Merton, *Raids on the Unspeakable* (New York: New Directions, 1966) 141-51; subsequent references will be cited as "*RU*" parenthetically in the text.

9. Thomas Merton, *The Geography of Lograire* (New York: New Directions, 1969).

10. See Bonnie Bowman Thurston, "Zen in the Eye of Thomas Merton's Poetry," *Buddhist-Christian Studies* 4 (1984) 103-17.

11. Also published in a limited edition as *The Ox Mountain Parable of Meng Tzu* (Lexington, KY: Stamperia del Santuccio, 1960) and as the final section of Merton's essay "Classic Chinese Thought" in Thomas Merton, *Mystics and Zen Masters* (New York: Farrar, Straus and Giroux, 1967) 65-68; subsequent references will be cited as "*MZM*" parenthetically in the text.

12. Thomas Merton, *The Way of Chuang Tzu* (New York: New Directions, 1965).

13. Thomas Merton, *The Asian Journal*, ed. Naomi Burton Stone, Brother Patrick Hart and James Laughlin (New York: New Directions, 1973) 309-17; subsequent references will be cited as "*AJ*" parenthetically in the text.

14. Thomas Merton, *Emblems of a Season of Fury* (New York: New Directions, 1963).

15. See, for example, the Islamic subjects in "The Moslems' Angel of Death" (*CP* 307-308) and "Song for the Death of Averroes" (*CP* 325-29), the experience of "satori" reflected in part 3 of "Macarius the Younger" (*CP* 321), and the Chinese influences in "Song: In the Shows of the Round Ox" (*CP* 311-13) and "A Picture of Lee Ying" (*CP* 322-24) as well as many ideas in "A Letter to Pablo Antonio Cuadra . . ." (*CP* 372-91).

16. Mircea Eliade, *The Sacred and the Profane* (New York: Harvest Books, 1959) 129; subsequent references will be cited as "Eliade" parenthetically in the text.

17. Thomas Merton, *Thoughts in Solitude* (New York: Farrar, Straus and Cudahy, 1958) 85; subsequent references will be cited as "*TS*" parenthetically in the text.

18. Allan M. McMillan, "Seven Lessons for Inter-faith Dialogue and Thomas Merton," *The Merton Annual* 15 (2002) 194; subsequent references will be cited as "McMillan" parenthetically in the text.

19. Thomas Merton, *The Seven Storey Mountain* (New York: Harcourt, Brace, 1948) 202.

20. Thomas Merton, "Poetry and the Contemplative Life," *The Commonweal* 46.12 (July 4, 1947) 280-86, subsequently included in Thomas Merton, *Figures for an Apocalypse* (New York: New Directions, 1947) 93-111 (subsequent references will be cited as "*FA*" parenthetically in the text); and "Poetry and Contemplation: A Reappraisal," *The Commonweal* 69 (October 24, 1958) 87-92, subsequently included in Thomas Merton, *The Literary Essays of Thomas Merton*, ed. Patrick Hart, OCSO (New York: New Directions, 1981) 338-54 (subsequent references will be cited as "*LE*"

parenthetically in the text).

21. Thomas Merton, *A Thomas Merton Reader*, ed. Thomas P. McDonnell (New York: Harcourt, Brace, 1962) 326; rev. ed. (Garden City, NY: Doubleday Image, 1974) 302.

22. Timothy Materer, "Merton and Auden: Setting the Borders of Religious Poetry," *Commonweal* 41.21 (February 27, 1970) 578; subsequent references will be cited as "Materer" parenthetically in the text.

23. Lynn R. Szabo, "The Sound of Sheer Silence: A Study in the Poetics of Thomas Merton," *The Merton Annual* 13 (2000) 208.

24. William H. Shannon, "Thomas Merton in Dialogue with Eastern Religions," in Patrick F. O'Connell, ed., *The Vision of Thomas Merton* (Notre Dame, IN: Ave Maria Press, 2003) 215; subsequent references will be cited as "Shannon" parenthetically in the text.

25. John Howard Griffin, *A Hidden Wholeness: The Visual World of Thomas Merton* (Boston: Houghton Mifflin, 1970) 50.

26. William M. Thompson, "Merton's Contribution to a Transcultural Consciousness," in Donald Grayston and Michael W. Higgins, eds., *Thomas Merton: Pilgrim in Process* (Toronto: Griffin House, 1983) 163.

27. Fred W. Herron and Michael J. Herron, "A World-Embracing Prophet: Catholic Imagination and the Transcultural Believer," *The Merton Journal* 14.1 (Eastertide 2007) 38, 39.

28. Paul Knitter, "Thomas Merton's Eastern Remedy for Christianity's 'Anonymous Dualism,'" *Cross Currents* 31.3 (Fall 1981) 290.

29. Thomas Merton, *Cables to the Ace* (New York: New Directions, 1968).

30. Peter Kountz, "The Significance of Thomas Merton as Artist-Writer (Some Reflections)," *Cistercian Studies* 12.4 (1977) 315.

From Violence to Silence:
The Rhetorical Means and Ends
of Thomas Merton's Antipoetry

Jeffrey Bilbro

You are not big enough to accuse the whole age effectively, but let us say you are in dissent. You are in no position to issue commands, but you can speak words of hope. Shall this be the substance of your message? Be human in this most inhuman of ages; guard the image of man for it is the image of God.

Thomas Merton, Prologue,
Raids on the Unspeakable[1]

Thomas Merton scholarship has continually been forced to confront the astonishing breadth of Merton's life and thought. As George Woodcock rightly states, "The images that emerge of [Thomas Merton] seem often bewilderingly multiple."[2] Efforts to piece together some of these images can, in addition to clarifying our conception of his immensely assimilative mind, deepen our understanding of each of these facets. In this paper, then, I bring together some of the seemingly disparate themes in Merton's oeuvre, tracing the motivation behind his use of antipoetry by demonstrating how this style of writing enabled him to put into practice his understanding of non-violence and his monastic emphasis on silence and Zen thought.

Merton wanted to couch his critique of Western power, and particularly of the United States government, in a style that would not partake of the hegemonic, anti-human, self-justifying rhetoric used by politicians and too many pacifists. So Merton sought an alternative rhetoric that would enable him to speak for peace and human rights with integrity, to speak in a way that valued other humans instead of reducing them, that opened space for contemplation instead of foreclosing dialogue. To achieve such a humane rhetoric, Merton rejected ideologically violent means of advocating for peace and embraced a form of antipoetry – a style of writing similar to that called "writing degree zero" by Roland Barthes – as a way to disrupt the self-justifying language of militant politicians and to open space for a Zen-like silence that might reconnect his readers to a deeper ground of being, a ground from which real dialogue might begin.

After briefly reading one of Merton's antipoems to indicate its distinctive traits, I will examine the way Merton developed his antipoetry in response to two other forms of rhetoric: the sensational, violent language of too many war protestors and a symbolic, meaning-laden language denatured by academics and politicians. Then, in order to better understand the rhetorical techniques Merton's antipoetry employs, I will draw from Roland Barthes' theories in *Writing Degree Zero* and Merton's response to them to clarify the way Merton's antipoetry operates and to identify four particular ways that Merton's poetry goes about its task of disrupting inhuman language and opening space for silence. Finally, I will return to two more of Merton's antipoems to demonstrate how they work out these four rhetorical techniques.

I

One of Merton's late poems, "Epitaph for a Public Servant,"[3] exemplifies the way he uses antipoetry to respond to obfuscating, violence-justifying language. As I will demonstrate later, this antipoetry can be characterized by four distinguishing traits: 1) an artificial, distancing style; 2) a refusal to communicate clear meaning; 3) a juxtaposition of words from normally discrete discourses; and 4) an attempt to leave the reader in silence. "Epitaph for a Public Servant" clearly fulfills these criteria, and a brief reading of this poem indicates the way Merton's antipoetry disrupts the decontextualized language of violence.

Merton wrote this poem in response to the trial of Adolf Eichmann, a Nazi official who oversaw the transport of Jews to concentration camps. The construction of the poem immediately distances the reader through its non-standard use of grammar and punctuation. Indeed, the poem contains almost no punctuation, having only a few closing punctuation marks, parentheses, and quotation marks. This unpunctuated construction causes the words and phrases to merge, allowing Merton to ambiguously blend the various discourses he draws from and refusing to allow the reader to become lost in the flow of the writing. Instead, readers must continually reinterpret the words they find in the poem, and this work foregrounds the fact that they are reading a constructed piece of writing, not receiving any clear meaning.

Merton repeatedly frustrates readers' attempts to find meaning by scrambling earlier phrases and repeating them in differing forms. Merton reproduces phrases from Eichmann and other figures at the trial, taking them out of context and then rearranging words as they are repeated throughout the poem. Space does not permit a close reading of the entire poem, but one example of this linguistic shuffling is Merton's use of Eichmann's statement that opens the poem: "'Not out of mercy / Did I launch this transaction'" (ll. 1-2). These words weave through the rest of the poem, appearing in other contexts that further confuse and complicate their already vague meaning:

> Not out of mercy
> A man
> With positive ideas
> (This transaction)
> A Christian
> Education
> (Not out of mercy) . . .
>
> "Not out of mercy did I
> Launch this"
> Christian education . . .
>
> "I ENTERED LIFE ON EARTH"
> To launch a positive idea . . .
>
> With this transaction
> In my pocket . . .
>
> To grant a mercy death
> Institutional care
>
> Not out of mercy
> Did I dare
>
> To launch an institution
> Or the gifted Leader's
> Solution
> Not out of mercy
> Did I dare (ll. 6-12, 15-17, 28-29, 34-35, 115-23)

This representative selection of Merton's use of the words in Eichmann's phrase demonstrates the way Merton takes Eichmann's obfuscating language and jumbles it further. His blending of quotations destabilizes and confuses any stable meaning one might try to construct and instead communicates the absurd confusion Eichmann began when he wrenched these words from their original contexts and twisted them in an attempt to justify heinous violence. Merton's antipoem simply extends this abuse of language.

Merton's confusion of meaning and juxtaposition of discourses mirrors his view of Eichmann's own statements at the trial. Eichmann speaks in a linguistic jumble ingrained into him through the official language he imbibed, as Merton has him say, "Official orders / Were my only language" (ll. 81-82). Eichmann's own statement, "'Not out of mercy / did I launch this transaction,'" juxtaposes religious, ethical language – "mercy" – with a business term – "transaction" – that covers over the reality of the horrible "transaction" Eichmann "launch[ed]." Merton follows this statement with a jarring move into the discourse of psychology, presumably drawing from a professional opinion on Eichmann's mental health: "Relations with father mother brother / Sister most normal / Most desirable" (ll. 3-5). But in light of Eichmann's actions, the reader is left wondering what is "normal" or "desirable" about Eichmann's personal relations if they allow him to "launch" such "transactions"; the juxtaposition of different types of professional language reveals the cavernous gaps between the meaning these official words seek to convey and the actual reality they are used to obscure. Merton soon returns to religious language, stating that Eichmann received "A Christian / Education," and quoting Eichmann's notorious claim that "'repentance is for little children'" (l. 30). If Eichmann's understanding of repentance is the result of a "Christian" education, then "Christian" and "repentance" begin to mean something quite shallow. Merton's conglomeration of discourses reveals the way "official" language has already stripped words of their meaning in order to justify what honest, clear words could not justify; Merton's poem, with its lack of punctuation and scrambled quotations, cannot be any more confusing than Eichmann's own official language, and the fragmentary construction of Merton's poem draws attention to the sinister, twisted nature of this language.

At the end of his poem, Merton combines Eichmann's last words with a classical reference and echoes from Eichmann's earlier statements:

> Gentlemen Adios
> We shall meet again

> We shall again be partners
> Life is short
> Art is long
> And we shall meet
> Without the slightest
> Discourtesy
>
> Repentance is
> For little children. (ll. 182-91)[4]

While Merton's poem leaves readers horrified, Merton avoids overtly condemning Eichmann. Indeed, in the presence of an official language that has denatured the words that could be used to condemn violence, Merton finds that the most powerful condemnation comes through a form of poetry that draws attention to this abuse of language, an abuse that enables violence and preemptively undercuts the language of moral judgment. Eichmann's own words, when repeated and combined, reveal the shocking inhumanity of the language that justified his commission of horrible acts. Having recited the inhuman, official language that enables violence, Merton leaves his readers in a resounding silence that gives them space to search within themselves for an answer to such atrocities, an answer that can only be found when this insidious jumble of words is silenced.

II

In order to reveal how Merton came to embrace antipoetry as a form for disrupting the violence-justifying speech of power, it is helpful to understand the development of his thinking regarding nonviolent rhetoric. Throughout his life, the violent, assertive stances of some pacifists troubled Merton because they operated from the same set of assumptions held by those in power. As Anthony Padovano explains, Merton feared that some pacifists verged toward fanaticism, wanting "victory as ardently as some militarists wanted triumph in armed conflict."[5] Merton establishes his differences from this style of pacifism in his essay, "Peace and Protest: A Statement," where he first declares, "I do not advocate the burning of draft cards" and then goes on to explain in detail the kind of protest he supports and the kind he condemns:

> [Dissent] must give a clear and reasonable account of itself to the nation, and *it must help sincere and concerned minds to accept*

alternatives to war without surrendering the genuine interests of our own national community. . . . There is considerable danger of ambiguity in protests that seek mainly to capture the attention of the press and to gain publicity for a cause, being more concerned with their impact upon the public than with the meaning of that impact. Such dissent tends to be at once dramatic and superficial. . . . What is needed is a *constructive dissent that recalls people to their senses, makes them think deeply, plants in them a seed of change, and awakens in them the profound need for truth, reason and peace which is implanted in man's nature.*[6]

Merton insists that constructive dissent is needed in the face of inhuman government actions, and he proposes two criteria by which to conduct this beneficial dissent: it must convey a clear alternative to violence, and it must not be threatening or superficial but rather humanizing, a term that for Merton draws attention to the image of God within each person. Such dissent, instead of adding to the existing noise and agitating people to superficial action, enables humans to contemplate a deeper truth and make judgments arising from the image of God inside them. Burning draft cards and other dramatic forms of protest fail to meet these criteria, in Merton's mind, because these protests simply escalate tension without opening space for an alternate form of discourse.

Consistent with his opposition to the burning of draft cards, Merton was initially alarmed when he heard in November 1965 that a man associated with the Catholic Worker Movement, Roger La Porte, had burned himself outside the UN headquarters as a protest against the Vietnam War. In response, Merton sent a telegram withdrawing from the Catholic Peace Fellowship.[7] Dorothy Day responded by explaining that although suicide was a mortal sin, she agreed with La Porte's intention. She called La Porte's death a "tragedy" but drew attention to the far greater tragedy of the Vietnam War.[8] While Merton decided to remain affiliated with the Fellowship, he continued to reject such violent forms of protest because, as James Forest explains, "he couldn't see in such actions the qualities of a genuinely non-violent movement."[9] As Merton writes in his essay "War and the Crisis of Language," these acts of violent protest, including "race riots and assassinations," are symptomatic of a loss of faith in language and are not beneficial in effecting peaceful change (*NVA* 235). Because those in power have twisted language and used it to justify unjustifiable acts, people wishing to dissent resort to violent acts, acts they hope might still have meaning even though their speech has been rendered ineffective: "The incoherence of language that cannot be trusted and the coherence of weapons that are infallible, or thought to be: this is the dialectic of politics and war, the prose of the twentieth century" (*NVA* 235). Merton goes on to expose the dangers of responding in this prose of force, regardless of the message it contains: "if you face an enemy with the conviction that he understands nothing but force, you will yourself necessarily behave as if you understood nothing but force" (*NVA* 243). This type of action only participates in a rhetoric in which words are useless and force stands as the only effective means of communication. Merton desperately wanted to speak out against the inhuman actions of his country, but this assertive, sensational rhetoric troubled him because it, like the speech of those in power, assumes that one's opponent is not a fellow human who can be engaged in reasonable dialogue.

So Merton sought other rhetorical means with which to advocate for humane peace. In particular, he looked for a way of writing poetry that would deepen the humanity of his readers instead of demeaning it. Merton dismissed most contemporary American poets as "esoteric American pontiffs."[10] As Ross Labrie explains, "[Merton] believed that the academic poets were caught in a sterile impasse in which they were reduced to experimenting with language instead of writing a poetry that was meaningful. He abhorred didacticism, and yet he also disliked an arid emphasis on technique."[11] Merton expresses his desire for a deeply meaningful poetry in his essay "Symbolism: Communication or Communion?" where he argues that symbols have lost their power to point "to the very heart of all being" because they have been denatured by scientific reductionism.[12] Humans have been reduced to the limits of a shallow, scientific discourse, and symbols are asked to operate simply as "indicative or quantitative signs," thus losing their former potency (*LL* 57). Symbols should express "union, understanding, and love among men" (*LL* 64), but because of man's "violent illness, a technological cancer," symbols currently have little depth (*LL* 79). Merton concludes his essay with a dire warning: "if the . . . monk . . . and the poet merely forsake their vestiges of wisdom and join in the triumphant, empty-headed crowing of advertising men and engineers of opinion, then there is nothing left in store for us but total madness" (*LL* 79). While this may seem like a final apology for symbolism, by the time Merton writes this essay, in 1965, he has increasingly begun to write antipoetry aimed directly at subverting the "empty-headed crowing" of his society. Symbolism may have once been an effective way of writing poetry, and Merton continues to write some symbolist poetry, but he finds that language's symbolic depth has been so eviscerated by political language that his first task must be to expose and silence this denatured language. Instead of merely adding his voice to the cacophony of solutions, Merton wants to enable his readers to realize their own guilt; each individual is complicit in Western injustice through their immersion in language and ideas, in "*simulacra*," that have been twisted to justify violence.[13] The beginning of a solution lies, according to Merton, in a silent realization of individual guilt: "When one has too many answers, and when one joins a chorus of others chanting the same slogans, there is, it seems to me, a danger that one is trying to evade the loneliness of a conscience that realizes itself to be in an inescapably evil situation. . . . None of us is free from contamination" (*FV* 145). Merton felt symbolist poetry was not the best medium for inducing this realization.

Critics have written about the shift in Merton's poetry away from symbolism, but previous studies have only begun to explain the way in which Merton hopes his antipoetry can achieve a kind of transcendence.[14] George Woodcock notes a move in Merton's poetry toward the absurd, and he offers a brief explanation of the nature of this change: "The anti-poems . . . abandon metre and poetic diction and imagery – and even Merton's earlier symbolist assumption that poetry primarily works by suggestion – for the poem as statement, even as journalism, reporting in a flat undramatic language facts that are at the same time so banal and so inhuman that they become the images of their own inherent horror" (Woodcock 143). Woodcock concludes his accurate description of Merton's antipoetry by claiming that it "was undisguisedly didactic" (Woodcock 143). In one sense Woodcock's imprecision is understandable – Merton blatantly shows the problems at the heart of current political and economic language – but "didactic" implies that Merton proclaims a single alternative message, and such definitive pronouncement is precisely what Merton avoids. Indeed, antipoetry operates merely as a parasite on other forms of language: it can say nothing positive but can only undermine the persuasive power of other forms of rhetoric. The only message Merton's antipoetry conveys is the inhuman, twisted nature of the contemporary political discourse.

David Cooper offers a more sustained analysis of Merton's antipoetry. He draws on the thinking of Herbert Marcuse, whom Merton read and admired, to posit Merton's antipoetry as an exercise in technological speaking: "a radically experimental, postmodern antipoetry notable for its lack of moral fervor or prophetic inspiration, a poetry that does not resist 'the mystifications of bureaucracy, commerce and the police state' but rather submits to such mystifications."[15] He analyzes one of Merton's books of antipoetry, *Cables to the Ace*, reading it as "a sustained Marcusian meditation on the dysfunctionalization of symbolic language in technological society – an antipoetry *qua* social criticism" (Cooper 261). Cooper rightly sees that Merton now employs a language stripped of symbolism, but Cooper partially mischaracterizes Merton's style, failing to see its efforts at transcendence, because he splits Merton into two personae, claiming that with his poetic self he "seemed more interested in parody than prophecy" while his somewhat separate, priestly self called for poets to prophesy (Cooper 259). Cooper's bifurcation is the result of a fundamental misunderstanding of Merton's goal in his antipoetry: the parody that Cooper notes is not the *telos* of Merton's antipoetry; rather, as we will see, Merton desires to bring readers to the place where they may be in a position to hear the deep prophecy of silence.

Some critics have recognized this silencing, humanizing goal of Merton's antipoetry. As George Kilcourse rightly claims, "What proves striking about antipoetry for Merton is the very positive effort on the part of the poet to reclaim the purity of poetic language. In that sense, despite the forbidding first impressions, it remains a humanistic, affirmative project."[16] Patrick O'Connell identifies the way these antipoems achieve their humanizing effect even more precisely in his discussion of *Cables to the Ace*: "by pushing the abuse of language to the point of absurdity, by exposing, not just parodying, the meaningless babble of contemporary discourse, the poet has cleared the way for a movement into the silence and emptiness of contemplation. . . . '[A]nti-poetry' can function as a *via negativa* that impels one to silence by inducing revulsion from its meaningless cacophony."[17] From this silence, readers may be able to finally realize deeper truth, truth usually drowned out by the deceptive clamor of our language.

This humanizing silence, for which Merton's antipoetry opens space, is valued by both Zen thought and Merton's Christian monastic tradition. Zen, as Merton explains, does not communicate a message but rather "an awareness that is potentially already there but is not conscious of itself. Zen is . . . realization, . . . awareness of the ontological ground of our own being here and now, right in the midst of the world."[18]   Merton was attracted to Zen because its "quest for direct and pure experience on a metaphysical level, liberated from verbal formulas and linguistic preconceptions" (*ZBA* 44), aligned with his desire to free his thoughts and the thoughts of his readers from the injustices enabled by the "verbal formulas" of power. This liberating, non-verbal awareness constitutes an essential part of all monastic life, as Merton writes in adumbrating the similarities between Eastern and Western monks: "It is the peculiar office of the monk in the modern world to keep alive the contemplative experience and to keep the way open for modern technological man to recover the integrity of his own inner depths."[19]   For Merton, this deepest part of man is silent: "the deepest level of communication is not communication, but communion. It is wordless. It is beyond words, and it is beyond speech, and it is beyond concept" (*AJ* 308). Only in this interior silence can the grounds for real peace be found; Merton believed that, as Victor Kramer writes, "Peace in the world can only exist . . . if man recognizes the core of his own being."[20] So the techniques of his antipoetry open a way for ultimate peace through a truth he learned through his monastic disciplines: the deepest, most prophetic communion possible comes through silence.

III

In order to understand the particular ways that antipoetry can unsettle a language of power and bring readers to an experience of prophetic silence, it is helpful to turn to Roland Barthes. Barthes, a Marxist when writing in the early 1950s, influenced both Marcuse and Merton. Merton wrote an essay on Barthes's 1953 book *Writing Degree Zero*, and although his essay was published in 1969,[21] Therese Lentfoehr dates its composition to 1964.[22] While it is unclear when Merton first read this book – making it difficult to determine whether Barthes influenced Merton's antipoetic style or rather articulated and confirmed it – Barthes' work and Merton's direct response to it provide a detailed explanation of why Merton turned to antipoetry and the way that this antipoetry operates.[23]

Barthes claims, in *Writing Degree Zero*, that the manipulative uses of language by those in power contributed to a recent shift in literature's view of language: authors no longer have the luxury of treating language as a simple recorder of thought but must consider the effects a denaturing language of power has had. Barthes identifies the distinguishing characteristic of this political language that Merton wanted to avoid mirroring: "[P]ower, or the shadow cast by power, always ends in creating an axiological writing, in which the distance which usually separates fact from value disappears within the very space of the word, which is given at once as description and as judgment."[24] Barthes goes on to claim that in political language, "the alibi stemming from language is at the same time intimidation and glorification: for it is power or conflict which produce the purest types of writing" (Barthes 20). Speaking of past actions within the discourses of politics, literature, or history with authority and completeness bestows causality on the narrative facts and, according to Barthes, allows the speaker to reduce "the exploded reality to a slim and pure logos, without density, without volume, without spread, and whose sole function is to unite as rapidly as possible a cause and an end" (Barthes 31). As Barthes explains further in his description of political writing, this straightforward, assertive type of writing can further oppression:

> Since writing is the spectacular commitment of language, it contains at one and the same time, thanks to a valuable ambiguity, the reality and the appearance of power, what it is, and what it would like to be thought to be. . . . We see here that the function of writing is to maintain a clear conscience and that its mission is fraudulently to identify the original fact with its remotest subsequent transformation by bolstering up the justification of actions with the additional guarantee of its own reality. (Barthes 25)

What Barthes describes is essentially a language used by power to justify power, and in being so used, language begins to lose its ability to question and unsettle power and instead slips into a tightly reduced logical circle.

Eichmann's language, from "Epitaph for a Public Servant," perfectly fits Barthes' description. Eichmann's statement, "Not out of mercy / Did I launch this transaction," assumes that his actions, while regrettable, were necessary. What is most remarkable about this statement is the enormity of what it leaves out; it is indeed "a slim and pure logos . . . whose sole function is to unite as rapidly as possible a cause and an end" (Barthes 31). Eichmann's conscience is clear because he believes he did what he had to. Even though he is "saddened" at his orders (l. 56), he imbibes the slim logic of the "official" language and learns to "forget / The undesirable Jew" (ll. 101-102) because, after all, "Who was I / To judge / The Master?" (ll. 96-98). Eichmann's language inseparably unites the facts he describes with the values given them by Nazi power; he has lost the ability to speak – to think – from outside the logic of this denatured language.

Merton talks about this phenomenon in his essay "War and the Crisis of Language" (*NVA* 234-47). Merton, like Barthes, focuses on language because, as David Belcastro claims, it is the manipulation of language that enables "the illusion of innocence and sanity to be maintained" (Belcastro 69). In his essay, Merton locates this manipulation in the trivialized language of both economic and political power. In advertising, Merton claims, "we have an example of speech that is at once totally trivial and totally definitive" (*NVA* 238). Merton offers an example of this kind of speech in the service of war and explains its cause and result:

> [A] U.S. major [in Vietnam] calmly explained, "It became necessary to destroy the town in order to save it." Here we see, again, an insatiable appetite for the tautological, the definitive, the *final*. It is the same kind of language and logic that Hitler used for his notorious "final solution." The symbol of this perfect finality is the circle. An argument turns upon itself, and the beginning and end get lost: it just goes round and round its own circumference. (*NVA* 238)

Merton claims this kind of language is not unique to the American government: "This is purely and simply the logic shared by all war-makers. It is the logic of *power*" (*NVA* 239). He explains with horrifying precision the reasoning behind this language and its sinister, invasive potency:

> The ambiguity of official war talk has one purpose above all: to mask this ultimate unreason and permit the game to go on. . . . [T]he language of escalation is the language of naked power, a language that is all the more persuasive because it is proud of being ethically illiterate and because it accepts, as realistic, the basic irrationality of its own tactics. . . . Yet the language itself is given universal currency by the mass media. It can quickly contaminate the thinking of everybody. (*NVA* 241)

What both Barthes and Merton describe is a language that is self-enclosed and self-justifying. It is perfectly logical, but its abstraction and the limited scope of its thought allow it to legitimate otherwise horrible actions.

This is the language used by the "sane" people of the world who, as Merton writes in his essay about Eichmann, "will have *perfectly good reasons*, logical, well-adjusted reasons, for firing the [first nuclear] shot" (*RU* 47). Because the language of modern society has been usurped by power, it can no longer speak truly about Christian, peaceful concepts like "justice, charity, love, and the rest" (*RU* 48). In *Orthodoxy*, written forty years before Barthes's book and sixty years before Merton's essay, G. K. Chesterton diagnoses the modern mind in similar terms. He likens the logic of the modern mind to the functioning of a madman's mind: "his mind moves in a perfect but narrow circle. A small circle is quite as infinite as a large circle, but . . . it is not so large. In the same way the insane explanation is quite as complete as the sane one, but it is not so large."[25] The politicians and advertisers whom Merton critiques have used language to justify their thinking in precisely this small way, and by doing so, they have reduced the ability of language to refer to anything larger, anything outside of their logical circle. Near the end of "War and the Crisis of Language," Merton describes the implications this use of language has for pacifist rhetoric:

> The effect of this, of course, is a vicious circle: it begins with a tacit admission that negotiation is meaningless, and it does in fact render the language of negotiation meaningless. War-makers in the twentieth century have gone far toward creating a political language so obscure, so apt for treachery, so ambiguous, that it can no longer serve as an instrument for peace: it is good only for war. But why? Because the language of war is *self-enclosed in finality*. (*NVA* 244)

Merton here makes a bold claim for those who, like him, want to advocate for peace: in the current political, linguistic climate, the language of negotiation can serve only war, not peace.

Merton and Barthes may seem to be overestimating the damage caused by the way political power brokers have used language, but Merton provides detailed evidence of how the United States government has used language in this fundamentally insane way. He argues that the Vietnam War was an attempt to make the declarations of the Pentagon into fact. While the war's failure demonstrated the falsity of their words, the Pentagon continued to act on its declarations, attempting to prove they were right after all:

> What needs to be noted is that the massive effort of the United States to gain acceptance for its own version of the Vietnam war by doing all in its power to turn that version into accomplished fact has had profoundly significant effects. . . . The *political language* of the United States, which was suspect before, has now been fatally denatured. It has probably lost all its value as intellectual currency. . . . Language has been distorted and denatured in defense of this solipsistic, this basically isolationist and sometimes even paranoid, attitude. (*NVA* 245-46)

Merton goes on to mourn the effects this use of language has had on the whole political discourse, tainting even the language of those who would speak for alternative courses to war and advocate against oppression:

> Revolt against this [contempt for humans] is taking the form of another, more elemental and anarchistic, kind of violence, together with a different semantic code. . . . It is . . . the violent language and the apocalyptic myth of the guerrilla warrior, the isolated individual and the small group . . . . [These revolts] are couched in the same terms of magic and witchcraft that assert something and then proceed to make it so in fact, thereby vindicating their own prophecy. . . . [F]lexible though [this revolt] might be in some respects, it remains another language of power, therefore of self-enclosed finality, which rejects dialogue and negotiation on the axiomatic supposition that the adversary is a devil with whom no dialogue is possible. (*NVA* 246-47)

These forms of political revolt fundamentally mirror the denatured language used by the United States government during the Vietnam War. While Merton would like to take hope at efforts to decentralize power – and its insidious language – he finds that those who rebel are unable to change the terms of the discourse and simply perpetuate a way of speaking that requires violence to make its pronouncements come true.

It is from this despair over the political, linguistic situation that Merton turns to antiwriting. Belcastro accurately summarizes Merton's motivation for this turn: "The world of commerce and politics had so contaminated language that any serious writer would have to resort to anti-language or, in the case of the poet, anti-poetry" (Belcastro 64). This antiwriting aims to jar the reader out of the relentless hamster wheel that political language has accustomed him to, as the antiwriter's first act is to foreground his own decision to step out of this linguistic circle. For, as Merton writes, if an individual were "a little more aware of his absurdities and contradictions, perhaps there might be a possibility of his survival" (*RU* 49). Chesterton offers a similar remedy for escaping the modern mind's tightly circumscribed logic: "A man cannot think himself out of mental evil . . . . He can only be saved by will or faith. The moment his mere reason moves, it moves in the old circular rut; he will go round and round his logical circle . . . unless he performs the voluntary, vigorous, and mystical act of getting out. . . . Decision is the whole business here; a door must be shut for ever" (Chesterton 26). Only through this decisive act of breaking the logical circle, Chesterton argues, can "all that is human" be saved (Chesterton 29). Merton's antiwriting desires to make this act not only possible but necessary by demonstrating the absurd chasm between reality and linguistic value, the chasm that political writing seeks to elide. If his readers realize the obfuscations and false equivalences that the language of power enacts, they may lose their faith in language's ability to justify itself and so begin to look beyond language to determine their system of values.

Merton explains how he, as a poet, hopes to contribute to a remedy for this linguistic disease: "[P]oets are perhaps the ones who, at the present moment, are most sensitive to the sickness of language – a sickness that, infecting all literature with nausea, prompts us not so much to declare war on conventional language as simply to pick up and examine intently a few chosen pieces of linguistic garbage" (*NVA* 234). And he declares that "it is the vocation of the poet – or anti-poet – *not* to be deaf to such things but to apply his ear intently to their corrupt charms" (*NVA* 237). Merton, then, listens carefully to the self-justifying language of power in order to expose its sinister workings.

In his essay on Barthes' *Writing Degree Zero*, Merton fleshes out the framework from which the antiwriter operates. He commends Barthes for understanding that any author proclaiming an authoritative message is not a truly subversive writer: "[Barthes] carries out an exemplary campaign of criticism against all forms of writing with a message, and particularly of writing with a political message" (*LE* 141). Merton's project of antipoetry, then, is not to

posit an alternative message to the justification of war being proclaimed by those in power; this would keep him confined inside
the logical circle of political negotiation. Instead, Merton's poetry is
designed to expose the inadequacies of all message-laden writing,
to lay bare the inevitable rift between the facts and the values that
are equated in political writing. Barthes claims that the "function
of writing is to maintain a clear conscience" (Barthes 25), so Merton
chooses an antiwriting that seeks an opposite result, a conscience
properly aware of its true guilt. Merton wants his antiwriting to
disable the blurring of reality and ideology that political writing
perpetuates and to forcefully trouble the consciences of his readers, requiring them to turn to something other than language by
which to calibrate their consciences.

Near the end of his book, Barthes offers some suggestions about
how this kind of subversive writing might operate. He explains
that one danger for writers who have become more self-conscious
about writing, and who seek to avoid perpetuating literature's
ideological service, is to so despair of literature that they eventually write themselves into agraphia, becoming silent in the face
of history. But Barthes offers an alternative, "writing at the zero
degree" (Barthes 76):

> The new neutral writing takes its place in the midst of all those
> ejaculations and judgments, without becoming involved in any
> of them; it consists precisely in their absence. . . . [W]riting is
> then reduced to a sort of negative mood in which the social or
> mythical characters of a language are abolished in favour of a
> neutral and inert state of form; thus thought remains wholly re-
> sponsible, without being overlaid by a secondary commitment
> of form to a History not its own. . . . [N]eutral writing in fact
> rediscovers the primary condition of classical art: instrumen-
> tality. But this time, form as an instrument is no longer at the
> service of a triumphant ideology; it is the mode of a new situ-
> ation of the writer, the way a certain silence has of existing. . . .
> If the writing is really neutral, and if language, instead of being
> a cumbersome and recalcitrant act, reaches the state of a pure
> equation, . . . then Literature is vanquished, the problematics
> of mankind is uncovered and presented without elaboration,
> the writer becomes irretrievably honest. (Barthes 77-78)

Thus neutral writing serves no ideology except an ideology of
non-power: the antiwriter writes not to authoritatively convey

a set of values but to expose the inability of language to remain absolutely honest to reality, particularly a language wielded by those in power. This exposure of the problematics of language is what Merton is after, and Barthes here expresses Merton's goal: Merton wants his antiwriting to be a way that "a certain silence has of existing." Instead of becoming mute himself, the antiwriter works to make all other voices mute. If Merton can write his readers into a distrust of language and a state of silence, then perhaps space will be opened up for a radically contemplative, human form of being that is grounded in a silence beyond speech.

IV

Throughout his essay on Barthes, Merton writes about the techniques of this form, and from what he says four distinct traits of his antipoetry can be identified. The first is its continual distancing of the reader; Merton claims that antipoetry asserts its constructedness, its artificiality, in order to keep the reader from being lulled into any false belief in the self-sufficient reality of language:

> When the choice [to write] is completely lucid, when the writer chooses simply to *write* and renounces all the rest ("message," "expression," "soul," "revolution"), then the writing itself stands out clearly as writing. A distance is established which reminds the reader not to get lost in the writer or in the writing, not to immerse himself in false complicities with the message or the emotion, not to get swept away by illusions of an inner meaning, a slice of life, a cosmic celebration, an eschatological vision. When the writing is just writing, and when no mistake about this is possible because the very writing itself removes all possibility of error, then you have "writing degree zero." (*LE* 142)

The refusal of zero degree writing to sweep the reader up in its flow and apparent meaning enables the reader to gain an awareness of the triviality of all writing: "when we read writing we need to realize that what we are doing is not experiencing the deep things of life, penetrating the esoteric meaning of human existence, or being swept out of ourselves by rapture: we are just reading writing" (*LE* 146). This statement of writing's triviality radically disrupts the weight of pronouncements of power by showing them to also be nothing more than writing.

If readers can become accustomed to reading antiwriting in a distanced, self-conscious way, they may be less prone to easily accept the value statements of any writing. This distrust of writing would frustrate the attempts of those in power to cast a pall of false values and deceptive ideology over society, as Merton explains in a message he wrote for Latin-American poets:

> It is the businessman, the propagandist, the politician, not the poet, who devoutly believes in "the magic of words."
>
> For the poet there is precisely no magic. There is only life in all its unpredictability and all its freedom. All magic is a ruthless venture in manipulation, a vicious circle, a self-fulfilling prophecy.
>
> Word-magic is an impurity of language and of spirit in which words, deliberately reduced to unintelligibility, appeal mindlessly to the vulnerable will. Let us deride and parody this magic with other variants of the unintelligible, if we want to. (*RU* 159)

Merton expresses here the doubts and heightened consciousness that antipoetry attempts to elicit towards writing by distancing itself from the reader in order to foreground the artificiality and manipulability of writing. Once this artificiality is recognized, linguistic justifications for violence lose much of their persuasive power.

Merton's statement here also addresses the second trait of antipoetry: unintelligibility. Not only does the antipoet cause doubts about the sufficiency of political or economic language to establish value, but he also refuses to allow his own voice to fill this absence of meaning. As Merton explains concerning Barthes' antiwriter, his "mere *decision to write* is what matters, not his decision to communicate a political message or share a human experience" (*LE* 143). Communication ceases to be the goal of writing in order to deeply unsettle any remaining faith in the power of language to mean simply:

> [T]he "writer" (if he is cool) does not try to communicate something to the rest of the world, but only to define correctly the relation between writing and the world.... He does something to society not by pushing against its structures – which are none of his business – but by changing the tune of its language and shifting the perspectives which depend on the ways words are arranged. He systematically de-mythologizes literature.

> What the writer owes society is, then, *to refuse to communicate* with the reader if the urge to communicate interferes with his writing. And what the reader will look for is precisely this refusal. This, at least, is what he will look for in "writing degree zero." (*LE* 144)

Merton's antipoetry, therefore, largely resists conveying a cohesive message and instead questions the connections between words, meaning, and social value. Merton desires to expose the "relationship between writing and the world" so that his readers will question all writing and refuse to uncritically accept the values embedded in any writing.

What words then does this antipoetry contain? Juxtaposed quotations that the poet arranges in order to parody them, the third trait of antipoetry. Merton's antipoetry jumbles together strings of political language, journalistic phrases, and the poet's own ironic commentary to produce an eclectic montage. The antiwriter draws on the structuralist understanding of the synchronic nature of language:

> The "writer" is conscious of words in synchronous interrelated systems (style, etc.) and if he knows what he is doing he can deliberately choose to subvert the systems by his use of words. It is here, and not in his doctrine, his "revolutionary message" or in a supposed "revolutionary style" that the writer really changes the world – (though he should be free of any obvious purpose to change anything). (*LE* 143)

Merton references Joyce's *Ulysses* as an example of a work that uses language from many discourses to subvert an artificial compartmentalization of language. But in his own writings, Merton demonstrates a more political aim that that of Joyce as he seeks to parody not genres of literature, primarily, but various political and economic languages of power.

The unsettling of these languages is not difficult because Merton sees the language of his society as so denatured that parody is no longer required: "[A]ntipoetry . . . freely draws on the material of superabundant nonsense at its disposal. One no longer has to parody, it is enough to quote – and feed back quotations into the mass consumption of pseudoculture. The static created by the feedback of arguments or of cultural declarations – or of 'art' into their own system – is enough to show the inner contradictions of the system" (*AJ* 118). Simply by pulling various political statements into the poetic genre and freeing them from the voice of power, he reveals the fissures contained in this language between the expressed values and the apparent reality. And these silent fissures contain the meaning the antipoet suggests: "The antipoet 'suggests' a tertiary meaning which is *not* 'creative' and 'original' but a deliberate ironic feedback of cliché, a further referential meaning, alluding, by its tone, banality, etc., to a *customary and abused context*, that of an impoverished and routine sensibility, and of the 'mass-mind,' the stereotyped creation of quantitative preordained response by 'mass-culture'" (*AJ* 286). Through the suggested meaning, the fissure between the statements and the context, the antipoet begins to achieve the final goal of Merton's antipoetry.

By creating distance between the reader and writing, by refusing to communicate to the reader, and by parodying different discourses to unsettle meaning, the antipoet jars the reader to distrust any voice that would establish final meaning, offering him instead a prophetic silence. Derision or parody is not the final goal of Merton's antipoetry: "it is better to prophesy than to deride. To prophesy is not to predict, but to seize upon reality in its moment of highest expectation and tension toward the new" (*RU* 159). This expectation is felt in a positive silence, a silence that finally overrides all the voices that clamor to provide value and meaning. In his essay on *Writing Degree Zero*, Merton draws on Barthes' claim that neutral writing allows a kind of silence to exist: "What Barthes says about writing . . . is a kind of quietism, if you like; but a deadly, Zenlike stillness out of which . . . there does nevertheless spring a certain inscrutable excitement" (*LE* 146). Merton would naturally find reason for excitement in a kind of writing that opened up space for silence; as a monk he continually sought greater room in his life for solitude and silence,[26] and his interest in Asian thought and particularly in Zen stemmed from its valuing of silence that enabled humans to find wholeness and grounding.[27] As Merton concludes in his "Message to Poets":

> Let us be proud of the words that are given to us for nothing; not to teach anyone, not to confute anyone, not to prove anyone absurd, but to point beyond all objects into the silence where nothing can be said.
> We are not persuaders. We are the children of the Unknown.
> We are the ministers of silence that is needed to cure all victims

of absurdity who lie dying of a contrived joy. (*RU* 160)

The ultimate goal of Merton's antipoetry, then, is not to show the absurdity of anything but instead to minister silence; the distancing and parody are merely employed to achieve this silent end. For Merton, because of his life as a monk and his understanding of Zen, this silence is not a negative absence but a place where humans become more human by confronting the God who is the source of their existence. In his essay "Creative Silence," he writes: "when we come face to face with ourselves in the lonely ground of our own being, we confront many questions about the value of our existence, the reality of our commitments, the authenticity of our everyday lives" (*LL* 39). The silence that Merton declares to be the goal of his poetry seems to be the most human response he has to the self-justifying, violent language of Western negotiation, and rather than attempting to persuade readers of a singular alternative message, Merton employs a nonviolent anti-rhetoric, one whose means and ends are both diametrically opposed to the coercive, clamoring language of power.

V

With this understanding of Merton's antipoetry, I want to return to his poetry and demonstrate the particular ways that he employs these techniques. Most of Merton's antipoetry, including the majority of *Cables to the Ace* and *The Geography of Lograire*, directly unsettles the language of economic and cultural power. Merton draws on quotes from advertising and other sources, using subversive repetition and a constant deferral of meaning to break readers from the stranglehold of this language and to expose the materialistic, anti-humanitarian values that America's cultural language simultaneously reinforces and justifies. While these constitute the majority of Merton's antipoetic project, because my focus is on the ways that antipoetry constitutes a nonviolent rhetoric, I will look at antipoems in which Merton silences language used to justify war and demonstrate how they employ the four traits of Merton's antipoetry.

In "Chant to Be Used in Processions around a Site with Furnaces" (*CP* 345-49), Merton writes from the perspective of a Nazi death camp commander. The poem was published during the Eichmann trial (1961),[28] but Merton employs a different, unnamed Nazi narrator.[29] The incredible effectiveness with which the Nazi regime used language to justify violence gripped Merton, leading him to write multiple poems that expose its insidious discourse. Like "Epitaph for a Public Servant," Merton writes this poem from the first person, a move that could hide the artificiality of the writing and effect a more direct connection to readers. The poem, however, has no punctuation, forcing readers to slow down in order to construct an interpretation, and preventing them from being swept into any flow of meaning. As the speaker develops his persona and his role as the administrator of a Nazi death camp becomes clearer, any connection the reader would be tempted to find with this narrator quickly evaporates.

The poem is broken up into stanzas that form a type of punctuation, but these serve less to order the words than to fragment the language. Throughout the poem, the speaker offers information in a flat, matter-of-fact tone, and his disconnected use of abstract, vague terms contributes to the reader's uncertainty about what exactly the commander is describing. As the poem nears its end, the speaker shifts to a justification of what he has done, but his Nuremberg defense fails to save him and he is hanged. He continues speaking from beyond death, however, and the poem concludes with a stanza that echoes Nathan's accusation of David: "Do not think yourself better because you burn up friends and enemies with long-range missiles without ever seeing what you have done" (¶ 35). While Merton speaks indirectly here to his Western audience through the Nazi commander, the effect is a direct condemnation, and it may have been excised from later, more "pure" antipoetry, like "Epitaph for a Public Servant" where Merton concludes in Eichmann's actual words. But in this poem also, Merton resists directly condemning the Nazi commander, and he refuses to didactically propose an answer to either Nazi or nuclear horrors. Even the concluding accusation does not convince readers of a particular solution but shames them to silence.

This poem's powerful effect comes largely through Merton's skillful blend of discourses, although in one sense, his work has been done for him; as he wrote to Nicanor Parra: "In truth this poem is composed almost in its entirety from the very words of the commanders of Auschwitz. It would be impossible to invent something more terrifying than the truth itself."[30] Merton skillfully chooses phrases that highlight the way violence-justifying language draws on religious and economic discourses in its efforts to bestow legitimacy on heinous crimes, effectively stripping these discourses of their original significance and exploiting language's susceptibility to ideologically motivated manipulation. All of the functions of the death camp operated by the speaker are described in industrial, economic terms: He "installed a perfectly good machine it gave satisfaction to many" (¶ 6); the people who were "invited" (¶ 12) were "disinfected with Zyklon B" (¶ 11); the winds that brought this "satisfaction" were "efficient" (¶ 17) and "made ends meet" (¶ 18). This last phrase has a further ironic significance in that its inversion – they met their end – is also applicable. This parodying of discourses extends even more jarringly to religious diction, which the first line of the poem invokes: "How we made them sleep and purified them" (¶ 1). The speaker clarifies this religious definition of his role, saying that although he chose not to become a priest, he "purified" the "human weakness" of those who came to him and so "remained decent" himself (¶ 3). And he claims that all the workers there were "self-sacrific[ing]" and "conscientious" (¶ 34). He describes the humans he killed as "votaries" (¶ 11) who were "bathed" (¶ 14). By using these economic and religious terms to describe and legitimate his actions, the speaker twists language to justify his actions. As Barthes puts it in his description of this kind of language, "the distance which usually separates fact from value disappears within the very space of the word, which is given at once as description and as judgment" (Barthes 20). Merton's antipoem demonstrates the unreliability of these words that attempt to provide ethical cover for inhuman actions; the commandant's descriptions of his actions as "good" and "decent" and "conscientious" are only true within the limits of his self-sufficient speech.

And this language of power reduces the truth of all discourse: "good," "decent," and "conscientious" are irrevocably tainted by the commandant's use of these words. If economic and particularly religious words can no longer be innocently used, Merton has no language to overtly condemn the actions of this man; the very terms that should demonstrate his inhumanity have been perverted in order to justify his actions.[31] And so Merton uses the title to convey his hope: "Chant to Be Used in Processions around a Site with Furnaces." In a chant, words are repeated to induce a meditative state, a state of deeper consciousness. Maybe these words that Merton brings together can serve this function; maybe his repetition of them will enable his readers to grasp sublingually the significance of what has happened in these death camps and to meditate on this in silence, the silence he shames them to in the poem's final accusation.

Merton's short book, *Original Child Bomb* (1962),[32] is a series of forty-one numbered statements about the events surrounding the dropping of the atomic bombs on Japan. The white space between the poem's sections and the Arabic numeral headings immediately register the poem's constructed, fragmentary nature. This awkward structure reminds the reader that the poem is an artificial conglomeration of facts and statements from many sources and prevents the reader from being carried away by the writing.

The fragmentary structure also contributes to the poem's unintelligibility. The poet never connects these bits of data and refuses to evaluate explicitly their moral content, choosing instead to let the facts and the words spoken by the government officials speak for themselves. This flat, reportorial tone, given the readers' knowledge of the event being described, exposes the horrific failure of the official language and enables readers to recognize the awful consequences of this failure. As Michael Higgins notes about this poem, "the discrepancy between the heinousness of the deed and the restrained recounting exacerbat[es] the mood of dread."[33] While Merton's antipoem does not communicate his attitude toward the bomb directly, it certainly conveys horror over the bomb's destruction. But Merton proposes no answer beyond this sense of horror, maintaining his commitment to only repeat and unsettle the answers already being offered. The last section is the only time the poet clearly speaks for himself: "Since that summer many other bombs have been 'found.' What is going to happen? At the time of writing, after a season of brisk speculation, men seem to be fatigued by the whole question" (#41). Merton's refusal to positively weigh in on this question constitutes his refusal to add his message to the current cacophony of voices; he simply disrupts the coherence of the existing voices.

Merton destroys the power of these voices by juxtaposing Japanese and American terms and religious and military discourses, and he relies on the instability this creates, even when presented in a journalistic tone, to disrupt language's justifying power. The title, *Original Child Bomb*, fuses the innocent-sounding, crudely literal translation of the Japanese description of the atomic bomb, "Original Child," with the explosive American word, "Bomb," to create an oxymoronic, unmeaning label. As the poem develops, Merton focuses on the religious words used in the government's language about the bomb: its test explosion was named "Trinity" (#13); those who saw it quoted the Bible to express their belief in its power (#15); one official, however, remained a "doubting Thomas" (#16); the bomb was called "Little Boy" (#22) and tucked "devoutly" into the "womb" of the "mother" plane, figuring the bomb as a Christ child (#26); the plane's base was called "Papacy" (#34). This confusion of religious language and military facts shows the hollowness of even spiritual words; what does "Trinity" mean in a church now that it also describes a nuclear explosion? Merton describes the events leading up to the bomb in a matter-of-fact, journalistic voice, and he deliberately reveals the gaps in meaning that this tone attempts to conceal. For instance, Merton states, "Admiral Leahy told the President the bomb would never work" (#2). The word "work" here provides the slippage in meaning that Merton wants to demonstrate; what must the bomb accomplish for it to "work"? "explode"? (#16); "demonstrate" power? (#5); "jeopardize the future of civilization"? (#3); "produce eternal peace"? (#3). The vastly different interpretations of "work" offered by various officials illustrate the uselessness of the language used by those in power to justly evaluate the "Original Child Bomb."

In the face of this obscuring language, as we have seen, Merton refuses to partake in the speculation about the future of the bomb. But he encodes his fear and his stance in the poem's subtitle: "Points for meditation to be scratched on the walls of a cave." If the potential horrors of the Cold War do happen, maybe Merton's sampling of official language can lead the few survivors to silence and, as in Plato's allegory, guide them toward a more genuine light. This meditation, this silence after the vacuity of language is exposed, may enable humans to regain their humanity after the violence caused by an obfuscating, reductive language.

VI

Merton has other poems that deal similarly with inhuman violence and the language that justifies it, poems such as "A Picture of Lee Ying" (*CP* 322-24). His antipoetic approach impressively charts a truly nonviolent rhetoric, which pacifists today still struggle to articulate. As Ellen Gorsevski writes in her 2004 book on nonviolent rhetoric, "It is vexing to evaluate rhetoric in terms of nonviolence and an orientation toward peacemaking when so much of the rhetorical tradition is steeped in the notion that might rules. Much has been written in the field of rhetoric about violence, but precious little has been written about rhetoric vis-à-vis nonviolence."[34] Merton, writing four decades earlier, found a powerful way to respond to a violent, persuasive rhetoric without falling into the same errors he wanted to condemn. His parasitic antipoetry acts as a destabilizing, questioning force that reveals the fissures inherent in the language of contemporary political power. Perhaps it is helpful to compare Merton's antipoetry to a modern technological innovation: active noise-canceling headphones. These headphones listen to ambient noise and broadcast it to the listener in the opposite polarity as the original sound, resulting in destructive interference and near silence. Antipoetry listens to the linguistic static of the culture and feeds it back into the culture in the opposite polarity – from art and not from a place of power – resulting in words that are out of phase and induce silence. In this way, Merton enacts his own humanity without attempting to assert it at the expense of other humans: his writing breaks the hegemonic aims of political writing and clears space for each person to begin meditating and living on the basis of his or her own humanity, a humanity which Merton believes transcends the limits of language and contains the image of God (see *RU* 6). Individuals no longer have to accept the statements of value that are issued to them by their political leaders; instead, Merton prompts people to question these values and to look elsewhere for truth and justice.

Merton's antipoetry is not meant, however, to be the sole rhetorical form used by those desiring peace. Merton implicitly recognizes the limits of his antipoetry by writing much prose and traditional poetry, writing that certainly contains a message. Antipoetry can only accomplish a negating task, and even in this it has weaknesses. One such limitation is its reliance on time-bound material; antipoetry's parasitic nature makes it contingent on transitory cultural phrases that later readers may not recognize. Labrie notes Merton's consciousness of this difficulty: "He was aware that the ephemeral nature of [the advertising materials from which he borrowed language] could undermine the integrity of his poetry, but he wrote to a friend in 1968 that he felt *Cables* still represented a right approach, even if 'dour' and 'perhaps shallow'" (Labrie 138). Merton's antipoetry may be dated, then, and new antipoetry may always be needed to destabilize the new language of political and economic power. Merton recognizes another potential weakness of antipoetry when he asks: "The only thing that remains to be explained is: how does the reader keep awake when reading such writing?" (*LE* 144). If the poet commits himself to unintelligibility, he may sentence himself to a dwindling audience. And Merton also concedes that the reader who has completely accepted the voices of society may not be affected by his antipoetry, although Merton does not feel responsible for this failure: "when [a reader's] supposed values are returned to him in irony, as static, he will not accept the implications. That is *his* problem" (*AJ* 118). In spite of these limitations, Merton chose to write antipoetry because perhaps some people are not too far gone, and perhaps it can enable some readers to achieve a "Zenlike stillness" (*LE* 146) that would open them to the deeper Word found in this silence.

Merton came to believe that effective discourse in the midst of war was only possible if the self-justifying "verbal formulas" of power were first broken. By revealing the gap between the truth found in the divine core of humanity and the truth claimed by a power-hungry language, Merton's antipoetry attempts to rehabilitate language for humble, respectful, and contingent use. Antiwriting induces a proper distrust of the ultimate sufficiency of language and enables humans to learn from what is said while remaining aware of the inevitable shortcomings of writing: its tendency to superimpose values on the facts it describes, its susceptibility to manipulation by those in political and economic power, and its final inability to fully express the image of God implanted in each person. With this awareness, readers can approach writing and language with an appropriate skepticism – looking for meaning while remaining aware of the ultimate failure of human language. This awareness continues to be vital in our global society where political jockeying and the frenzied race for economic dominance perennially abuse and manipulate language to serve the interests of those in power. Poets are still needed who can "point beyond all objects into the silence where nothing can be said" (*RU* 160). And perhaps Merton's own antipoetry can continue to provide the space for positive stillness in a clamoring society; perhaps it will continue to plant "a seed of change [that] awakens in [humans] the profound need for truth, reason and peace which is implanted in man's nature" (*NVA* 68).

Endnotes

1. Thomas Merton, *Raids on the Unspeakable* (New York: New Directions, 1966) 6; subsequent references will be cited as "*RU*" parenthetically in the text.

2. George Woodcock, *Thomas Merton, Monk and Poet* (New York: Farrar, Straus, Giroux, 1978) 1; subsequent references will be cited as "Woodcock" parenthetically in the text.

3. Thomas Merton, *The Collected Poems of Thomas Merton* (New York: New Directions, 1977) 703-11; subsequent references will be cited as "*CP*" parenthetically in the text.

4. While Hippocrates is the original source of Merton's phrase, "Life is short / Art is long," Primo Levi, an Auschwitz survivor, also wrote a poem for Eichmann that includes this allusion: "Or will you at the end, like the industrious man / Whose life was too brief for his long art, / Lament your sorry work unfinished, / The thirteen million still alive?" (Primo Levi, *Collected Poems*, trans. Ruth Feldman and Brian Swann [London: Faber and Faber, 1992] 24).

5. Anthony T. Padovano, *The Human Journey: Thomas Merton, Symbol of a Century* (Garden City, NY: Doubleday, 1982) 65.

6. Thomas Merton, "Peace and Protest: A Statement," in Thomas Merton, *The Nonviolent Alternative*, ed. Gordon C. Zahn (New York: Farrar, Straus & Giroux, 1980) 68 (emphasis added); subsequent references will be cited as "*NVA*" parenthetically in the text.

7. Thomas Merton, *The Hidden Ground of Love: Letters on Religious Experience and Social Concerns*, ed. William H. Shannon (New York: Farrar, Straus, Giroux, 1985) 285.

8. See Paul Elie, *The Life You Save May Be Your Own: An American Pilgrimage* (New York: Farrar, Straus & Giroux, 2003) 379-81; subsequent references will be cited as "Elie" parenthetically in the text. See also Woodcock, who rightly notes, "Merton was in total sympathy with those who opposed the war in Vietnam, though . . . he did not always agree with their methods or their policies" (134).

9. James H. Forest, "Thomas Merton's Struggle with Peacemaking," in Gerald Twomey, ed., *Thomas Merton: Prophet in the Belly of a Paradox* (New York: Paulist Press, 1978) 43.

10. Thomas Merton, *Conjectures of a Guilty Bystander* (Garden City, NY: Doubleday, 1966) 119.

11. Ross Labrie, *The Art of Thomas Merton* (Fort Worth: Texas Christian University Press, 1979) 110; subsequent references will be cited as "Labrie" parenthetically in the text.

12. Thomas Merton, *Love and Living*, ed. Naomi Burton Stone and Brother Patrick Hart (New York: Farrar, Straus, Giroux, 1979) 55; subsequent references will be cited as "*LL*" parenthetically in the text.

13. Thomas Merton, "Events and Pseudo-Events: Letter to a Southern Churchman," in Thomas Merton, *Faith and Violence: Christian Teaching and Christian Practice* (Notre Dame: University of Notre Dame Press, 1968) 152; subsequent references will be cited as "*FV*" parenthetically in the

text. See also David Joseph Belcastro, "Chanting on the Rim of Chaos: Sane Language in an Insane World," in Angus Stuart, ed., *Across the Rim of Chaos: Thomas Merton's Prophetic Vision* (Stratton-on-the-Fosse, Radstock, UK: Thomas Merton Society of Great Britain and Ireland, 2005) 68: "Merton eventually extends the indictment of 'war criminal' to include the entire western world" (subsequent references will be cited as "Belcastro" parenthetically in the text).

14. See Malgorzata Poks, "Thomas Merton's Poetry of Endless Inscription: A Tale of Liberation and Expanding Horizons," *The Merton Annual* 14 (2001) 184-222. In this essay, Poks argues for a more cohesive understanding of Merton's oeuvre. In her terms, Merton's movement toward antipoetry constitutes an "evolution rather than [a] rupture" (185) in his poetic style, but even so, it remains important to understand why this shift was a needed evolution for Merton.

15. David D. Cooper, *Thomas Merton's Art of Denial: The Evolution of a Radical Humanist* (Athens: University of Georgia Press, 1989) 259; subsequent references will be cited as "Cooper" parenthetically in the text.

16. George A. Kilcourse, *Ace of Freedoms: Thomas Merton's Christ* (Notre Dame: University of Notre Dame Press, 1993) 170.

17. Patrick F. O'Connell, *"Cables to the Ace,"* in William H. Shannon, Christine M. Bochen and Patrick F. O'Connell, *The Thomas Merton Encyclopedia* (Maryknoll, NY: Orbis, 2002) 38.

18. Thomas Merton, *Zen and the Birds of Appetite* (New York: New Directions, 1968) 47; subsequent references will be cited as *"ZBA"* parenthetically in the text.

19. Thomas Merton, *The Asian Journal*, ed. Naomi Burton Stone, Brother Patrick Hart and James Laughlin (New York: New Directions, 1973) 317; subsequent references will be cited as *"AJ"* parenthetically in the text.

20. Victor A. Kramer, *Thomas Merton: Monk and Artist* (Kalamazoo, MI: Cistercian Publications, 1987) 92.

21. Thomas Merton, "Writing as Temperature: Roland Barthes," *Sewanee Review* 77 (Summer 1969) 535-42; reprinted as "Roland Barthes – Writing as Temperature" in Thomas Merton, *The Literary Essays of Thomas Merton*, ed. Patrick Hart, OCSO (New York: New Directions, 1981) 140-46 (subsequent references will be cited as *"LE"* parenthetically in the text).

22. Thérèse Lentfoehr, *Words and Silence: On the Poetry of Thomas Merton* (New York: New Directions, 1979) 97 (subsequent references will be cited as "Lentfoehr" parenthetically in the text); the headnote in *Literary Essays* dates the essay to September 1968 (140).

23. Paul M Pearson, "Poetry of the Sneeze: Thomas Merton and Nicanor Parra," *The Merton Journal* 8.2 (2001) 3-20. Pearson traces the relationship between these two antipoets but argues that Merton's "an-

tipoetic style initially developed independently of Parra's influence" (7), so while this Latin-American poet provides confirmation for Merton's style, he cannot be seen as its source.

24. Roland Barthes, *Writing Degree Zero*, trans. Annette Lavers and Colin Smith (New York: Hill and Wang, 1977) 20; subsequent references will be cited as "Barthes" parenthetically in the text.

25. G. K. Chesterton, *Orthodoxy* (San Francisco: Ignatius Press, 1995) 24; subsequent references will be cited as "Chesterton" parenthetically in the text.

26. See Elie 316-17, and John F. Teahan, "The Place of Silence in Merton's Life and Thought," in Patrick Hart, ed., *The Message of Thomas Merton* (Kalamazoo, MI: Cistercian Publications, 1981) 91-114.

27. See *ZBA* 139-41 and Bonnie Bowman Thurston, "Zen in the Eye of Thomas Merton's Poetry," *Buddhist-Christian Studies* 4 (1984) 104-107.

28. *The Catholic Worker* 28 (July 1961) 4; *Journal for the Protection of All Beings* 1 (1961) 5-7.

29. See Lentfoehr 44.

30. Thomas Merton, *The Courage for Truth: The Letters of Thomas Merton to Writers*, ed. Christine M. Bochen (New York: Farrar, Straus and Giroux, 1993) 213.

31. As Belcastro claims concerning this poem, "Language had been sufficiently distorted for profit and power to be ineffective any longer for telling the truth" (63).

32. Thomas Merton, *Original Child Bomb* (New York: New Directions, 1962); *CP* 293-302.

33. Michael W. Higgins, *Heretic Blood: The Spiritual Geography of Thomas Merton* (Toronto: Stoddart, 1998) 169.

34. Ellen W. Gorsevski, *The Geopolitics of Nonviolent Rhetoric* (Albany: State University of New York Press, 2004) 178.

The Geography of Lograire as Merton's Gestus – Prolegomena

Małgorzata Poks

I. Pre-texts: How the Poet Has Changed His Address[1]

1

In a journal entry dated February 8, 1968 is found an interesting note about Thomas Merton's pre-Gethsemani novel, which he was just preparing for publication. Originally entitled *Journal of My Escape from the Nazis* (finally published as *My Argument with the Gestapo*),[2] it contains passages of wordplay and surreal experimentation. This note deserves attention in the context of Merton's growing dissatisfaction with his writings. While most of the old stuff seems to him useless and trivial, this novel – somewhat surprisingly – passes the mark as "one of my best." What is at stake here? A celebrated writer and acclaimed spiritual master whose signature style is recognizable all over the world decides to release his – rather uneven – juvenile novelistic attempt and, as if that was not risky enough, elevates it over his canonical writings? Surely, it is not aesthetics, depth of insight, or spiritual maturity he has in mind. No, but the book feels authentic and somehow relevant. As Merton puts it, "it comes from the center where I have really experienced myself and my life. It represents a very vital and crucial – and fruitful – moment of my existence. Perhaps now I am returning to some such moment of breakthrough."[3] Caught in a predetermined model of monastic life, imprisoned within the image of a successful spiritual author, neurotic and depressed about his future and the future of the world, the Merton of the late 1960s was hungering for authenticity. Not accidentally was the last decade of his life heavily marked by existentialism, which is evident even on the level of the language he used. His journal entries from that period often feature such terms as "process," "event," "encounter," "the foolishness of the Cross."

The 1960s brought fascination with the Jewish theology of encounter.[4] In 1965 a chance meeting with some French-speaking students occasioned the following reflections:

The thing about the encounter was whether or not they got anything out of it, it was a revelation of Christ to *me* – just because they were human, open, frank, sincere, interested in ideas, and in a situation where they were fully exposed to risk and possibility. A meeting of possibilities resulting in new ideas, new directions for all of us . . . . The theology of "encounter" is not just a phrase. What else is the Acts of the Apostles? The whole life of the Christian is "The Acts of the Apostles."[5]

Encounters happen to us every day, challenging us to grow. God's Word, too, is an event rather than a fixed message whose content has been determined once and for all by Bible scholars and theologians. As an event, the Word continues to be spoken and in the changing circumstances of our lives it continues to disrupt our "little securities," those little idols that tend to replace the living God. As the main place where the Word is spoken, the institutional Church should be the first to register this dynamism of growth and change. To be true to her mission, Merton claims, the Church must therefore become the

scene of encounter, the [place] of openness, where possibilities are kept free and clear, where the word can be spoken (not according to a predetermined pattern or clever manipulation, but simply *spoken*). And where it is spoken, there is the eschatological event, the freedom of grace, a freedom that breaks through all the artificialities of predetermination and prejudice and in fact acts right across all the accepted patterns of society. (*DWL* 267)

Poetry is another privileged sphere of encounter with the Word. With some necessary modifications, the above statement can be read as Merton's declaration of the poet's obligation to follow the living Word of the moment. As amply evidenced by his *oeuvre*, rather than imprisoning himself within a "safe" and tested style or artistic identity, Merton felt obliged to grow in all areas of his creative life. He frequently insisted that the zealous protagonist of *The Seven Storey Mountain* that many wanted him to remain was – a persona, a mask of someone long dead. The newer Merton, forced to abandon or revise his old and somewhat narrow ideas, humbled and confused by a number of irresolvable contradictions within himself, was realizing the provisional status of human judgment and cognition. Already in a journal entry in 1961 he introduced a telling corrective to the popular idea of the Last

Judgment understood as "the cruel candid shot of you when you have just done something transient but hateful. As if this could be truth," he noted. The final act of the universal drama was more likely to be "a patient, organic, long-suffering understanding of the man's whole life, of *everything* in it, all in context" (*TTW* 180). This important realization underpins Merton's new experimental poetry, which is inclusive, contextual, open-ended, written by an embodied human being whose identity has been formed by and in opposition to a number of influences, in response to a variety of encounters, at an intersection of roots and routes.[6]

For some time it had been dawning on Merton that he needed a new language to express his changed awareness, that his old style would no longer be adequate. "How often is speech an excuse for remaining within, on the grounds that one 'has communicated,'" he wrote at the beginning of 1964, acknowledging the artist's right to refuse to communicate along predictable lines, if authenticity is at stake. "The artist who recognizes and loves his own style," he continues, becomes his own style and loses "contact with the world," whereas "the style is only a by-product of that contact" (*DWL* 61-62). Merton's recognition of style as formed and re-formed in the process of encountering the world was largely influenced by his readings in Maurice Merleau-Ponty. Through this French philosopher came also the appreciation of the body – not merely the intellect – as a tool of cognition. Rather than simply an apparatus making "use of pre-existing signs to express a meaning which is 'there'" (*DWL* 62), the body actively explores and *makes* sense of the world by all its acts and gestures. The meaning is not simply "there." Meditating on Merleau-Ponty's ideas, Merton found it deeply religious that the body should be "art and full of art" and that "[c]orporeity is style" (*DWL* 63). In a way, being a compulsive notebook writer and journal keeper, he had been experiencing this truth all his life. "How true it is that I think with my hands," he admitted in 1965. "Jotting things down, writing and rewriting, Drawing (not often)" (*DWL* 346) helped him to slow down the tempo of reading and to think his way through complex problems. The resulting interim reports from consciousness he recorded in his journals reveal the dynamics of the *process* of becoming, as well as the depth of his *encounter* with the world. Those journals, which Merton frequently numbered among his best writings, felt authentic. So did *Journal of My Escape from the Nazis,* which as a semi-autobiographic novel depicts a narrator-protagonist seeking elucidation of life through the process of writing. In the last decade of his life Merton adopted an experimental poetics that seemed an extension of "thinking with [his] hands."

2

The refusal of closure characteristic of the new, exploratory poetics, employed most consistently in his two book-long prose poems,[7] *Cables to the Ace* and *The Geography of Lograire*, seemed more consonant with the new reality governed by Einstein's relativity and Heisenberg's uncertainty principle. Many academics were involved in a serious critique of language as a tool of understanding and expressing reality, and Merton, too, was registering the impact of the "linguistic turn" in the humanities – a way of thinking that denied language transparency by problematizing the relationship between the word (the signifying), the concept it names (the signified), and the world the signified refers to (the referent). Already Martin Heidegger's analysis of being in *Being and Time* (1927) had brought to light the fact that we are "always already" shaped by the presuppositions we inherit. The implication of this discovery is that words neither imitate nor express reality, but *shape* consciousness and perception: it is not man that speaks language, but language that speaks man, as Heidegger famously claimed in his 1950 essay,[8] thus introducing a corrective on the Adamic myth of linguistic transparency. Having learned a language, we *live* in it and our perceptions are once and for all determined by its inner logic. Rather than seeing reality "as it is," we see through the distorting mirror of concepts, while "pure reality" remains forever inaccessible. A society that mistakes concepts for reality is idolatrous, and Merton was particularly alert to such spiritual malaise. Observing the world from his monastic enclosure, he witnessed the rapid disappearance of the real and the triumph of the sign without origin. Although Merton's essay "War and the Crisis of Language,"[9] published in 1969, antecedes the French sociologist Jean Baudrillard's influential *Simulations* (1981),[10] it clearly indicates how close Merton was to the bottom line of Baudrillard's dissection of consumer society and his famous conclusion that the world is being remade in the image of our desires.

An important consequence of the scholarly community's interrogation of language was the realization that the language we speak helps to tame the strangeness of the world by organizing reality into a coherent, meaningful whole. Reducing difference to sameness and explaining the strange by means of the familiar, it constructs for its users a "safe" dwelling place in a world which is dangerous, unstable, possibly also meaningless in itself. Human beings crave sense, but even a modest grasp of life's purpose and direction often seems impossible. Yet, what eludes us in our day-to-day existence becomes available the moment the chaotic flux of reality gets organized into a coherent narrative, thanks to rhetorical and troping devices of language. This explains at least two facts: why human beings are compulsive storytellers and, equally importantly, why the stories we tell often clash with one another, depending on the storytellers' presuppositions about the world. Contrary to popular belief, it is not only creation myths or ancient chronicles, not only journals, diaries, or fables, that record this all-too-human struggle to make sense of life by means of constructing narratives. Even the discourse of science is not free from the subjectivism and constructivism that rule all human discourses. Moreover, the findings and theories of biology, physics, history, theology, etc. are likewise structured as narratives, their raw data "emplotted" or arranged into stories within the limited number of generic deep-plot structures available in a given culture.[11] After all, scholars too are *situated* subjects who actively project their intuitions and prejudices onto their research. On top of that, they work under certain overarching frameworks called paradigms, which are culture-specific and subject to change. In consequence, objective "scientific" knowledge is a myth nobody takes seriously anymore.

Merton seems to have been reaching this awareness partly independently of sophisticated theoretical considerations, the latter rather confirming and articulating in words what he was already experiencing "in the flesh." Nowhere is his attitude of ambiguity, ambivalence, and doubt towards so-called metanarratives more pronounced than in *The Geography of Lograire*, one of the two poems (along with *Cables to the Ace*) Merton "regret[ted] less" (*OSM* 156) than most of the writings he had done. It is in *Geography* that we see how hard he struggles against the abuses and limitations of his white "Christian"[12] culture and the metanarratives of progress or racial superiority that seemed to legitimate its dominance over the whole world. Hard as he tries, however, he cannot completely disavow his membership in it. What the blacks, cast in the role of New Testament publicans, say to Christ who joins them at the table in the final fragment of "Queen's Tunnel" (the "North" canto of *Ge-*

ography) applies to Merton as well: "You have become a white man and it is not so simple at all" (*CP* 516).

This brings me back to the question of nomenclature. Shakespeare's Juliet, in love with a man who bore the name of the enemy, dismissed words as mere air, as nothing, but the dismissal did not save Romeo's life. That words do kill is a well-known truth, especially when they happen to replace reality. "The error of racism," writes Merton in early 1965, "is the logical consequence of an essentialist style of thought" (*DWL* 200). The rigidity of definitions that "defin[e] you and me forever without appeal" (*DWL* 201) (as "White," "Negro," "Red," etc.) appeared to Merton as a form of epistemological violence. To dismantle an unjust system one first had to dismantle the language that grounded it. "Rendre imprévisible la parole n'est-il pas un apprentissage de la liberté?"[13] mused Merton, copying this phrase from Gaston Bachelard on the first page of his notebook containing the greater part of his *Geography of Lograire*.

3

In "The Author's Note" which opens this long prose poem, Merton evokes "an urbane structuralism" (*CP* 458) as his procedural method. Importantly, he rated this unfinished poem highly, expecting that work on it would bring him the much desired breakthrough. The note of February 8, 1968, with which I started this essay, continues: "*Geography of Lograire* may in parts have some of the same sardonic vitality [as *Journal of My Escape*], but with much more involvement and complexity" (*OSM* 51).

It is to be regretted that the depth of Merton's expertise in non-religious and non-spiritual fields, including critical theory, has so far been underestimated and understudied. When seen in the context of his 1968 essay "Roland Barthes – Writing as Temperature,"[14] Merton's "late" poetry appears as a truly responsive encounter with structuralism and other current linguistic and literary theories. That essay also shows Merton as a perceptive reader and commentator of one of the subtlest of twentieth-century French intellectuals, whose work was only just being translated into English. "Writing as Temperature" is a review of Barthes' first book, *Writing Degree Zero*, written in 1953 and published in America in 1968. At the time when Merton was writing it, Barthes (1915-1980) was lecturing on the sociology of signs, symbols, and representations at various French institutions. Inspired by Ferdinand de Saussure's idea of semiology as a science of signs, he had been exploring ways of extending the linguistic structuralist analysis to larger cultural contexts. His *Mythologies* (1957) was a study of cultural "myths" or ideological propositions that permeate mass culture. His book *On Racine* (1963) applied the structuralist method to the study of the staging of Racine's dramas in the traditional French theatre. Controversial in France,[15] the book was hailed by Merton as "a masterpiece of literary criticism, the power and impact of which may not be fully felt by one who has not had to study Racine in a French Lycée" (*LE* 146). Not only was Merton well read in French literature, he was also quick to appreciate the revolutionary character of the literary theories emanating from Paris as well as their potential to subvert accepted categories of reading and writing. Calling Barthes "one of the most articulate and important literary critics writing today in any language" (*LE* 140), Merton demonstrated truly prophetic insight.

In the last decade of his life Merton was drawn to the minimalist painting of Ad Reinhardt; he was also reading Alain Robbe-Grillet's anti-novels, translating the Chilean Nicanor Parra's antipoems and writing his own, as well as making other "anti-art" experiments (Zen photography, calligraphic drawings). Under these circumstances he could not fail to be impressed by Barthes' theorizing of writing as *gestus*. In "Writing Degree Zero" Merton defines *gestus* as "the chosen, living, and responsible mode of presence of the writer in his world" (*LE* 144). "The authentic *gestus* of writing," he goes on to expound Barthes's theory,

> begins only when all meaningful postures have been abandoned, when all the obvious "signs" of art have been set aside. At the present juncture, such writing can hardly be anything but antiwriting. The writer is driven back to the source of his writing, since he can no longer trust the honesty of his customary dialogue with the rest of society. (*LE* 145)

At the heart of Barthes's theory lies the idea of writing as an act which is free from any message, does not attempt to raise consciousness or express the writer's emotions. Like Brecht's *Verfremdungseffekt* in theatre, writing establishes a distance between the reader and itself.[16] In "Writing as Temperature" Merton explains how Barthes adapted de Saussure's idea of semantic fields to literature. The fact that words constantly migrate from one field to another has an impact on all the words in the relevant systems, and this in turn affects language users' understanding of reality. Knowing this, the writer can manipulate words in such a way as to question or subvert the system. "It is here," explains Merton, "and not in his doctrine, his 'revolutionary message' or in a supposed 'revolutionary style' that the writer really changes the world – (though he should be free of any obvious purpose to change anything)" (*LE* 143). Responsible to their writing only, writers do not try to influence or transform society. Instead, they use words carefully and responsibly, attempting to demythologize or just "define correctly the relation between writing and the world" (*LE* 144). If they succeed in this task, they succeed in changing the society, precisely because they have transformed the way we perceive things. Such writing, however, is the exact opposite of "poetic writing," as Merton crucially points out. Rather, in a writing so construed, "language no longer 'violates the abyss' but slides away from us across an icy surface." To prove the point, he evokes Barthes' understanding of Robbe-Grillet's silence as a language "which irremediably establishes the limits of the object, not its 'beyond'" (*LE* 145-46).

Merton was not new to Robbe-Grillet, the French *nouveau roman* author. *Cables to the Ace* opens with an epigram from Robbe-Grillet, which proclaims the subversive value of language: "La mise en question du monde dans lequel nous sommes ne peut se faire que par la forme et non par une anecdote vaguement sociale ou politique" (*CP* 394),[17] which can be translated as: "Questioning the world in which we live can be done only by means of form, not by an anecdote with a vaguely social or political content." It does not seem likely that this epigram was meant as a complete break with Merton's earlier, more politically and socially conscious writing. He remained appreciative of Ernesto Cardenal and other Latin American poets who fought for a better world with their pens, if not openly with a gun. Likewise, his own poems on Eichmann, *Original Child Bomb* (about the bombing of Hiroshima) or the 1963 collection of verse *Emblems of a Season of Fury* continued to testify to his involved stance toward the problems of the world. But Merton was also seeing the other side of the coin: his own style was becoming a bankable convention and so artistic development could only come at the price of radical transformation. It was time to abandon the self-fabricated image of an articulate spiritual author who knew (what arrogance!) how to save the world, resist the penchant for flag-waving, and chose the authentic *gestus* of writing "by which alone the writer gives evidence that he is alive"

(*LE* 145) – and hope that he was right when he wrote in his review of *Writing Degree Zero* that a language-conscious writer, choosing words with deliberation, can bring the system down (*LE* 143).

II. The First Opening Up of a Dream

This long poem is organized into four cantos according to the four cardinal points of the compass: South, North, East, and West, with "Prologue: The Endless Inscription" (*CP* 459-62) opening the whole work. It is this prologue I wish to focus on in this part of my essay to demonstrate how the concept of writing as *gestus* works and how it can serve to open up a rewarding reading of Merton's (deconstructive) poetic testament.

Consisting of eighteen numbered sections of unequal length, the prologue begins abruptly:

Long note one wood thrush hear him low in waste pine places
Slow doors all ways of ables open late
Tarhead unshaven the captain signals
Should they wait? (1.1-4)

Reading and rereading the above, one begins to realize that, rather than organizing words and ideas in a customary, linear fashion, Merton invites the reader into a dense semantic field. The opening section already fully exposes us to the dramatic, polyvalent world of Merton's *Geography* in which meanings are always provisional, unstable, ideologically informed, made and unmade by the very discourse that legitimizes them; in which language endlessly forms and re-forms, inscribes and re-inscribes the world. The poem's coherence is not metaphorical but associational. Metonymy seems to be its dominant trope. But the title – "The Endless Inscription" – also alludes to Merton's changed epistemology, one that privileges process over the finished "product" of knowing. Throughout the poem the speaking voice assumes a stance that is epistemologically non-violent: involved in the world, shaped by and in opposition to events, he nevertheless withholds judgement and tries not to impose his interpretations or cognitive categories on reality. Far from a drive to mastery over the text (most characteristic of Merton's earlier, "new critical" verses), the poet lets the writing guide him to meanings he cannot anticipate in advance. Letting go of systems, words, projects, attachments – as in the Eckhartian/ Heideggerian concept of *Gelassenheit*[18] – he becomes a catalyser rather than originator of meanings.

So *Geography* starts with a question: "Should they wait?" But who are "they"? Where and what are "they" waiting for? These, however, are difficult questions. Places, times and identities are fluid; they blend into each other and transform so that the archetypal pattern, a basic "design" governing our geography – as well as Merton's *Geography* – might emerge. This is a universal "design of ire" or violent passion. Organizing human reality the world over into predictable patterns of oppression and exploitation, this "design" results from human uncontrollable, unbounded desires: "Desire desire O sign of ire" (10.1) mourns the poet. After all, the geography as we know it today has been shaped by greed and will to power resulting in endless conquests, wars, human sacrifice, ethnocentric violence, imperialism, colonialism, and postcolonial domination. As a consequence, the cardinal points of the compass no longer designate *geographical* reality only; the division of the modern world into the rich North/West and the impoverished, "exotic" South/East is also *ideological* and an abiding result of centuries of oppression of non-white, non-Christian populations.

Realizing this, it is easier to situate the above-quoted fragment in the overall geography of desire. The scene is set for a sinister deal. Most probably, the captain of a slave ship is waiting for a fresh consignment of slaves and the deal is to be transacted in a solitary place under the cover of night. The word "ables" brings to mind able-bodied males, probably crew members or those involved in the slave trade. Equally convincingly, however, the "ables" of the fragment can refer to the slaves themselves, whose able bodies are likely to fetch good price at the slave market; or, alternatively, whose build and physical strength predestine them for impressment[19] into the navy (able seamen) where they will have to fight against their racial/tribal brothers. To complicate things further, the word is a homophone of Abels, the plural of the name of Cain's brother from the Old Testament parable, which seems to suggest that, ultimately, the manifold designs of "ire" are reducible to this most archetypal (for a Westerner, anyway) story of fratricidal violence. In the larger human family any act of aggression is always directed against a brother or a sister, and it is obvious that no society is free of aggression. When the prologue's section nine refers back to the opening scene, by showing "Tarhead slaver captain selling the sables / To Cain and Abel by design" (9.2-3) a simplistic victim/victimizer dichotomy is called into question only to be finally dismantled. Additionally, the image, which evokes the whole history of slavery, an institution as old as the human race itself, also reveals Merton's determination to critique popular cultural "myths" circulating in the mass society of his day and unmask false representations of reality by reaching to the roots of the problems that created them. In May 1960 he wrote in his journal: "You can be in a Trappist monastery and never become a Southerner. But I am becoming a Kentuckian and a conscious one."[20] But being a Southerner meant piercing the various mystiques of the South, including the mystique of violence and racial oppression as, supposedly, more peculiar to that region than to others. In the American cauldron of racial riots and the Civil Rights Movement, thinking in terms of right=black / wrong=white was an easy temptation to a liberal-minded intellectual. Naturally, simplifications are not without value, as they facilitate human beings' orientation in the world and help us to act more effectively. But this does not change the fact that they distort the image of the world beyond recognition. If we are to live peacefully as one human family, the suppressed complexity and polyvalence of the real has to be reclaimed. Thus, Merton's writing as *gestus* begins to manifest its subversive power in this project of retrieval, which, however, was not realized as a *project* – an idea conceived beforehand and projected onto the poem. Merton is saying familiar things once again (he "is driven back to the source of his writing"), but the way he is doing it precludes "preaching" a message and taking sides (since the writer "can no longer trust the honesty of his customary dialogue with the rest of society" [*LE* 145]).

Coming back to the problem of slavery, however, it is sometimes forgotten that "that peculiar institution," as it was euphemistically called in the American South, had not been invented by Europeans at the dawn of the age of explorations and discovery, but had existed since time immemorial. It was known to the Old Testament peoples, African civilizations and the Muslim world, the indigenous populations of pre-Columbian Americas, the peoples of Asia and Oceania, as well as pre-Christian Europe. Slave-lords were of all racial and cultural backgrounds, which idea Merton alludes to by using "tarhead" as a modifier for the slaver captain, thus initiating a process of dismantling a series of culturally sanctioned but often mutually contradictory oppositions: in Western epistemology black used to be associated with stain, sin, Satan, therefore also with Cain; while white would naturally correlate with purity, saintliness, therefore with the innocent Abel and ultimately with Christ, whose cruel death Abel's sacrifice seemed to prefigure. On the other hand, blacks were the unquestionable victims of white oppression in Africa or the New World, where they were often brutally tortured and murdered by innumerable white "Cains." Characteristically, Merton makes both Cain and Abel buy "the sables by design," reclaiming the complexity of historical experience, and, by the same token, taking a soberly ironical perspective on the supposedly inherent racial difference as concerns cruelty and greed. It is in this perspective that the figure of the captain becomes archetypal of any leader plotting the manifold "designs of ire." Once he is a "tarhead" slaver, at other times he is more like the homebound Odysseus – the cunning protoplast of modern Europeans – or a captain of "the hated navy" the speaker's "family ancestor the Lieutenant" (7.6) was forced to serve. Obviously, Merton is playing his Celtic card here, introducing himself into the poem as doubly inscribed in the process of victimization: a son of a New Zealand father of Welsh ancestry and an American mother of an Anglo-Saxon background, he was partly oppressed Celt, partly Germanic invader: "Two seas in my self Irish and German / Celt blood washes in twin seagreen people" (5.4-5), says the poem's speaker. By identifying with the family ancestor impressed into the English navy, he is siding with the world's oppressed and no doubt *com-passion*-ately watching the Lieutenant as the latter "[f]rom the square deck cursed / Pale eyed Albion without stop" (7.7-8).

This victimized-victimizer pattern is ubiquitous, although it is never essentialized. There is a Cain and an Abel within *every* human being. Section 12 reads:

Wash ocean crim cram crimson sea's
Son Jim's son standing on the frigate
Jim Son Crow's ocean crosses a span
Dare heart die Spanish ram or Lamb Son's Blood
Crimson's well for oceans carnate sin sign
Ira water Ira will not wash in blood
Dear slain son lies only capable
Pain and Abel lay down red designs
Civil is slain brother sacred wall wood pine
Sacred black brother is beaten to the wall
The other gone down star's spaces home way plain (12.1-11).

In this shorthand image temporal and spatial references conflate, inscribing instances of fratricidal violence within a universal naval history. The oceans of the world are crimson with blood. Whether "Jim Crow" or plain Jim, their sons are all Christs – God's sons – whose blood ("Lamb Son's Blood") stains the waters with an abiding mark of sin ("carnate sin sign"). The vicious circle never stops. When another "dear son" of man is slain, the orphaned ones cry out for blood and plot further vengeance: "Pain and Abel lay down red designs." Against culturally-motivated expectations, Abel is not more innocent than Cain. It is already obvious that Merton uses those two easily recognizable names as counters in his revisionist history of human relations. In the postlapsarian world one-sided radical innocence is not possible and Abel's malice frequently surpasses Cain's. But the opposite is also true: seen from the Paschal perspective of renewal of everything in Christ, Cain's goodness can equal his brother's. Having reclaimed the reverse side of the well-known (which often means *imperfectly* known) story and having suggested that good and evil interpenetrate, perhaps even condition each other, Merton can finally bid farewell to what he once called "the last vestiges of the pharisaical division between the sacred and the secular."[21] The termination of Manichean thinking, which frequently mars the Christian message, requires that the founding myth of dualism be abolished in an intuition of a *redeemed* world, i.e., wholly *reconciled* to God in Christ. The chasm between "sacred" and "secular" has been closed by the Paschal Lamb. The "civil brother" slain in the temple of the natural world ("sacred wall wood pine") and the "[s]acred black brother . . . beaten to the wall" are really one.

In the poem's optics, slavery – the treatment of human beings as possessions which can be freely disposed of by their owners – appears as the quintessential transgression against the idea of universal brotherhood. In Merton's immediate cultural context, that practice was most intimately associated with the exploitation of Africans by their white "brothers." Yet, section 13 introduces the ancient kingdom of Dahomey (now the Republic of Benin) as "father of Africa pattern" in an effort to reclaim a more balanced vision of the issue:

> Dahomey pine tar small wood bench bucket
> Under shadow there wait snake
> There coil ire design father of Africa pattern (13.1-3).

One of the principal slave states in west Africa, Dahomey also practiced massive human sacrifice. In modern times, though, instead of offering its war captives as sacrifice to ancestor spirits, the country's rulers would rather trade them for firearms with European slavers. Thus, Dahomey's slave trafficking on a commercial scale seems to function in the poem as a correlate of the original sin, as suggested by the presence of the snake. The then-recent theories claiming Africa as the cradle of human life might have added another connection between Dahomey and the scene of the Fall. Had racial solidarity been maintained and had Africans refused cooperation with white slavers, much suffering might have been avoided; possibly even the infamous Middle Passage might have failed as a commercial venture. This is not to claim that Merton indulges in speculations of "what might have been." But such speculations are prompted by the gravitational pull of associations suggested by the poem's work of condensation.[22] What else can be the significance of the section's cryptic ending: "Dead rope hang cotton over captain branch" (13.6), which seems to tie in a shorthand fashion the founding transgression against brotherhood with lynching and present-day hate-crimes as its end-results?

Cotton imagery, weaved throughout the prologue as a metonymic reminder of the exploitative slave labor on Southern plantations, never lets the reader forget the American contribution to the shameful "design." Little wonder that, like Dahomey in the days of its glory, the American Deep South would also prove capable of sacrificing people in the name of caste privilege, even if they happened to belong to the "right" race, as evidenced by the murder of three civil rights workers, two of them white, in Mississippi, in June 1964.[23] The resulting situation is an incredible confusion: "Snake and tarheel minister and bat / And blood and ram and Isaac done in a dare" (14.4-5). It is no longer within human power to redeem it, and so the poem's speaker resorts to prayer. "Hallow my Savior the workless sparrow" (17.1), he begins, evidently desiring some eschatological reversal. Section 17 continues:

Closes my old gate on dead tar's ira slam
Gone far summer too far fret work blood
Work blood and tire tar under light wood
Night way plain home to wear death down hard
Ire hard down on anger heel grind home down
Weary is smashed cotton-head beaten down mouth
When will they all go where those white Cains are dead? (17.2-8)

Images of an end of the old order are prominent: the "old gate" closes and violence seems to have exhausted itself ("dead tar's ira slam"). The "summer" of the second line may contain an allusion to the annual American "long hot summers" of race riots, which started in 1964 in the Watts district of Los Angeles and lasted until 1968 when a riot broke out in Washington, DC, after the assassination of Martin Luther King, Jr. That summer had gone "too far" in the work of blood and the collective number of casualties seemed to have tired death herself ("wear death down hard"). The lines that follow bring associations with Genesis 3:15 and God's promise to humankind of an eventual triumph over evil. God says to the serpent: "I will put enmity between you and the woman, and between your offspring and hers; He will strike at your head, while you strike at his heel." Ire, anger – attributes of the archetypal serpent – let loose among humans, accomplish the second part of the prophecy: the heel of the human race is being crushed or "ground down hard." The image of a "cotton-head" – a choice example of metonymy and synecdoche combined – evokes slave labor on the one hand, and, on the other, the snake/serpent tempter responsible for the atrocities of slavery, whose head is smashed ("cotton-head beaten down mouth") the moment human relations are being finally restored to health. The return home – understood as an initial oneness of the human family – becomes possible.

But is this interpretation not guilty of cultural overdetermination? Instead of being inscribed in the Western culture's chain of signification, section 17 could be reinscribed in terms of cultures marginalized by colonial domination. In such reinscription, the verses would actually contain a *call* to increase violence against oppressors in order to exhaust death, wear it down, as it were, in preparation for the long awaited eschatological era. This interpretation sounds logical in the context of Cargo cults, to which Merton devotes so much space in *Geography*. Originating in New Guinea and Melanesia, but developing along analogous lines in other geographical latitudes as well, those messianic movements would cluster around charismatic leaders (another realization of the captain figure) who insisted on removal – which sometimes amounted to murdering – of all whites from their territory. The disappearance of "white Cains" was seen either as a precondition for or a consequence of the return of ancestors, and with their return the much desired Cargo was to flow in, the possession of which would re-establish the marginalized peoples' sense of dignity.

"When will they all go where those white Cains are dead?" seems, therefore, more likely to be asked from a non-white perspective, but the question has relevance for everyone regardless of cultural or racial background, as it concerns the end of oppression and the beginning of a new, just world. Merton merely echoes this obsessive question about the advent of the messianic kingdom, but he is wiser than to speculate about the likely answer. He knows that both secular and religious attempts at instituting justice and peace for all inevitably degenerate into even more oppressive regimes. The poem ends on this cryptic note: "Sign Redeemer's 'R' / Buys Mars his last war" (18.1-2). Religiously motivated wars are obviously among the worst. Yet, one wonders. Can "last war" mean what it does, i.e., not simply the latest, but the final one? Having just surveyed a panorama of atrocities perpetrated by members of the human family on one another, and realizing that human desire is not ever likely to be controlled by administrative measures, does the text suggest that violence can eventually have redemptive value; that out of it redeemed times can emerge? Or shall we read the lines as indicating that the Messiah himself, and in his own time, will finally redeem the destructiveness of human history? Perhaps such expectations are only wish projections of desperate humanity unable to bear the Nietzschean eternal return of the same? The ending is as undecided as the whole body of "the endlessly inscribed" *Geography of Lograire*, an unfinished poem, "a purely tentative first draft of a longer work in progress, in which there are, necessarily, many gaps," as Merton admits in the "Author's Note" (*CP* 457).

III. Conclusion: In Praise of the Plural

Merton intended *Geography* as part of the ongoing process every poet is involved in: that of "building" or "dreaming" the world which "is at once his" and "everybody else's" (*CP* 457). Rather than either purely personal or purely universal, the poem is a confluence of both and situates him at an intersection of countless encounters with people, places, texts, and ideas. In the scope of about a hundred and fifty pages Merton inscribes himself within the text, and by the same token re-inscribes the world. The full text of this exciting, dense, and challenging poem reveals an interesting aspect of Thomas Merton, yet an aspect hardly inconsistent with the other Mertons we know so well – with the possible exception that his heightened awareness of the ideological implications of style and his use of language to critique a number of essentialist positions (religious orthodoxy, Eurocentrism, etc.) constitute the poem's point of gravity around which everything revolves. By allowing the free interaction of a number of voices, both dominant and oppressed, without authorial commentary, Merton's *Geography* presents a revisionist history: it reveals the limitations and contradictions of power discourses and reclaims repressed perspectives.

The monologism of the dominant Western culture is cleverly subverted and ultimately dismantled by the fact that the poem juxtaposes several, highly contradictory accounts of cross-cultural and/or interfaith encounters. On the one hand, there are the rational, apparently "objective" accounts of Western explorers reaching new lands and exotic cultures; of ethnographers and archeologists studying "primitive" societies; of Christian missionaries working among native pagans; of guardians of religious orthodoxy uprooting heresy. But these stories clash with alternative versions of the same encounters told from the "other's" point of view: that of tribal South Africans, the Maya jaguar priest, Native American Ghost Dancers, members of an English antinomian sect, Melanesian "Cargo" cultists, or the medieval Islamic scholar from Morocco, Ibn Battuta, who left an engaging travel narrative depicting his journeys to Asia and Africa – a narrative which presents a full-blooded alternative to the European adventurers' accounts of traveling West (see Clifford 11). Having said that, it is possible to argue that *Geography* can be called a text in a Barthesian understanding of the term: reading it can be compared to taking a stroll on a busy day and being at once bombarded by a variety of half-identifiable, half-registered impressions: "what [the stroller] perceives," writes Barthes in an essay of 1971, entitled "From Work to Text," "is multiple, irreducible, coming from a disconnected, heterogeneous variety of substance and perspectives" (Leich 1472). The combination of impressions, moreover, is absolutely unique to this one experience of walking-reading. Obviously, Barthes had already proclaimed the death of the Author and freed the process of reading from paternalistic supervision. Unlike the *work* (which "has nothing disturbing for any monist philosophy . . . ; for such a philosophy, plural is the evil"), the *text* is best seen in the light of Mark 5:9: its name is Legion. A crucial explanation of the provocative claim follows: "The plural of demoniacal texture which opposes text to work can bring with it fundamental changes in reading, and precisely in areas where monologism appears to be the Law" (Leich 1473).

The Merton of the 1960s, rebelling against paternalism and the stunting influence of father figures on spiritual growth,[24] would naturally want the reader to be his partner in their common effort to understand, and would no doubt respect the reader's right to read the text of his ambiguous work in progress against the grain, "without the inscription of the Father" (Leich 1473). In *Geography*, Merton himself is such a reader as much as he is a writer. He often reads against the explicit intentions of the texts he uses or quotes from, bringing out their suppressed implications. Even if the sources he incorporates are "orthodox," in the sense of cohering to an accepted body of belief, his reading renders them para-doxical in the strict etymological sense of the term (see Barthes in Leich 1471-72).

Endnotes

1. In "Prologue" to *Cables to the Ace*, the long "antipoem" published in 1968, Merton explicitly announces his changed poetics in the following words: "The poet ... has changed his address and his poetics are on vacation. He is not roaring in the old tunnel" (*The Collected Poems of Thomas Merton* [New York: New Directions: 1977] 395 [subsequent references will be cited as "CP" parenthetically in the text]). Obviously, Merton's writing as *gestus* manifests itself in the most radical way first in *Cables* and only later in *The Geography of Lograire* – published in 1969. My point in this essay, however, is to use the concept of *gestus* instrumentally to suggest an angle of approach to the dense and unconventional poetics of the latter poem, and not to document the minute chronology of Merton's experiments with style.

2. Thomas Merton, *My Argument with the Gestapo: A Macaronic Journal* (Garden City, NY: Doubleday, 1969).

3. Thomas Merton, *The Other Side of the Mountain: The End of the Journey. Journals, vol. 7: 1967-1968*, ed. Patrick Hart (San Francisco: HarperCollins, 1998) 51; subsequent references will be cited as "OSM" parenthetically in the text.

4. In November 1960 he was reading Abraham Heschel's *God in Search of Man*; see Thomas Merton, *Turning Toward the World: The Pivotal Years. Journals, vol. 4: 1960-1963*, ed. Victor A. Kramer (San Francisco: HarperCollins, 1996) 66; subsequent references will be cited as "TTW" parenthetically in the text.

5. Thomas Merton, *Dancing in the Water of Life: Seeking Peace in the Hermitage. Journals, vol. 5: 1963-1965*, ed. Robert E. Daggy (San Francisco: HarperCollins, 1997) 266-67; subsequent references will be cited as "DWL"

parenthetically in the text.

6. The idea of "roots and routes" as constitutive of cultural and personal identity comes from James Clifford, *Travel and Translation in the Late Twentieth Century* (Cambridge, MA: Harvard University Press, 1997) 11; subsequent references will be cited as "Clifford" parenthetically in the text.

7. The first extensive attempts at writing "antipoetical" poetry were obviously "Chant to be Used in Processions around a Site with Furnaces" (published in 1961) (*CP* 345-49) and *Original Child Bomb* (New York: New Directions, 1962) (*CP* 291-302).

8. Martin Heidegger, "Language," *The Norton Anthology of Theory and Criticism*, ed. Vincent B. Leich (New York: W. W. Norton, 2001) 1121-34; subsequent references will be cited as "Leich" parenthetically in the text.

9. Thomas Merton, *Passion for Peace: The Social Essays*, ed. William H. Shannon (New York: Crossroad, 1995) 300-14.

10. Jean Baudrillard, *Simulations*, trans. Paul Foss, Paul Patton, Philip Beitchman (New York: Semiotext(e), 1983).

11. Hayden White is a vocal proponent of "the poetics of history," but his theory can be easily extended to the "poetics" of other scientific discourses: see Hayden White, *Metahistory: The Historical Imagination in Nineteenth-Century Europe* (Baltimore: John Hopkins University Press, 1973).

12. The inverted commas imply that what Merton rejects are the abuses and distortions of Christianity, especially in its alliance with power elites, and not the religion itself.

13. James Laughlin, "Notes on Sources" for *The Geography of Lograire* (*CP* 595). The phrase means: "Rendering the word unforeseeable, isn't this the beginning of liberty?"

14. Thomas Merton, *The Literary Essays of Thomas Merton*, ed. Patrick Hart, OCSO (New York: New Directions, 1981) 140-46; subsequent references will be cited as "*LE*" parenthetically in the text.

15. Raymond Picard, a Racine scholar at the Sorbonne, wrote a reply to it entitled *New Criticism or New Fraud?* (Pullman: State University of Washington Press, 1969).

16. Significantly, Barthes was already drifting towards a poststructuralist theory of textuality – summarized in his 1971 essay "From Work to Text" – which defines text as a process, a signifying field to be entered by the reader in order to activate the free play of the signifier, i.e., the dissemination and disruption of meaning rather than its coherence. Had Merton lived a few years longer, he would not have been surprised by this development.

17. For a very interesting recent exposition of Merton's experimental

poetics in *Cables* see Robert L. Davis, "Sacred Play: Thomas Merton's *Cables to the Ace,*" *The Merton Annual* 20 (2007) 243-64.

18. The concept of *Gelassenheit* was originally developed by Meister Eckhart, but Heidegger's appropriation of the term gave it currency in twentieth-century philosophy; it plays a crucial role in section 84 of *Cables to the Ace* (*CP* 452).

19. I am consciously using the term "impressment" rather than "conscription," which is more common in the American usage, to allude to the historical practice (alive especially in the British Navy up to 1814), of compelling people to serve in the military, usually without notice.

20. Thomas Merton, *A Search for Solitude: Pursuing the Monk's True Life. Journals, vol. 3: 1952-1960,* ed. Lawrence S. Cunningham (San Francisco: HarperCollins, 1996) 391.

21. On September 11, 1965 Merton writes: "Here [in the hermitage] I see my task is to get rid of the last vestiges of a pharisaical division between the sacred and secular, and to see that the *whole* world is reconciled to God in Christ, not just the monastery, nor only the convents, the churches, and the good Catholic schools" (*DWL* 294).

22. I use Sigmund Freud's term consciously to suggest parallels between Merton's poetics and the work of dreams.

23. Merton refers to this event several times in his journal (see *DWL* 133, 177, 235).

24. In *Woods, Shore, Desert,* Merton rebels against the imposing, solemn authority of monastic superiors, preferring a partnership of seekers: "Brother rather than father. Partnership in seeking to understand our monastic vocation" (*OSM* 93).

Thomas Merton's Ecopoetry:
Bearing Witness to the Unity of Creation

Deborah Kehoe

From his school days to his last days on earth, from Greenwich Village to Gethsemani, Thomas Merton was a poet. What began as youthful literary ambition grew over the years into an outlet for his maturing spirituality and created a body of work exhibiting an extraordinary range of style and tone, from derivative to experimental, from playful to deeply serious. Within the covers of his voluminous *Collected Poems*,[1] audiences can read the story of Merton's celebrated, lifelong soul search. Its pages ring out with a voice perpetually dissatisfied with conclusions, that of a mystical pilgrim pursuing truth and the unifying vision.

In *The Seven Storey Mountain*, Merton claims that he did not produce any good poetry until after he became a Catholic, attributing his success to his newborn desire at the time to tell people of the love of God in a language that was not "hackneyed or crazy."[2] While the entire body of Merton's post-conversion writing speaks to readers of the love of God and testifies that all creation lives in relationship, many of his most stirring challenges to a fragmented world are indeed found in the poetry, work which charts the monastic author's progress along the contemplative path and displays his deepening insight into the interplay between God and nature.

As celebrations of the mysterious unity of creation and all that such appreciation implies, certain of Merton's poems assume a renewed vitality when read within the context of today's widening demand for environmental stewardship. No longer marginalized, this concern now manifests itself in an increasing body of literature and has received attention in religious statements across the denominations, from the evangelical call for "creation care" to the Vatican's recent declaration that environmental irresponsibility is a sin.[3] As is the case with many social and political topics, Merton, over forty years ago, was ahead of his time in his embrace of this issue. His personal, creative, and theological writings all manifest an ecological conscience often at odds with the times in which he lived and wrote. He allied himself with the early, urgent, and often vilified nature guardians, most notably Rachel Carson, a sympathy which Merton scholars confidently speculate would be thriving today. Monica Weis, for example, asserts: "Were Merton alive today, I have no doubt that he would be in the vanguard of contemporary nature writers and environmentalists."[4] Also, Kathleen Deignan writes that Merton left a legacy "for modern people who labor toward a rebirth of our consciousness of and identity with creation, as an urgent spiritual and ecological necessity."[5] Such assessments and conjectures find compelling support in the vast array of those works which can broadly be called Merton's nature poems, poems so prophetic in their "greenness" that they justify the new and timely label of *ecopoetry*.

Still a fluid term, *ecopoetry* prompts a wide range of possible interpretation and application. Notable seminal studies, however, offer some solid ground from which to begin to explore specific illustrative works. *Ecopoetry: A Critical Introduction* is one such study which provides useful descriptive summaries. For example, Bernard Quetchenbach explains that the ecopoet "is a kind of missionary, motivated by a fierce devotion to a subject matter that is . . . absolutely crucial to the poet's well-being and . . . to [that of] the world at large."[6] Additionally, J. Scott Bryson identifies the key defining traits of ecopoetry as "a humble appreciation of wildness," "ecocentrism," and "skepticism toward hyper-rationality and its resultant over-reliance on technology" (*Ecopoetry* 7). These features named by Bryson serve as a point of departure from which to revisit selected poems by Merton and to re-examine them as pre-existing examples of an emerging category of poetry.

Humility in the formal, prescribed life of the Benedictine monk is the product of sustained spiritual exercise. The monk's way to humility is through devoted observance of the *Rule* of Saint Benedict wherein that particular virtue is broken down into twelve degrees or steps. According to Merton's explanation to his novices, the first degree of humility is to remember constantly and with awe the eternal presence of God.[7] Merton frequently speaks from such a disposition in his poems, many of which feature images of the natural landscapes amid which he led his monastic life and those which flourished in his inclusive imagination. Many of these poems express the poet's awe in the presence of a Christ-infused wildness and his awareness of his own inexplicably unique part in the continuum.

An early example of this reverent response to nature is the poem "Song: Contemplation" (*CP* 157-59). The opening stanzas contain a series of exclamatory lines in which the speaker apostrophizes the world around him: "O land alive with miracles!" and "O country wild with talent" (ll. 1, 7). He goes on to acknowledge the land's power to inspire wonder and praise in the earthbound observer: "Is there an hour in you that does not rouse our mind with songs?" (l. 8). In language echoing Gerard Manley Hopkins' poetics of *instress*, the poem exudes the speaker's rapture as he regards, if only in momentary apprehension of its brilliance, the splendor of nature:

> Lo, we have seen you, we have seized you, wonder,
> Caught you, half held you in the larch and lighted birch:
> But in that capture you have sailed us half-mile-high into the air
> To taste the silences of the inimitable hawk: (ll. 22-25).

The speaker further proclaims that the source of this overwhelming glory is the truth that "Christ and angels walk among us, everywhere" (l. 18). Here, as throughout much of his poetry, Merton avows that in the natural world one beholds the Incarnation of Christ, a view which Dennis O'Hara argues can be interpreted as a "portent" of Merton's affinity for what would later be called eco-theology.[8] The poet's assurance of Christ's transfiguring presence in nature ultimately takes "Song: Contemplation" from celebration of the landscape of his earthly existence to exultation in the power of prayer to lift one beyond the limits of the material world:

> But in the dazzled, high and unelectric air
> Seized in the talons of the terrible Dove,
> The huge, unwounding Spirit,
> We suddenly escape the drag of earth (ll. 40-43).

Yet, in this poem, as in many of those which Lynn Szabo classifies under the similarly worded heading "Songs of Contemplation,"[9] the first stage of the poet's transcendence is his humble appreciation for the wildness which encompasses him.

Like all of his successful poems, "Song: Contemplation" demonstrates Merton's faith in the capacity of poetry to evoke experiences which prose can only relate. "Poetry can go where prose cannot," Merton can be heard explaining to his novices in the recorded conference titled *Natural Contemplation*.[10] In *The Art of Reading Poetry*, Harold Bloom explains this peculiar ability when he writes that poetry expands human understanding through "strangeness," a quality he defines by quoting Owen Barfield, author of *Poetic Diction: A Study in Meaning*:[11]

> [Strangeness] arises from contact with a different kind of consciousness from our own, different, yet not so remote that we cannot partly share it, as indeed, in such a connection, the mere word "contact" implies. Strangeness, in fact, arouses wonder when we do not understand: aesthetic imagination when we do.[12]

As Bloom puts it, consciousness is to the poet what marble is to the sculptor – the raw material and medium of expression. Through words born of a broadened awareness and crafted to stimulate alertness in others, the poet invites the reader to share in strangeness. Authoritative readers, such as Anthony Padovano, familiar with the full range of the Merton canon, and sensitive to its modulations, have remarked on the singularly "unguarded" tone audible in his poetry,[13] a tone which suggests that the poet has made direct contact with the creatively energizing *strangeness* of God. "Song: Contemplation" effectively illustrates this moment of connection in words which pulse with life as if they come straight from the heart of a man fully engaged in what Merton famously referred to as the cosmic dance.[14]

In "Night-Flowering Cactus" (*CP* 351-52), the poet relies on his inner eye to capture the sacred strangeness of the natural world. Through his imagination, he responds to the wonder of untamed, uncontrollable, and largely unseen processes of nature and bears witness to the oneness of all creation by assuming the voice of a cactus which blooms rarely and only in the silent darkness of the desert, requiring no observer or admirer to complete or confirm the significance of its existence:

> I know my time, which is obscure, silent and brief
> For I am present without warning one night only (ll. 1-2).

The poem is remarkable for the audacity of much of its imagery, suggestive descriptions which, as Lynn Szabo notes, are usually "reserved for sexual and spiritual encounter of orgasmic resonance,"[15] most readily illustrated by the depiction of the cactus opening itself in preparation for the long-awaited ejaculatory release of the "all-knowing bird of night" (l. 25).[16] The central event of the poem is portrayed in diction rich with both sensual and sacramental connotations:

> When I come I lift my sudden Eucharist
> Out of the earth's unfathomable joy
> Clean and total I obey the world's body
> I am intricate and whole, not art but wrought passion
> Excellent deep pleasure of essential waters
> Holiness of form and mineral mirth: (ll. 10-15).

This re-creation of the intimate merger of poet, nature, and Christ leads the reader into what Szabo calls "the nexus of holy mysteries" (Szabo, "Sound" 221), a holiness which derives from the sacrificial humility upon which the poem focuses, from the utter absence of any ego-driven need for recognition on the part of nature, to the contemplative poet's complete submission to her unknowable ways.

"Night-Flowering Cactus" poses a question and topic for reflection not uncommon in literature throughout the ages: what is the rational mind to make of nature's splendid curiosities, particularly those which involve "wasted beauty"? In his poem "Night Blooming Cereus,"[17] twentieth-century African-American poet Robert Hayden offers a work of striking complement and counterpoint to Merton's poem. Like "Night-Flowering Cactus," "Night Blooming Cereus" expresses awe at the spectacles of nature. Yet, unlike Merton's poem, Hayden's piece speaks in the voice of a detached spectator, whose impression of the singular event begins in repulsion at the serpentine appearance of the plant and evolves into silent recognition of the eternal, but incomprehensible significance of its marvelous blossoming. The speaker and his companion do not possess a connection with nature, nor, at first, even with each other (although one assumes by virtue of the epithet "my dear" that they are intimately related). Their initial reactions are not of one accord and only gradually merge into conscious agreement that they must in some way celebrate what they are watching. By contrast, the poet of "Night-Flowering Cactus" is from beginning to end at one with the secret intelligence of nature, the transformative force which arises from and parallels the reconciling death and resurrection of Christ.

Like "Night-Flowering Cactus," "O Sweet Irrational Worship" (*CP* 344-45) pays tribute to the majesty of nature expressed not in the voice of an observer but of a participant; here, the speaker moves out into his surroundings with what Ross Labrie describes as "a Keatsian negative capability, temporarily becoming . . . one with an environment that draws him into the wider circle of being."[18] Unlike the lavish tropes of "Song: Contemplation" and "Night-Flowering Cactus," the vision of this poem opens and unfolds in minimal phrasing:

> Wind and a bobwhite
> And the afternoon sun. (ll. 1-2)

The spare quality of the poem's style befits the speaker's humble acceptance that he is but a small and "nameless" yet integral part of all creation, a reality which no questioning can demystify:

> By ceasing to question the sun
> I have become light,
>
> Bird and wind. (ll. 3-5)

Genuine, but inexpressible, understanding is possible only through total and joyful surrender to the irrationality of the love that brought the universe into being and arranged it according to a benevolent ordering principle:

> I am earth, earth
> My heart's love
> Bursts with hay and flowers.
> I am a lake of blue air
> In which my own appointed place
> Field and valley
> Stand reflected. (ll. 20-26)[19]

Just as the wordless spaces of "O Sweet Irrational Worship" are filled by the ecstasy of the speaker and evoke kindred feelings in the reader, critics have noted similar effects in the work of prominent contemporary ecopoets such as Mary Oliver. Laird Christensen, for example, writes the following description of Oliver's style: "It is not so much the words of a poem that enact . . . experiences in the reader's mind but rather the constellations of emotions and implications that accrue to those words and flicker through the spaces between them." The result of such dynamics, Christensen continues, is the poet's recreation of "the numinous intersection of the self and the natural world."[20] Laird's observations readily apply as well to the elliptical poetry of Merton, who eventually arrived at the belief that "good poetry is fifty percent silence,"[21] a philosophy of composition of which "O Sweet Irrational Worship" is but one example.

By compressing language in this way, the poet diverts attention from any self-contained, individual presence in the poem in order to accentuate the awesome power and free-flowing unity of the world as a whole. Such selflessness as the foundation of a holy existence is a recurring tenet in Thomas Merton's writing and teaching, not only for a monk but also for a poet, as he indicates in an early journal entry in which he quotes William Blake's assertion that a "poet's humility is to write 'in fear and trembling.'"[22] Merton later emphasizes that a humble soul is also a grateful soul, realizing its utter dependence on a loving God who does not deny His creatures anything they *really* need – if one accepts that all anyone *really* needs is God's grace. "Thanks for everything. I have no complaints"[23] are the words of the perfect prayer of humility which Merton taught his novices.

For object lessons on how to *live* such a prayer, Merton frequently turned to the wilds of nature. In the tape recording entitled *Does God Hear Our Prayer?* he extols the non-human universe's way of following God's will – by not striving to be anything more than what it was created to be.[24] Also, in *New Seeds of Contemplation*, employing that aphoristic style which characterizes much of Merton's most memorable prose, he announces: "A tree gives glory to God by being a tree," a deceptively simple concept, the logic of which he explains: "The more a tree is like itself, the more it is like Him. If it tried to be like something else which it was never intended to be, it would be less like God and therefore it would give Him less glory" (*NSC* 29). His desire for his own life to exhibit such an immediacy of existence uncomplicated by the demands and distractions of a false self – a characteristic impulse which Ross Labrie calls Merton's "romantic primitivism" (Labrie 90) – enlivens much of his most forceful poetry in which he depicts animals, plants and elements fulfilling their mysterious purpose in the world without the dissatisfaction or self-importance that the comforts and privileges of civilization can induce.

"The Turtle," a poem found in *The Way of Chuang Tzu*, Merton's collection of imitations of the verse teachings of ancient Chinese philosopher Chuang Tzu, offers a charming and instructive example. The poem narrates how Chuang Tzu, holding a bamboo pole and fishing on the banks of the Pu River, is visited by representatives of royalty. When they inform him that he has been named Prime Minister, Chuang declines their offer in favor of a life unencumbered by artificial gifts. He tells them the story of how a turtle was once removed from its home in the mud and dressed and housed as a god, only to end up as a venerated but empty shell. When his visitors agree that such was not the best life for a turtle but apparently do not understand the story's implications for their own lives, Chuang dismisses them through a statement of solidarity with the humble creatures of the earth:

> "Go home!" said Chuang Tzu.
> "Leave me here
> To drag my tail in the mud!"[25] (ll. 31-33)

The poem suggests that such a choice as Chuang's is inscrutable to princes, vice-chancellors, and other bearers of "formal documents," who neither appreciate the purity of a natural existence nor see that the sterile trappings of status are as potentially deadly for a human being as they would be for a turtle removed from its rightful environment.

On a deeper level, the poem implies that such pursuits and preferences regarding station and lifestyle are misguided because they offend humility, which Michael Casey, in *A Guide to Living in the Truth: Saint Benedict's Teaching on Humility*, defines as "above all, a respect for the nature of things, a reluctance to force reality to conform to subjective factors within ourselves."[26] To read "The Turtle" as ecopoetry is to remark how it subtly denounces the world's tendency to impose upon the things of nature – including perhaps oneself – the whims of human will and exposes how false and consequently self-destructive such projections often are.

The offense of forcing nature to meet subjective demands is the charge contemporary ecologists and animal welfare advocates level against industrial meat producers on the oxymoronically-named "factory farms" which not only contaminate the earth's soil, water, and air but assault nature more egregiously than unsustainable extraction, irresponsible consumption and environmental pollution do all together. The practice distorts natural order for commercial gain on a staggering scale, by confining living beings in unconscionably crowded settings not even remotely resembling their natural habitats, as if they had no need to breathe fresh air, touch the earth or nurture their offspring. In short, they are reduced to the status of production units manufactured and maintained according only to the laws of economics.

This outrage is the theme of Matthew Scully's *Dominion: The*

Power of Man, the Suffering of Animals, and the Call to Mercy. Scully condemns equating dominion with a license for ruthless tyranny over animals which, like humans, received their lives from the hand of a loving God and therefore possess a unique destiny beyond mere service to human appetite. Scully writes: "Whatever measure of happiness [the animals'] Creator intended for them, it is not something to be taken lightly by us or to be withdrawn from them wantonly or capriciously."[27] Furthermore, such arrogant callousness on the part of human ego ultimately turns back upon itself, as John Elder in *Imagining the Earth: Poetry and the Vision of Nature* points out: "Unwillingness to recognize spirit in the earth and its creatures finally wounds the same human beings who pursue such insensitive dealings with their world."[28] Implicit in the work of both writers is a belief that compassion for the suffering of animals is far from sentimentality; it emanates from the purest depths of the human soul and reveres the sacred connection between all creatures and their Creator.

That Merton would at least in part concur with both Elder and Scully is a safe conclusion for anyone familiar with Merton's many accounts of his relationship with animals, such as that found in his correspondence with Czeslaw Milosz dated May 6, 1960. In response to Milosz' charge that Merton essentially romanticizes and overlooks the brutality and misery found in nature, Merton offers a simple response, disarming in its recognition that nature, like all of creation in its fallen state, contains harsh realities, dark mysteries on which he elects not to dwell, opting instead to cherish the equally real, deep and peaceful bond possible between human and non-human beings: "[N]ature and I are very good friends, and console one another for the stupidity and the infamy of the human race and its civilization."[29]

The poem "The Joy of Fishes" (*WCT* 97-98; *CP* 910-11) another paraphrase from *The Way of Chuang Tzu*, illustrates this emotional kinship, as the poet assumes the sage voice of Chuang Tzu and testifies that a life lived in harmony with its assigned environment is a delightful life and that the bliss of animals is a condition with which the observer properly attuned to his own environment may on a spiritual level connect. Walking with a companion along the river and watching the fish dart and leap, Chuang identifies their behavior as "their happiness" (l. 7), a phrase which calls to mind the Romantic poet William Wordsworth's phrase "glad animal movements,"[30] and suggests that *joie de vivre* creatures often spontaneously exhibit when they are free to be themselves. When challenged by his companions as to how he could possibly know this, Chuang answers:

"I know the joy of fishes
In the river
Through my own joy, as I go walking
Along the same river." (ll. 33-36)

Because he bypasses the path of purely systematic reasoning that can alienate humans from one another, from nature, and from their own capacity for joy, Chuang perceives, identifies with and ultimately shares the happiness of his fellow beings.

"The Joy of Fishes," like many of Merton's poems, illustrates what Ross Labrie recognizes as the poet's ability to set aside the "privileged view of the ego" and shift his "center of perception" in the direction of "a dispersed yet unified field" (Labrie 35). In ecopoetics, this quality is known as *ecocentrism*. Although the term does not appear in many Standard English dictionaries, if one distills the various explanations found in contemporary political and philosophical dictionaries written for non-specialists, it can be broadly defined as a view of the natural world that refuses to privilege any single organism over another. Matthew Humphrey, for example, in the online *Political Dictionary*, writes that *ecocentrism* implies an ethical belief in the "equality of intrinsic value across human and non-human nature," or to compress it into one loaded phrase, "biospherical egalitarianism."[31] The obvious similarity between *ecocentrism* and *egocentrism* invites ready comparison of the two *isms*. The exchange of a single letter makes for a dramatic change in perspective and renders an apparent contradiction: there is no center of the universe; the "center" is everywhere, a paradox which tempts one to conclude that the neologism might have gratified the contemplative and paronomasial sides of Thomas Merton.

To view the literary career of Thomas Merton through eco-centric lenses is to see throughout his books, letters, and essays evidence of a writer who wanted to "write about everything,"[32] who recognized the holiness of "living and growing things, of in-animate beings, of animals and flowers and all nature" (*NSC* 30). It is to note in his journals an ongoing record of reverence for the creatures with which he shared his home in the hills and fields of rural Kentucky, a touching compassion for their vulnerability, such as the following entry reveals: "A tiny shrew was clinging to the inside of the novitiate screen doors, trapped in the house! I took her up and she ran a little onto my sleeve and then stayed fixed, trembling. I put her down in the grass outside and she ran away free."[33] Finally, it is to trace in his long and winding odyssey as a poet his growing awareness of the intricate web of life and the incalculable importance of every strand, an appreciation inherent in his enthusiastic identification with kindred writers along the way, Gerard Manley Hopkins and the phenomena of *inscape* (the uniqueness of every created entity in the universe) and *instress* (the conscious apprehension of that singularity); Rainer Maria Rilke and the poetry of natural contemplation; and Chuang Tzu and his enigmatically rendered teachings in holism.

In *The Way of Chuang Tzu*, rather than apply his poetic gifts to original works, Merton adopts the ancient voice of Chuang Tzu to render in modern English a series of poems containing both subtle and straightforward versions of what can be interpreted as lessons in ecocentrism. "Great and Small" (*WCT* 87-90; *CP* 879-81), for example, summarizes the poems' radical and guiding holistic philosophy:

> When we look at things in the light of Tao,
> Nothing is best, nothing is worst. . . .
> It can seem to be "better"
> Than what is compared with it
> On its own terms.
> But seen in terms of the whole,
> No one thing stands out as "better." (ll. 1-2, 5-9)

In "Where is Tao?" (*WCT* 123-24; *CP* 929-31), a related poem from the same collection, the poet confronts the human tendency to make value distinctions among the things of this world. The poem's controlling idea is summed up in the speaker's response to the title question asked by his companion, Master Tung Kwo:

> Why look for Tao by going "down the scale of being"
> As if that which we call "least"
> Had less of Tao? (ll. 21-23)

In the face of the questioner's persistence, Chuang descends the chain of being, affirming with every perceived regression the full presence of that mysterious and sacred essence known as Tao, until he brings the Socratic session to a halt with an abrupt scatological reference, beyond which the curiosity of the questioner apparently can go no further, so he falls silent. Sensing in his audience a readiness for truth, Chuang chides his friend for his shortsightedness and offers to accompany him to a realm where all distinctions and limitations disappear, the palace of Nowhere, an epithet immortalized in Merton studies by James Finley's durable analysis of Merton's concept of the True Self, the indestructible identity of beings dwelling in indivisible union with all others as the mystical body of Christ.[34]

"Where is Tao?" challenges the characteristically Western habit of hierarchical categorizing and is especially vivid in its images of what most people would readily dismiss as vermin and filth, a predictable reaction but one which Thich Nhat Hanh (the Buddhist monk whom Merton called his brother[35]) indirectly rebukes in *Living Buddha, Living Christ* where he holds that the circle of respect for life should embrace the minute and even microbial beings of the world and suggests that while the practical needs of existence may reasonably require their control, their destruction is still a form of loss.[36] Taking a view that inclusive, extending one's reverence for life to insects and even bacteria, demands that the human ego throw away its entrenched, cultivated notions of superiority and take on an ecocentric disposition, a feat possible only through extraordinary or supernatural means, such as compassionate mindfulness or contemplative prayer.

As a contemplative, Merton recognized the human need for solitude, silence, and simplicity; furthermore, he also realized that the world largely does not value these things because it does not properly understand them. As has been amply documented, his dramatic embrace of the monastic life originated in pious contempt but blossomed into loving concern for the noisy, frenetic and sometimes misguided lot of humanity with whom he shared an indissoluble bond.

One persistent source of distress for Merton was society's relationship with technology. While some accounts depict him as a recalcitrant Luddite, a more accurate picture reveals his prophetic judgment regarding the popular overreliance on mechanization and artificial intelligence to provide labor-saving devices and status symbols. While Merton knew that engineering advances could relieve needless hardship in the world, he also saw the imminent threats posed by a naïve misconception of progress. His writings frequently point out the damage to the world's individual and

collective mind, body and soul wrought by its widespread commitment to mindless "improvement." His journals also reveal a
sustained reflective interest in the ideas of eminent thinkers such
as Jacques Ellul concerning the negative impact of technology on
humanity.[37] The intensity of Merton's passion for this issue can
be found in *Conjectures of a Guilty Bystander*, where he inveighs
against society's devotion to technology for its own sake: "We
have not even begun to plumb the depths of nonsense into which
this absurd error has plunged us." He sums up the effects of this
absurdity in one dire conclusion: "[W]e contemn and destroy our
own reality and the reality of our natural resources."[38]

Just as he did with other profoundly disturbing social injustices
or follies which occupied his mind, Merton turned to poetry for an
outlet, not merely to vent his disdain for this particular variety of
destructive human behavior but also to convey hope for reconciliation between civilized culture and nature. Merton's late-career
accomplishment, the anti-poetic *Cables to the Ace*,[39] comprising
a series of 88 numbered items characterized by multi-tonal and
multi-lingual discourse and dialectic, is a prime example. In its
Whitmanesque expansiveness, *Cables to the Ace* displays in a single
piece all of J. Scott Bryson's defining features of ecopoetry.

The work's ecopoetic affinity derives primarily from the poet's
fervent rejection of the misplaced values of Western culture, a
denunciation delivered in a *tour de force* of irony, a steady stream
of associations and correlatives mocking the attitudes and hollow
language of a thoroughly consumerist society which subjugates
nature to unnatural ends. Cable 13 illustrates:

> And the cart wheel planet
> Goes down in the silos of earth
> Whose parkways vanish in the steam
> Of ocean feeling
> Or the houses of oil-men
>
> Go home go home
> And get your picture taken
> In a bronze western
> An ocean of free admissions
> To the houses of night
> To the sandy electric stars
> And the remaining adventures
> Of profiteers. (*CA* 9; *CP* 403)

As Cable 8 suggests, not only does this electric culture despoil nature for material gain; it virtually bows down before the artificial and possibly unforgiving god of technology:

> Write a prayer to a computer? But first of all you have to find out how It thinks. *Does it dig prayer?* . . . How does one begin: "O Thou great unalarmed and humorless electric sense . . ."? Start out wrong and you give instant offense. You may find yourself shipped off to the camps in a freight car. (*CA* 5-6; *CP* 399-400)

The anti-poetic quality of *Cables to the Ace* takes on an added dimension with its occasional perversions of familiar romantic poems. These debasements intensify the speaker's attack on modern society's disavowal or exploitation of traditional romantic concepts, such as the spiritually healing virtue of nature which William Butler Yeats' "The Lake Isle of Innisfree" celebrates. In Yeats' poem, the speaker announces in the manner of an Irish Henry David Thoreau that he will "arise and go" to the wilds of County Sligo where he will have a simple and peaceful life.[40] Cable 61 with its echoes of a popular cigarette commercial which appropriates the splendor of nature for lethal purposes turns Yeats' lyrical musing on its head:

> I will get up and go to Marble country
> Where deadly smokes grow out of moderate heat
> And all the cowboys look for fortunate slogans
> Among horses' asses. (*CA* 40; *CP* 434)

The zeal with which Merton delivers these cultural critiques evokes Bernard Quetchenbach's summary profile of the ecopoet as one who writes with the passionate commitment of a missionary or prophet. In this regard, Merton also anticipates the description offered by John Elder in his introduction to *Imagining the Earth*, where he delineates the ecopoetic movement in contemporary American poetry:

> The attentiveness to nature distinguishing today's American poetry often expresses itself as hostility toward Western civilization. . . . A solitary voice from the mountains calls upon the community to renew itself; a socially eccentric impulse makes possible a more balanced culture, concentric with the planet. In their imaginative passage from estrangement to transformation

and reintegration, poets enact a circuit of healing. (Elder 1)

While the voice of Merton's work calls out (sends cables, as it were) from the marginalized setting of a monastic cloister (or "island," as the speaker refers to it in his final stanza [*CA* 60; *CP* 454]) and does so with a wit periodically sharp enough to draw blood, it simultaneously channels the unifying energy of God's grace. As Lynn Szabo puts it, "[Merton] attacks cherished beliefs and the icons of a material culture but he does so in order to open them into the wholeness of the Hidden Ground of Love."[41] The truth of Szabo's observation can be seen in those cables which appear throughout the work as if by pentimento effect, in which the sardonic wordplay is replaced by straightforward expressions of awe and humility, a voice in perfect harmony with the created world. With its vivid sensory images of nature, Cable 10 is one example:

> Warm sun. Perhaps these yellow wild-flowers have the minds of little girls. My worship is a blue sky and ten thousand crickets in the deep wet hay of the field. My vow is the silence under their song. I admire the woodpecker and the dove in simple mathematics of flight. Together we study practical norms. The plowed and planted field is red as a brick in the sun and says: "*Now my turn!*" Several of us begin to sing. (*CA* 6; *CP* 400)

These cables resonate with what might be called an anti-anti-poetic voice and anchor the work with statements of faith in the saving sacrifice of Christ, whose Incarnation in the dimension of time and nature is depicted in Cable 80:

> Slowly slowly
> Comes Christ through the garden
> Speaking to the sacred trees
> Their branches bear his light
> Without harm (*CA* 55; *CP* 449).

While Robert Lax, Merton's longtime friend, to whom the work is formally dedicated, is logically identified as the "ace" of the title, scholars such as George Kilcourse also equate the ace with the one to whom the majority of Merton's work is always dedicated, Jesus Christ.[42] This ace is the Christ of Cable 80, God immanent in "trees" and "cornfields," who "weeps into the fire" for fragmented humanity's lack of consciousness regarding His sacred and reintegrating presence and whose tears ultimately extinguish the consuming effects of that negligence.

In the introduction to a collection of essays on poetry writing, former U.S. Poet Laureate Louise Glück writes: "The world is complete without us. Intolerable fact. To which the poet responds by rebelling, wanting to prove otherwise."[43] To which Thomas Merton presumably would respond: it is intolerable because it is not true. No view of the world which permits exclusion or division can be called *complete*. This presumption finds support in the following comparison by Dennis O'Hara of the spiritual ecology of Thomas Merton with that of "geologian" Thomas Berry: "Like Berry, [Merton] prescribed a spirituality that would recognize and foster humanity's true place in creation, calling forth the authentic self of each person that we might 'enter by love into union with the Life Who dwells and sings within the essence of every creature and in the core of our own souls.'"[44]

More than just rebels, poets, according to Merton, today must "fill the role of monks"[45] and bring the world to humble recognition that all life is one interconnected body made holy by the Creator in whose love everything has its origin. The long poetic career of Thomas Merton consistently attests to this belief and remains his most highly charged medium for revealing the truth that self-reliance is a deception, and separateness is an illusion. He is the poet to whom Glück alludes: the one who proves the intolerable otherwise.

Endnotes

1. Thomas Merton, *The Collected Poems of Thomas Merton* (New York: New Directions, 1977); subsequent references will be cited as "*CP*" parenthetically in the text.

2. Thomas Merton, *The Seven Storey Mountain* (New York: Harcourt, Brace, 1948) 237.

3. John Thavis, "Social effects of sin greater than ever, says Vatican official," *Catholic News Service*, March 10, 2008 [accessed March 14, 2008].

4. Monica Weis, "Dancing with the Raven: Thomas Merton's Evolving View of Nature," in Patrick F. O'Connell, ed., *The Vision of Thomas Merton* (Notre Dame, IN: Ave Maria Press, 2003) 152.

5. Thomas Merton, *When the Trees Say Nothing: Writings on Nature*, ed. Kathleen Deignan, CND (Notre Dame, IN: Sorin Books, 2003) 40.

6. Bernard W. Quetchenbach, "Primary Concerns: The Development of Current Environmental Identity Poetry," in *Ecopoetry: A Critical Introduction*, ed. J. Scott Bryson (Salt Lake City: University of Utah Press,

2002) 248; subsequent references will be cited as *"Ecopoetry"* parenthetically in the text.

7. Thomas Merton, *The Rule of Saint Benedict: Initiation into the Monastic Tradition* 4, ed. Patrick F. O'Connell (Collegeville, MN: Cistercian Publications, 2009) 176-77.

8. Dennis Patrick O'Hara, "'The Whole World . . . Has Appeared as a Transparent Manifestation of the Love of God': Portents of Merton as Eco-Theologian," *The Merton Annual* 9 (1996) 90-117.

9. Thomas Merton, *In the Dark before Dawn: New Selected Poems*, ed. Lynn R. Szabo (New York: New Directions, 2005) 75-102.

10. Thomas Merton, *Natural Contemplation* (Kansas City: Credence Cassettes, 1988) [AA2077].

11. Owen Barfield, *Poetic Diction: A Study in Meaning* (1928; London: Faber & Faber, 1952).

12. Harold Bloom, *The Art of Reading Poetry* (New York: Perennial HarperCollins, 2005) 55.

13. See Jonathan Montaldo, "Spirituality, Scholarship and Biography: An Interview with Anthony T. Padovano," *The Merton Annual* 10 (1997) 293-94.

14. Thomas Merton, *New Seeds of Contemplation* (New York: New Directions, 1961) 296; subsequent references will be cited as *"NSC"* parenthetically in the text.

15. Lynn Szabo, "The Sound of Sheer Silence: A Study in the Poetics of Thomas Merton," *The Merton Annual* 13 (2000) 221; subsequent references will be cited as "Szabo, 'Sound'" parenthetically in the text..

16. For an extended explication of "Night-Flowering Cactus," with thorough investigation of the symbolic dimensions of the flower, see Patrick F. O'Connell, "Nurture by Nature: Emblems of Stillness in a Season of Fury," *The Merton Annual* 21 (2008) 134-42; subsequent references will be cited as "O'Connell" parenthetically in the text.

17. Robert Hayden, "Night Blooming Cereus," in *Contemporary American Poetry*, ed. A. Poulin, Jr. (Boston: Houghton Mifflin, 1985) 203-205.

18. Ross Labrie, *Thomas Merton and the Inclusive Imagination* (Columbia: University of Missouri Press, 2001) 35; subsequent references will be cited as "Labrie" parenthetically in the text.

19. O'Connell offers an in-depth reading of the speaker's "problematic" identification with the natural world in this passage (128-34).

20. Laird Christensen, "Pragmatic Mysticism of Mary Oliver" (*Ecopoetry* 139).

21. Thomas Merton, *Lyric Poetry* (Kansas City, MO: Credence Cassettes, 1991) [AA2460].

22. Thomas Merton, *Run to the Mountain: The Story of a Vocation. Journals, vol. 1: 1939-1941*, ed. Patrick Hart (San Francisco: HarperCollins,

1995) 37 [10/1/1939].

23. Merton, *Natural Contemplation.*

24. Thomas Merton, *Does God Hear Our Prayer?* (Kansas City, MO: Credence Cassettes, 1988) [AA2071].

25. Thomas Merton, *The Way of Chuang Tzu* (New York: New Directions, 1965) 93-94 (subsequent references will be cited as "*WCT*" parenthetically in the text); *CP* 918-19.

26. Michael Casey, *A Guide to Living in the Truth: Saint Benedict's Teachings on Humility* (Liguori, MO: Liguori Press, 1999) 18.

27. Matthew Scully, *Dominion: The Power of Man, the Suffering of Animals, and the Call to Mercy* (New York: St. Martin's Press, 2002) 2.

28. John Elder, *Imagining the Earth: Poetry and the Vision of Nature* (Athens: University of Georgia Press, 1996) 163-64; subsequent references will be cited as "Elder" parenthetically in the text.

29. Thomas Merton, *The Courage for Truth: Letters to Writers*, ed. Christine M. Bochen (New York: Farrar, Straus, Giroux, 1993) 65.

30. William Wordsworth, "Lines Composed a Few Miles above Tintern Abbey," *William Wordsworth: Favorite Poems* (New York: Dover, 1992) 23.

31. http://www.encyclopedia.com/The+Concise+Oxford+Dictionary+of+Politics/ publications.aspx?pageNumber=12.

32. Thomas Merton, *A Search for Solitude: Pursuing the Monk's True Life. Journals, vol. 3: 1952-1960*, ed. Lawrence S. Cunningham (San Francisco: HarperCollins, 1996) 45 [7/17/1956].

33. Thomas Merton, *A Vow of Conversation: Journals 1964-1965*, ed. Naomi Burton Stone (New York: Farrar, Straus, Giroux, 1988) 93 [11/2/1964].

34. James Finley, *Merton's Palace of Nowhere: A Search for God through Awareness of the True Self* (Notre Dame: Ave Maria Press, 1978).

35. Thomas Merton, *Faith and Violence: Christian Teaching and Christian Practice* (Notre Dame, IN: University of Notre Dame Press, 1968) 106-108.

36. Thich Nhat Hanh, *Living Buddha, Living Christ* (New York: Riverhead Books, 1995) 92.

37. Thomas Merton, *Dancing in the Water of Life: Seeking Peace in the Hermitage. Journals, vol. 5: 1963-1965*, ed. Robert E. Daggy (San Francisco: HarperCollins, 1997) 159, 161, 163, 274, 342.

38. Thomas Merton, *Conjectures of a Guilty Bystander* (Garden City, NY: Doubleday, 1966) 222.

39. Thomas Merton, *Cables to the Ace* (New York: New Directions, 1968); subsequent references will be cited as "*CA*" parenthetically in the text.

40. William Butler Yeats, *The Collected Poems of W. B. Yeats* (New York:

Macmillan, 1956) 39.

41. Lynn Szabo, "'Hiding the Ace of Freedoms': Discovering the Way(s) of Peace in Thomas Merton's *Cables to the Ace*," *The Merton Annual* 15 (2002) 110.

42. George A. Kilcourse, *Ace of Freedoms: Thomas Merton's Christ* (Notre Dame: University of Notre Dame Press, 1993) 178.

43. Louise Glück, "The Best American Poetry, 1993: Introduction," *Proofs and Theories: Essays on Poetry* (New Jersey: Ecco Press, 1994) 91.

44. Dennis Patrick O'Hara, "Thomas Merton and Thomas Berry: Reflections from a Parallel Universe," *The Merton Annual* 13 (2000) 223.

45. Thomas Merton, *Poetry and Imagination* (Kansas City, MO: Credence Cassettes, 1987) [AA2124].

Pivoting toward Peace:
The Engaged Poetics of Thomas Merton
and Denise Levertov

Susan McCaslin

In what ways is poetry transformative; how and to what extent can it pivot us toward peace? Both Denise Levertov (1923-1997) and Thomas Merton (1915-1968) grappled with these questions in their art and lives. On their respective journeys, neither poet abandoned the longing for an integral vision in which contemplation and action are unified. Both left a legacy of poetry that includes overtly political poems as well as more subtly lyrical and meditative ones that enact peace by offering glimpses of a world in which self and other are so deeply intertwined that war makes no sense. In many of their most contemplative poems, the poem itself becomes an incarnation of the longing for justice and peace, a microcosm of ecological balance between inner and outer worlds. Another way of saying this is that the poem, poised between the interiority of the poet and the turmoil of the outer world, creates an alternative order, a place of high energy discharge that can bring about both individual and social transformation.

Though Merton found his religious vocation in monasticism mid-way through his life, and Levertov made her way to an ecumenical Catholic Christianity in the last decade of hers, the two poets share striking commonalities. Levertov was born in England, and Merton in France, but both eventually became Americans. Both were prolific in prose and poetry and drawn to the political poets of Latin America, though the influences on Merton's writing were more European and Levertov's more American. In addition, they eventually shared the same publisher in James Laughlin at New Directions.

Since the 1950s, Levertov had been associated with the Black Mountain school of poetics, American poets of the avant-garde that included Robert Creeley, Ed Dorn, and Robert Duncan, all grounded in the free verse movement inspired by William Carlos Williams. Her early neo-Romanticism had evolved into a poetry and poetics of political and social engagement by the time she published her collection of essays, *The Poet in the World*.[1] Merton, who originally sought escape from the world by entering a Trappist monastery in Kentucky in 1941, gradually moved beyond his early renunciation of society and began to integrate the social and political into a more holistic vision.

Culturally rich and eclectic family heritages shaped both writers. Levertov's father was a Hasidic Russian Jew who converted to Christianity and became an Anglican priest, and her mother, a Welsh woman, was steeped in Celtic lore. Merton's parents were bohemian artists who roamed from place to place in Europe during the early years of their marriage. His father, Owen Merton, was from New Zealand, and his mother, Ruth Jenkins Merton, an American Quaker who, like Levertov's mother, also had Celtic roots. Levertov writes of herself: "Among Jews a Goy, among Gentiles a Jew . . . among school children a strange exception whom they did not know whether to envy or mistrust – all of those anomalies predicated my later experience."[2]

Merton lost both parents when young. In his mid-twenties in 1941, he sought stability in monasticism by joining the Abbey of Gethsemani, a monastery of Cistercian monks in Kentucky, but remained intellectually expansive, as evidenced in his far-ranging correspondence and self-revelatory posthumously published journals. Though Levertov remained for most of her life outside institutional religion, both poets were liminal writers, people with an outsider's sense of dwelling at the margins.

In addition to having family heritages that inspired their creativity, both poets set lyrical poems of deep interiority in their collections beside more engaged political poems. In fact, single poems often interweave both voices, which become complementary since they stem from a unified base in experience. Levertov shifts from an early focus on mythopoetic themes to poems of more public concern; yet these two aspects of her work remain side by side throughout her canon. For instance, "A Tree Telling of Orpheus," in which she retells the story of Orpheus charming the creatures and trees, appears in the same 1970 volume as "A Marigold from North Vietnam."[3] Like Merton, Levertov argues in the '60s that poets especially, as guardians of language, must take responsibility for the ethical impact of their words in the public sphere. In fact, her break with her mentor, poet Robert Duncan, was in part due to his resistance to her emerging political activism.[4] Both Merton and Levertov, then, stood as witnesses to injustice, speaking out publicly, whether through Merton's *Cold War Letters*, originally circulated in mimeographed form,[5] or Levertov's involvement in rallies and protests against the Vietnam War, nuclear testing in New Mexico, and more recently, the first Gulf War in Iraq. "Picket and pray" became her motto in her later years.

Both artists also explored throughout their lives a mystical-contemplative spirituality. Merton's dramatic conversion to Catholicism occurred in his mid-twenties, but his faith passed through many metamorphoses. Though he lived half his life at the monastery, his outward pilgrimages took him to places as diverse as Cuba, New York, and, at the end of his life's journey, India, Sri Lanka and Thailand. His concurrent inward pilgrimage led to inter-spiritual engagement with other religious traditions such as Sufism and Buddhism. In contrast, Levertov's Christian orientation emerged more gradually and flowered much later in life, as she converted to Catholicism in 1984. In her last essays, Levertov speaks of her journey as a pilgrimage. In 1991, she writes: "But more and more, what I have sought as a *reading writer*, is a poetry that, while it does not attempt to ignore or deny the ocean of crisis in which we swim, is itself 'on Pilgrimage' . . . in search of significance underneath and beyond the succession of temporal events: a poetry which attests to [a] deep spiritual longing."[6]

While writing the poem, "Mass for the Day of St. Thomas Didymus"[7] (traditionally the doubting saint), she discovered she had moved unconsciously from observer to worshipper, for she states, "The experience of writing the poem – that long swim through waters of unknown depth – had been also a conversion process."[8] Though Levertov carved a longer trajectory than Merton toward Catholicism in its most universal sense, both writers' works trace the arc of a pilgrimage.

Given Merton's and Levertov's shared spiritual and social passions and milieu, it seems inevitable that their lives should intersect. Merton was reading Levertov in 1961, when he wrote his friend, Latin American poet Ernesto Cardenal: "There is a very fine new poet, Denise Levertov. I forget whether you translated some of her work or not. She is splendid, one of the most promising."[9] In 1967, Levertov sent a letter to Merton requesting his written support in a Vietnam War protest, and he responded positively, initiating their short correspondence over matters political and poetic.

Merton's and Levertov's first and only face-to-face encounter occurred on December 10, 1967, where she joined him, photographer Ralph Meatyard and his wife, and Kentucky poet Wendell

Berry and his wife Tanya at the Abbey of Gethsemani. After her visit, Merton wrote in his journal: "Rainy. Denise Levertov was here with Wendell Berry. . . . They came up to the hermitage and spent the afternoon. I like Denise very much. A good warm person. She left a good poem ('Tenebrae') and we talked a little about Sister Norbert in San Francisco who is in trouble about protesting against the war."[10]

Merton's premature death in Bangkok exactly one year later must have shocked Levertov, cutting short a friendship that would surely have flourished. It is evident from her subsequent poems and writings that Merton remained a continuing influence, and was a seminal influence in her movement toward Christianity. Her poem "On a Theme by Thomas Merton" (1992) reflects her ongoing respect for his work.[11] And her remarks earlier in 1984 acknowledge him as one of the premier religious writers not only of her generation but of the ages:

> I see nothing detrimental to my own poetry in the fact that I participate in the Eucharist or that I read Julian of Norwich, Bonhoeffer, or Thomas Merton without skepticism. I am ecumenical to a degree no doubt scandalous to the more orthodox. . . . [I]f I discover spiritual fellowship and an active commitment to my political values I take it where I find it.[12]

Again, as late as 1990, she invokes Merton as a model and inspiration for her growing faith: "If . . . a Thomas Merton . . . could believe, who was I to squirm and fret, as if I required more refined mental nourishment than [his]?"[13]

A number of Levertov's later, more explicitly religious poems echo or directly cite Merton, who becomes to her a kind of posthumous mentor. For instance, in *Breathing the Water* (1984), Levertov's poem, "I learned that her name was Proverb," is what she calls in her note to the poem "a spinoff" of a line from Merton.[14] The source of the title, she writes in a note, "comes from the dream which Thomas Merton recounted in a letter to Boris Pasternak quoted in a review by Father Basil Pennington of Michael Mott's biography of Thomas Merton" (Levertov, *Breathing* 85). Levertov's note bears citing in order to indicate the depth of her serious study of Merton after his death. She was following avidly reviews, biographies, and correspondence related to him.

Levertov's note on her "spinoff" from Merton also reveals their shared fascination with the figure of Proverb-Sophia or Divine

Wisdom (Hagia Sophia), which can be traced through Merton's journals, poems, and correspondence beginning in 1958 when he wrote of his archetypal dream experience of Sophia-Wisdom, the feminine divine figure who appeared to him as "a young Jewish girl. . . . I asked her her name and she says her name is Proverb."[15] In the October 23, 1958 letter to Boris Pasternak that Levertov mentions, Merton clearly links his often-quoted experience of identifying with the divine in "ordinary" people at the corner of Fourth and Walnut in Louisville to this figure of Proverb:

> One night I dreamt that I was sitting with a very young Jewish girl of fourteen or fifteen, and that she suddenly manifested a very deep and pure affection for me and embraced me so that I was moved to the depths of my soul. I learned that her name was "Proverb," which I thought very simple and beautiful. . . . A few days later when I happened to be in a nearby city [Louisville] . . . I was walking alone in the crowded street and suddenly saw that everybody was Proverb and that in all of them shone her extraordinary beauty and purity and shyness, even though they did not know who they were and were perhaps ashamed of their names – because they were mocked on account of them. And they did not know their real identity as the Child so dear to God who, from before the beginning, was playing in His sight all days, playing in the world. (*CT* 90)

Merton's and Levertov's common focus on the figure of Wisdom from Proverbs 8 and the Hebraic wisdom tradition is connected to their shared image of God as a feminine presence of peace and mercy in the world.

Before Levertov embraced the Christian mystical, sophianic traditions and an intentional spiritual practice of her own, she struggled with the question of whether or not a poetry of peace is even possible in times of violence. In her address "Poetry and Peace," at a conference at Stanford University in 1989 on the theme of "Women, War and Peace," Levertov was confronted with a question from the audience proposing that poets should bring images of peace to the world.[16] Her continuing rumination over this question led to the following poem entitled "Making Peace" (Levertov, *Breathing* 40):

> A voice from the dark called out,
>   "The poets must give us

imagination of peace, to oust the intense, familiar
imagination of disaster. Peace, not only
the absence of war."

But peace, like a poem,
is not there ahead of itself,
can't be imagined before it is made,
can't be known except
in the words of its making,
grammar of justice,
syntax of mutual aid . . . .

A line of peace might appear
if we restructured the sentence our lives are making,
revoked its reaffirmation of profit and power,
questioned our needs, allowed
long pauses. . . .

A cadence of peace might balance its weight
on that different fulcrum; peace, a presence,
an energy field more intense than war,
might pulse then,
stanza by stanza into the world,
each act of living
one of its words, each word
a vibration of light – facets
of the forming crystal. (ll. 1-12, 17-30)

Peace is "not there ahead of itself" because for Levertov it must be forged in the alembic of our lives. True peace is not a quietist state but one that emerges from inner silence that leads often to action, and discovers its form in the world. So if a poet writes words that call for personal and collective transformation, the poet herself must be willing to get involved and put herself, not just her work, on the line. She writes: "When words penetrate deep into us they change the chemistry of the soul, of the imagination. We have no right to do that to people if we don't share the consequences."[17]

Poets who share these political consequences, forging what Levertov called "engaged" poems and entering the arena of activism, however, must also be careful, according to Levertov, not to fall into the didactic. She was aware of how assuming a public voice can often lead poets into polemic and propaganda:

Good poets write bad political poems only if they let themselves write deliberate, opinionated, rhetoric, misusing their
art as propaganda. The poet does not *use* poetry, but is at the
service of poetry. To *use* it is to *misuse* it. A poet driven to speak
to himself, to maintain a dialogue with himself, concerning
politics, can expect to write as well upon that theme as upon
any other. He can not separate it from everything else in his
life. But it is not whether or not good "political" poems are a
possibility that is in question. What is in question is the role
of the poet as observer or as participant in the life of his time.
(Levertov, *Essays* 136-37)

In answer to the question of whether political poetry can be truly
poetic she writes in "Poetry, Prophecy, Survival": "A poetry of anguish, a poetry of anger, of rage, a poetry that, from literal or deeply
imagined experience, depicts and denounces perennial injustice and
cruelty in their current forms, and in our peculiar time warns of the
unprecedented perils that confront us, can be truly a high poetry,
as well wrought as any other."[18] Her response is that poetry that
rages against injustice is a "high poetry" if it is highly evocative,
well crafted, and emerges from the life experience of the artist.

Levertov also remarks on why poetry, as opposed to discursive
prose, is particularly effective as a catalyst for peace in her essay
"Paradox and Equilibrium" (1988):

We humans cannot absorb the bitter truths of our own history,
the revelation of our destructive potential, *except* through the
mediation of art (the manifestation of our other, our constructive potential). Presented raw, the facts are rejected: perhaps
not by the intellect, which accommodates them as statistics,
but by the emotions – which hold the key to conscience and
resolve. (Levertov, *Essays* 141)

Here she argues that poetry can be, in fact, more effective than
discursive prose because it emerges from the depths of the soul,
transforming raw emotions through the fires of the creative imagination.

Both Merton and Levertov craft poems that resist injustice,
many of which are commentaries on particular historical events.
Such poems draw on the devices of irony, satire, and parody often
associated with the Hebraic prophetic voice of rage and denunciation. Levertov's poem "Prologue: An Interim" is a call for imagina-

tive attention, empathy with the suffering of others. That which is witnessed compels moral response:

> But we need
> the few who could bear no more,
> who would try anything,
> who would take the chance
> that their deaths among the uncountable
> masses of dead might be real to those who
> don't dare imagine death.
> Might burn through the veil that blinds
> those who do not imagine the burned bodies
> of other people's children.[19]

She associates this stance with that of the prophets of ancient Israel:

> And this brings one to a very important factor which is shared by poets and prophets: prophetic utterance, like poetic utterance, transforms experience and moves the received to new attitudes. . . . We also need direct images in our art that will waken, warn, stir their hearers to action; images that will both appall and empower. (Levertov, *Essays* 148-49)

Merton's similarly political poem, "Chant to Be Used in Processions around a Site with Furnaces" (from *Emblems of a Season of Fury,* 1963[20]), is an example of a prophetic poem that both "appall[s] and empower[s]" in Levertov's sense. It uses corrosive irony, startling juxtapositions, understatement, and a flat, dehumanized tone, to lay open the inner workings of the bureaucratic mind and its complicity with systemic evil:

> How we made them sleep and purified them

> How we perfectly cleaned up the people and worked a big heater

> I was the commander I made improvements and installed a guaranteed system taking account of human weakness I purified and I remained decent

> How I commanded

> I made cleaning appointments and then I made the travellers sleep and after that I made soap (*CP*, 345-346).

Merton's anti-chant is chilling because of its use of a Nazi war criminal persona, the language of mechanization and abstraction, passive voice, and euphemism ("sleep" for "die"). The speaker's self-absorption (repeated use of "I") and delusional thinking ("I did my rightful duty as commanded") plunges the reader into a clinical hell. The poem reminds us how easily we can become dehumanized if we give ourselves over to a system that would dehumanize others. Yet the poem simultaneously empowers us to maintain an inner vigilance against such a moral descent.

During the Cold War, both Merton and Levertov wrote compellingly on the implications of what Hannah Arendt called "the banality of evil" in the context of the Eichmann trials. Both were critical of the war-hungry bureaucracies in the United States that kept alive the hatred of "the other" in the name of resisting Communism. Levertov wrote a poem called "During the Eichmann Trial" (from *The Jacob's Ladder*, 1961[21]), which employs the figure of Eichmann to speak to the potential in each of us for betrayal of our common humanity: "He stands / isolate in a bulletproof / witness-stand of glass, / a cage, where we may view / ourselves, an apparition" (ll. 66-70).

Much later, in the '90s, demonstrating another strategy, Levertov's "Witnessing from Afar the New Escalation of Savage Power" (Levertov, *Train* 80) offers a poetic-political experience of the effects of the first Gulf War. The poem depicts devastation in one woman's life due to a bombing raid that compels engagement with her suffering. Its well-wrought lines shock the reader, yet avoid mere rant:

> There was a crash and throb
> of harsh sound audible
> always, but distant.
> She believed
> she had it in her
> to fend for herself and hold
> despair at bay.
> Now when she came to the ridge and saw
> the world's raw gash
> reopened, the whole world
> a valley of steaming blood,
> her small wisdom
> guttered in the uprush;

> *rubbledust, meatpulse* –
> darkness and the blast
> levelled her. (*Train,* 80)

We are told that the elderly woman had "tended a small altar, / kept a candle shielded there" (*Train,* 80) but could not ward off through her simple faith the violence brought about by human hate. The stunning image of the "world's raw gash" reminds us that "the whole world" is affected by the "leveling" that crushes the spirit in all.

Such poems open new ways of witnessing, imagining others' pain. Seeing deeply can lead to empathy or compassion; compassion to transformed ways of being in the world. If witnessing from within compels action, then Merton's and Levertov's explicitly political poems need to be revived in the context of our current global conflicts. Their engaged political poems disturb us, while the more contemplative poems gently pivot us toward peace by pointing to another way of being in the world that, if enacted in many, could lead to social transformation.

Both Merton and Levertov composed more subtle peace poems by drawing from the natural world to enact a shift in perception. Their legacy is a poetic of praise through a contemplative vision of the world. In *Contemplation in a World of Action,* Merton writes: "The contemplative life should liberate and purify the imagination which passively absorbs all kinds of things without our realizing it; liberate and purify it from the influence of so much violence done by the bombardment of social images."[22] Contemplative poetry counters the bombardments of the culture, its abuses of language, its steady onslaught of advertising and propaganda that turns us into thoughtless consumers and makes us complicit in the machinery of war. Reading poetry can become an act of contemplative attention that evokes contemplative states in its hearers and readers. As Levertov insists, the more celebratory sort of peace poem offers a counterbalance to the poems of outrage:

> But we need also the poetry of praise, of love for the world, the vision of the potential for good even in our species which has so messed up the rest of creation, so fouled its own nest. If we lose the sense of contrast, of the opposites to all the grime and gore, the torture, the banality of the computerized apocalypse, we lose the reason for trying to work for redemptive change. . . . To sing awe – to breathe out praise and celebration – is as

fundamental an impulse as to lament. (Levertov, *Essays* 144)

Ultimately, these twin poles of the prophetic and the celebratory coexist in an authentic poetics of peace. Some poems emphasize the outrage and others the praise, while others encompass the two within a single poem. The peace poetry of Levertov and Merton is a poetry of ecological awareness in the largest sense. That is, if ecology can be defined as the study of the ways in which all things are interconnected and perceived as part and parcel of a larger, purposive, unified and therefore sacred whole, then a poetry and poetic that enters this field of interconnection with contemplative attention is one that might bring healing to the collective psyche. In one way, all poetry that raises consciousness past dualistic, either-or, them-us thinking is peace poetry. Such poetry is inherently ecological because it keeps us from seeing our fellow humans or the natural world as resources to be exploited or objectified. It grounds us in community and in the cosmos or larger order of things. True peace poetry leads to a de-centering of ego and an encounter with a more authentic and expansive self. Such poetry is essential because it gives us more than notions and concepts, speaking out of direct experience to the heart. Peace poems can redirect us to lived experience where faith and doubt are held in a field of mystery.

In her last years, when she lived near Seattle, Levertov spoke of a Northwestern poetry of wilderness that "gives rise to a more conscious attentiveness to the non-human and to a more or less conscious desire to immerse the self in that larger whole."[23] She found herself drawn to poems which "approach spiritual longing and spiritual experience in a way that is more direct, since it is frankly about the quest for or the encounter with God" (Levertov, *Essays* 11).

Two astonishingly beautiful ecological/spiritual peace poems are Merton's "Night-Flowering Cactus" (*CP* 351-52) and Levertov's "To Live in the Mercy of God." Both identify with the flood of beauty and love that is the divine Oneness manifesting in and through both humans and the natural world. Both poets recognize the complex mystery of nature, how it can be an expression of clashing powers striving for survival, as well as a unified ground of Being. In their most mystical nature poems, they focus on this spiritual dimension of nature. In Merton's poem, spirit manifests from a point of nothingness within a cactus that blooms only one night each year:

> I know my time, which is obscure, silent and brief
> For I am present without warning one night only. . . .

> When I come I lift my sudden Eucharist
> Out of the earth's unfathomable joy
> Clean and total I obey the world's body
> I am intricate and whole, not art but wrought passion
> Excellent deep pleasure of essential waters
> Holiness of form and mineral mirth:

> I am the extreme purity of virginal thirst. . . .

> He who sees my purity
> Dares not speak of it.
> When I open once for all my impeccable bell
> No one questions my silence:
> The all-knowing bird of night flies out of my mouth.

> Have you seen it? Then though my mirth has quickly
>   ended
> You live forever in its echo:
> You will never be the same again. (*CP*, 351-352)

This is one of Merton's most deeply mystical poems, for it voices both the inner gnosis of the mortal, individual poet as well as the divine feminine presence and principle immanent in the world, Sophia or Holy Wisdom. The night-flowering cactus emerges from the virgin point of nothingness within the holy ground of silence beyond all our categories and utters her beauty from the depths, "clean and total." To identify even for an instant with this sacramental grace is to participate in a timeless unity where there is no more war within the self. The listener is not merely accosted by purity, but invited to be "the extreme purity of virginal thirst" which is longing for union with the Absolute. The sacramental emphasis on nature as "Eucharist" suggests that the human soul and the natural world, when perceived from this awareness, are a theophany or manifestation of the divine. Like Rilke's famous poem, "Archaic Torso of Apollo,"[24] which ends, "You must change your life," the conclusion of Merton's poem calls forth in the reader a transformation that is at once moral, emotional, rational and spiritual.

Similarly, in Levertov's "To Live in the Mercy of God,"[25] a waterfall pouring through a west coast rain forest becomes a metaphor for the Divine Mercy:

> To live in the mercy of God.
>
> To feel vibrate the enraptured
>   waterfall flinging itself
>   unabating down and down
>   to clenched fists of rock.
>   Swiftness of plunge,
>   hour after year after century,
>   O or Ah
>   uninterrupted, voice
>   many-stranded.
>   To breathe
>   spray. The smoke of it.
>   Arcs
>   of steelwhite foam, glissades
>   of fugitive jade barely perceptible. Such passion –
>   rage or joy?
>   Thus, not mild, not temperate,
>   God's love for the world. Vast
>   flood of mercy
>   flung on resistance. (*Sands*, 128)

These last lines seem a deliberate echo of Merton's words spoken as the "Voice of God" at the end of *The Sign of Jonas*: "*I have always overshadowed Jonas with My mercy, and cruelty I know not at all. Have you had sight of Me, Jonas My child? Mercy within mercy within mercy.*"[26]

Levertov's late poem on divine mercy likewise establishes the Eros of the divine as it woos its recalcitrant human creation. The issue in both poems is whether we choose to open ourselves or resist the flow of mercy. Whether speaking out against injustice or opening silently to grace, the contemplative poems of Merton and Levertov can move us toward peace. Indeed, in the work of these two significant religious poets of the mid- to late twentieth century, the simultaneous opening to the Spirit and resistance to injustice are twin aspects of a single motion.

Endnotes

1. Denise Levertov, *The Poet in the World* (New York: New Directions,

1973).

2. Denise Levertov, "Autobiographical Sketch," in *Denise Levertov: New & Selected Essays* (New York: New Directions, 1992) 260; subsequent references will be cited as "Levertov, *Essays*" parenthetically in the text.

3. Denise Levertov, *Relearning the Alphabet* (New York: New Directions, 1970) 81-85, 67.

4. See *The Letters of Robert Duncan and Denise Levertov*, ed. Robert Edward Duncan, Robert J. Bertholf and Albert Gelpi (Stanford, CA: Stanford University Press, 2004). The breach between Levertov and Duncan was complex, but in part the result of Duncan's public criticism of Levertov's political activism during the Vietnam War. The correspondence between them reveals that he felt her political engagement against the war in both writings and acts (protests, rallies, etc.) compromised her integrity as an artist.

5. Thomas Merton, *Cold War Letters*, ed. William H. Shannon and Christine M. Bochen (Maryknoll, NY: Orbis, 2006).

6. Denise Levertov, "Some Affinities of Content" (*Essays* 4).

7. Denise Levertov, *Candles in Babylon* (New York: New Directions, 1982) 108-15.

8. Denise Levertov, "Work That Enfaiths" (*Essays* 249).

9. Thomas Merton, *The Courage for Truth: Letters to Writers*, ed. Christine M. Bochen (New York: Farrar, Straus, Giroux, 1993) 127 [10/14/61]; subsequent references will be cited as "*CT*" parenthetically in the text.

10. Thomas Merton, *The Other Side of the Mountain: The End of the Journey. Journals, Vol. 7: 1967-1968*, ed. Patrick Hart (San Francisco: HarperCollins, 1998) 22.

11. Denise Levertov, *Evening Train* (New York: New Directions, 1992) 113; subsequent references will be cited as "Levertov, *Train*" parenthetically in the text.

12. Denise Levertov, "A Poet's View" (*Essays* 244).

13. "Work that Enfaiths" (Levertov, *Essays* 250-51).

14. Denise Levertov, *Breathing the Water* (New York: New Directions, 1987) 51; subsequent references will be cited as "Levertov, *Breathing*" parenthetically in the text. Levertov in a note defines a "spinoff" as "a verbal construct which neither describes nor comments but moves off at a tangent to, or parallel with, its inspiration" (85-86).

15. Thomas Merton, *A Search for Solitude: Pursuing the Monk's True Life. Journals, vol. 3: 1952-1960*, ed. Lawrence S. Cunningham (San Francisco: HarperCollins, 1996) 176.

16. Denise Levertov, "Poetry and Peace: Some Broader Definitions" (*Essays* 154).

17. Denise Levertov, "The Poet in the World" (*Essays* 136).

18. Denise Levertov, "Poetry, Prophecy, Survival" (*Essays* 143-44);

variants of this piece were presented orally on two or three different occasions in the early 1980s.

19. Denise Levertov, *To Stay Alive* (New York: New Directions, 1971) 27.

20. Thomas Merton, *Emblems of a Season of Fury* (New York: New Directions, 1963) 43-47; Thomas Merton, *The Collected Poems of Thomas Merton* (New York: New Directions, 1977) 345-49; subsequent references will be cited as "*CP*" parenthetically in the text.

21. Denise Levertov, *The Jacob's Ladder* (New York: New Directions, 1961) 61-66.

22. Thomas Merton, *Contemplation in a World of Action* (Garden City, NY: Doubleday, 1971) 347.

23. "Some Affinities of Content" (Levertov, *Essays* 6).

24. Rainer Maria Rilke, *The Selected Poetry of Rainer Maria Rilke*, ed. and trans. Stephen Mitchell (New York: Random House, 1982) 61.

25. Denise Levertov, *Sands of the Well* (New York: New Directions, 1996) 127. All subsequent references to this volume will appear in parentheses in the text as *Sands*.

26. Thomas Merton, *The Sign of Jonas* (New York: Harcourt, Brace, 1953) 362.

Shadows and Pathways:
Four Unpublished Poems by Thomas Merton

Lynn Szabo

When unpublished writings of Thomas Merton come to light or into hand by the courtesy of the findings of scholars, the bequests of friends or the cataloguing of archived materials, one is tempted to enthusiasm at the thought that something of the yet unknown Merton will be added to the seemingly replete corpus of his work. Although rarely the case, such writings often show themselves worthy of consideration for the part they play in our understanding of his process as a writer of significance in twentieth-century America. They also show the flaws and the frustration that accompanied his genius and its search for expression, sometimes providing the template for creativity in the context of spiritual formation, especially in the absence of mentors and peers in the cloistered monastic environment in which Merton often had to work out his poetics and aesthetics.

Recently, the editors of *The Merton Annual* were given a sheaf of unpublished and uncollected compositions and drafts from the archives at Bellarmine University. Some of the writings were poems that might have been written when Merton was a schoolboy in England and published in the *Oakhamian;*[1] others had been assigned to *Jester*[2] at Columbia University when Merton was a student there but they had not been included in Merton's *Collected Poems.*[3] When asked to peruse these materials, I decided that they would be an interesting study should I take them on their own merits and attempt to provide some insights about their origins and interpretations. What follows is that attempt, along with several items selected for their first publication in this volume. Those that have not been included have appeared in final drafts in Merton's published poetry or are drafts that are clearly not complete and were either discarded or set aside for future editing. In some cases, my comments include a discussion of drafts that need further scholarly work and careful editing but the value to readers is to know that they exist as a representation of his mind and typewriter at work in the extended process of his synthesis of life, art and the monastic vocation, to all of which he was allegiant.

"True Love's Novice" (44 ll.), dated October 3, 1943 (Feast of St. Thérèse of the Child Jesus, as Merton notes at the bottom of his typescript), offers the reader a template for what would become "The Image of True Lovers' Death," included in *A Man in the Divided Sea* (1946).[4] Dedicated to Jesus, Mary, Joseph, St. Bernard and St. Thérèse, as was common for Merton's writings of this period, the unpublished manuscript is in three sections headed by lower case Roman numerals, whereas the published poem is separated into two sections by a short line of asterisks. Its earlier structure elaborates the poet narrating a tale in which Frater Louis has "escaped through all his doors and windows / Leaving his body here" (ll. 3-4). Its metaphor is a study of Merton's battles of conscience, will against reason, God before the world, and spirit over body. The police have come to carry him away, pressing charges over the "mess [his] garden's in!" (l. 23). But Fr. Louis has left behind "sin" to find peace and grace, "where he sits, with God, and takes his rest" (l. 40). In the expiation of the Eucharist, "The false detectives vanish with a cry" (l. 27) as "The bells for sweet Communion fall like dew" (l. 23) and Frater is "gone to hide his whole delight / In somebody else's joy" (ll. 32-33). In the peace and grace where he dwells, he "bleeds . . . on a daily Cross / With Christ in the strong joys of [His] Eucharist" (ll. 43-44). Merton's identification with Christ's death becomes a symbolic metaphor in some of his most powerful poetry, notably "For My Brother: Reported Missing in Action, 1943."[5]

Some of the pivotal differences between this draft and the published poem are found in the voicing given to the poem's speaker. Merton's narrative resonates with the novice who seeks prayer and contemplation – the abandonment of the mind's concerns, denoted as "this rational flesh" (l. 30). The version of this poem that was subsequently published shows considerably more strength of voicing than its earlier draft, particularly in its speaker's movement from Frater Louis as protagonist to one who is an unidentified, more universalized, yet anonymous, brother monk. Unfortunately, the addition of several verbose explanatory verses in the middle of the latter version compromises the narrative integrity of the poem. The highly liturgical language and unevenness of diction reflect many of Merton's early poems, leaving us with a fuller understanding of his evolving monastic aesthetics and only occasional memorable lines. The ironies of spiritual naïveté and its attendant struggles foreshadow the tones and themes of *The Seven Storey Mountain* and the early triumphalism that precedes Merton's later hard-won spiritual integrity and the path to its "hidden wholeness" (*CP* 363). Neither of these versions is particularly potent in spite of their subject. They demonstrate the Merton who wanders about in words, painting the images but without enough care to the individual strokes comprised by careful diction choices. Although the earlier draft indicates in his handwriting several changes in the text and the published verses portray their characters more dramatically, his attempts to revise leave behind evidence of impatience and haste even though they indicate his desire to find the better expression.

Of interest particularly because they add to a considerable number of poems engaged with disasters and adventures at sea and their attendant water imagery are two drafts, a study of which would amplify the themes of Merton's poetic corpus. "Derelict," annotated "to be reworked," and "A Remark on a Situation," as "unfinished," are both weaker expressions of the apocalyptic genre, oft-confusing and lacking the thematic coherence required even of the Surrealists. "Derelict" (58 ll.) depicts events portrayed in a world absent of God. Its desperate characters, "blue-black" (l. 26) with oil, have been forced to jump ship and are awaiting rescue as their motorized life rafts "ride low in the water / Loaded like hampers at a picnic" (ll. 27-28). These figures serve as allegorical representations of hopelessness and calamity. The language of the poems is in keeping with the verbosity, overuse of simile and grasping for poetic statement of a number of Merton's early poems. "Derelict," as its name indicates, portrays an ocean liner hopelessly abandoned and adrift at sea, "Ports open, fires out, all the belts and boats / Gone" (ll. 2-3). One senses eeriness akin to that of the silent Titanic's lifeboats awaiting rescue "While their own fair continent / Seeks them with radios" (ll. 29-30). The story has the despairing agony of the passengers who see land that "would hug [them] all home . . . / . . . cheer [them] in" (ll. 39, 41), only to find that "the land [their] Providence" (l. 44) "withdrew its orisons" (l. 34) and that "The prayers that came so close without success / . . . left those lifeboats dancing / In the track of the giddy sun" (ll. 41-43). The timbre and rising action of the poem resembles Stephen Crane's "The Open Boat" (1897), a classic expression of American naturalism in fiction. In contrast to Crane's godless setting, Christ appears in Merton's draft, but ineffectually – "the storms came up and beat the ship like Christ / And bore Him away with bleeding eyes / To drown His image in the wild, offended sea" (ll. 56-58).

"A Remark on a Situation" (34 ll.), even more dramatically apocalyptic in its war with antichrist, offers its characters a more hopeful eschatology in that their triumphant "clean[ness]" (l. 23) allows them to leave their attackers "condemned" (l. 28); to "come out the other side / Where the light is" (ll. 31-32). The situation of the poem is introduced in its weak first line as "The tightest experience of all." Full of Biblical allusion, the narrative depicts high war drama in which "Engineers were digging in the smoke" (l. 2) and "Somebody remarked: 'See that eleven year / Old Jew, well, that's him / That's antichrist'" (ll. 6-8). The survivors, "Like sparrows, like the killed children of Bethlehem / . . . slipped [the attackers'] snare" (ll. 27-28). From the antipodes, in this case a compelling metaphor, the survivors rally with their lights and chariots, bringing their own "new wars" (l. 30). The rhetoric is reminiscent of "Figures for an Apocalypse" in the collection of the same title (1947).[6] Although one must respect Merton's end-of-page note that the work is "unfinished," its better part was perhaps yet to come or has appeared elsewhere in stronger phrasing or images, in such poems as "The Landfall"(*FA* 88-90; *CP* 190-92) and "Christopher Columbus."[7]

Dated October 1, 1948, "Visit to Louisville" (181 ll.) (with the header "Work in Progress") records Merton's first visit to Louisville in seven years, according to his journal entries of August 13 and 14, 1948.[8] The poem provides a profound contrast to the famous Louisville epiphany of March 18, 1958, recounted in his private journal entry of the following day,[9] and later with significant revisions in *Conjectures of a Guilty Bystander*.[10] The reason for Merton's unwanted trip was to serve as an interpreter for Dom Gabriel Sortais, who had been summoned to the Good Shepherd convent by the French-speaking Mother General of the Order who was visiting from France. For this propitious occasion, they were taken in a senator's car and dressed in civilian black suits. A somewhat resentful Merton portrays the event and the city in the tones of *contemptus mundi* he had embraced in his early years at Gethsemani. The poem, written in seven segments,[11] including many rhyming and slant-rhymed lines and a tone of impatient irritation, creates a disdainful view of urbanity and worldliness and even the convent chapel itself, very Baroque with its "altar bigger than a pagoda . . . . There they have kept His wings in a cage like a casino" (ll. 100, 106). His distress is clearly outlined:

"[I] prayed (O Love!) but prayed (O Love!) to You / Although it was an afternoon at Deauville" (ll. 111-12).

> Everywhere there was optimism without love
> And while most of the people had new clothes and
>   seemed to smell of haircuts
> They could not agree to be beautiful: . . . .
> If they could wash the stains of war off the warehouses
> And let a little respiration through that satin sky!
>   (ll. 20-22, 33-34)

Even a civic celebration seems a menace to him:

> Five armies were locked in battle
> On Fourth Street, by the big Hotel
> And bands tuned up the trumpets of their dusk
> While another August committed suicide. (ll. 131-34)

In profound contrast to this feast day which celebrates the poverty of St. Clare, Merton is understandably overwhelmed by this initial return to the secular, very material world. He experiences a kind of culture-shock that is relieved only by his return to the pastoral tranquillity of the Kentucky countryside and nature's intimate language of simplicity where:

> The flowering tobacco
> Swims along forever under the moon
> Like a sea of pachyderms . . .
> The little cow is in the barn
> The mules and the horses are gone
> And the children are already sleeping (ll. 169-71, 175-77).

This unpublished draft deserves serious attention in that it situates Merton in Louisville during the time of his turning away from the world just as the epiphany there in 1958 does the same in marking his "turning toward the world."[12]

The shadows and pathways of Merton's legacy as a poet/monk will be long, even if narrowly cast, in the future of literary conversations in America, becoming the focus of readers and scholars who see in his writings the unique character of a twentieth-century monastic whose poetry far exceeds the bounds of his cloistered life.

Endnotes

1. Thomas Merton, "Lines to a Crafty Septuagenarian"; "On the

Musical Propensities of VI Classical"; "*Dies Orationum.*"

2. Thomas Merton, "Window" (*Jester*, March 1938); "Pastoral for Maytime" (*Jester*, May 1941).

3. Thomas Merton, *The Collected Poems of Thomas Merton* (New York: New Directions, 1977); subsequent references will be cited as "*CP*" parenthetically in the text.

4. Sections 2 and 3 of "True Love's Novice" were incorporated in revised form into "The Image of True Lovers' Death" in Thomas Merton, *A Man in the Divided Sea* (New York: New Directions, 1946) 68-69; *CP* 100-102.

5. Thomas Merton, *Thirty Poems* (Norfolk, CT: New Directions, 1944) [7-8]; *CP* 35-36.

6. Thomas Merton, *Figures for an Apocalypse* (New York: New Directions, 1947) 13-28 (subsequent references will be cited as "*FA*" parenthetically in the text); *CP* 135-48.

7. Thomas Merton, *The Tears of the Blind Lions* (New York: New Directions, 1949) 15-18 (subsequent references will be cited as "*TBL*" parenthetically in the text); *CP* 206-209.

8. Thomas Merton, *Entering the Silence: Becoming a Monk and Writer. Journals, vol. 2: 1941-1952*, ed. Jonathan Montaldo (San Francisco: HarperCollins, 1996) 223-24.

9. Thomas Merton, *A Search for Solitude: Pursuing the Monk's True Life. Journals, vol. 3: 1952-1960*, ed. Lawrence S. Cunningham (San Francisco: HarperCollins, 1996) 181-82.

10. Thomas Merton, *Conjectures of a Guilty Bystander* (Garden City, NY: Doubleday, 1966) 140-42.

11. The second of these sections appears in revised form as "The City after Noon" in *Tears of the Blind Lions* 22-23; *CP* 212-14; and material from Sections I, VI and VII are incorporated into Sections III, IV and V, respectively, of "How to Enter a Big City" in Thomas Merton, *The Strange Islands* (New York: New Directions, 1957) 17-20; *CP* 225-28. A study of these revisions would provide an essay of its own in compositional analysis.

12. Thomas Merton, *Turning Toward the World: The Pivotal Years. Journals, vol. 4: 1960-1963*, ed. Victor A. Kramer (San Francisco: HarperCollins, 1996).

Four Unpublished Poems

Thomas Merton

A Remark on a Situation

The tightest experience of all.

Engineers were digging in the smoke.
Twisting the wires' well ravelled
Warning: thought suddenly rebounded
Like the waves off an explosion.

> (Somebody remarked: "See that eleven year
> Old Jew, well, that's him,
> That's antichrist.")

Pylons bent their knees,
Towers bowed down,
Reverend buildings split open
And knelt down upon the massed bandits.
Live wires shot some of the unwise
With the juice of their own false gospel.

Many kings went out
And killed themselves behind their own grandstands.
Great swine fell from their liners
And drowned among pearls.

When death came boiling through our broken teeth,
O Christ, in that hour without issue
And breath lay crushed between walls,

Our laughter conquered their treachery
For we were still clean.
Our dead tongues had made prayers out of their hell
Our broken hands wrung songs
Our of the hide of blasphemy.

Like sparrows, like the killed children of Bethlehem
We slipped their snare and left them condemned,

Went down to get our lights, our chariots
Our own new wars in the antipodes.

We have come out the other side
Where the light is, not bloodsmelling night, nor see
Nine stars shining like the eyes of the dead men
Whose hopes have rusted with their swords.

(unfinished)

***

Derelict

The big ship leans sideways on the waves without caps,
Ports open, fires out, all the belts and boats
Gone. Hopes trail all around her
In the oily water.
She drifts in no great danger.
We are leagues away from land.

Wind cries like a kitten on the stricken bridge,
Waits for many clocks to talk
But time tells no more bells.
The news printed in those instruments
Is all accounted lost.
No man comes to understand.

Not a living creature
Between the green tables
Where the lady passenger wanted to touch the drum.
The radical steward
Who talked behind the 'cellos
And the hundreds at shuffleboard
The fat men with brown caps
The lady at the captain's table
And the mother of twelve
And the mother of none

All dwell in little boats
Grazing the independent pastures of the sea.
The craters of white poppies
Are full of blue-black people.
The motor-boats ride low in the water
Loaded like the hampers at a picnic.

While their own far continent
Seeks them with radios,

Feels the air about their heads
The wind of their mighty blue liberty.
All around the lost masts
That influence has wept, implored.
(Mother, brother, sister, friend, creditor cry: "Come home!")
There were no ears to apprehend.
Wires had gone sterile,
Minds were not at home.

At last the land withdrew its orisons,
Drank back its pleas to their first fountains,
The prayers that came so close without success,
And left those lifeboats dancing
In the track of the giddy sun.

The bad gulls battled round the land our Providence
Where the towers with steam halos
And the hailing tugs
Would hug us all home
By the firm island's wall

Where docks come out to meet our ways
With boxes full of fellowmen
To cheer us in, to the long land.

But now with fainter and fainter cries
We laid our heads upon our arms
And the children moaned
The ladies repented and wept.
We did not change our treachery until too late.
By then the liner was well gone
With her galley full of buns.

We were not proud of our death
When the thirty first night came down
They threw the dry bottles out
To wander on the loathsome sea.
They vanished in the foul dawn.
Winds scattered our little boats.

Our message ended with a cry.

Then the storms came up and beat the ship like Christ
And bore Him away with bleeding eyes
To drown His image in the wild, offended sea.

***

JMJBT.

Oct. 3, 1943

True Love's Novice

Do not ask for Frater Louis,
Seek him no more:
He has escaped through all his doors and windows,
Leaving his body here.

He was a useless shepherd
So to forsake his flocks
And run away with robbers
To hang upon a public Cross!

He never tilled his vineyard,
And look: it is a jungle.
Not one temporal grape!
Good riddance to our little brother.
This defection is no loss:
The sheep and grapes will prosper, both.
Maybe the war will stop.

ii

It happened when they came to find our frater:
The men from the police,
And knocked at his five doors
With stern accusing face:
"Come out here, little brother,
And view our spurious badges,
While we convince you of sin:
(The mess your garden's in!)"

Before they cleared their throats
Or knocked, or rang again

iii

And thus, the day begins.
The false detectives vanish with a cry.
The bells for sweet Communion fall like dew among the shepherds.
The land sings softly, with the waking sky:

"No longer seek your Frater in this rational flesh,
For he has thrown his mind away
And gone to hide his whole delight

In somebody else's joy.

"Shepherd, he'll make your gladness a disguise to cloak his
        laughter:
Look to the substance of your best desires,
And you will find him praying there.

"The grace in your pure heart
Is this poor sinner's sweet abode:
The peace in your clean breast,
Is where he sits, with God, and takes his rest:

And in your peaceful breast
He hides and keeps his holy house,
And bleeds there, on a daily Cross,
With Christ in the strong joys of your Eucharist.

Feast of St. Therese of the Child Jesus, 1943

***

jhs
WORK IN PROGRESS   Oct. 1 1948

Visit to Louisville

On the Feast of St Clare, when all the Poor Clares pray,
All the pleasures in the world could not destroy my holiday,
For after I said Vespers to the whirling country
Glory over a bridge, "Laudate" in a boarding-house town,
We broke into the gunmetal city through a cemetery,
Heard the muffled swearing of two to four skyscrapers
The people came out into the sun
Covered all over with black powder
And began to attack one another with statements
Or to ignore one another with horror.
Red and yellow birds flew around the gas stations
To the tune of many bells.
It was nice the way they let the young ladies down out of the
        windows
On the end of ropes. Customs have not changed.
I saw a very rich man racing down the street in an automobile
Chasing the slaves up on to the sidewalk in order to knock them
        down.

Yet things as a whole were not exceptionally fast.
Young clerks full of sandwiches and old men with medicine
        under their skin
Were all approaching death at the rate of some thirty five miles
        an hour.
Everywhere there was optimism without love
And while most of the people had new clothes and seemed to
        smell of haircuts
They could not agree to be beautiful:
And as they walked down the streets they shadowed themselves
        from store to store
Shrinking from the little grey guy who is always turning on the gas
Or jumping out of a window.

                         ii
What if the wild confinement were empty
And the felons were free to come home?
I saw the Ohio River whom I love,
I saw the wide river, but only between buildings.
And o! The other bank was green.
What if the wild confinement were empty
And the mortgages were all gone!
If they could wash the stains of war off the warehouses
And let a little respiration through that satin sky!
What if the wild confinement were empty
And the lunatic pigeons were once again sane!

What a universe my tears betray
On St Clare's Day, on St Clare's Day!
Where the children of love are not yet born
And the fathers of destitution run
With horse, bottle and gun
To burn my river with their rum.
What a deluge my tears betray
On St. Clare's Day
When the little children lie naked in the manger;
Is there none to entertain the stepdaughter's ranger
Or Mother's anger or father's wager
With horse, bottle and feathers
They have set fire to the bloody weather!

What if the wild contentment were full

And the furlongs were free to go farming?
I saw the river's daughters overwhelm a hill
And the wide river made all places plain,
And the saints on the other green bank
Of Ohio's brown, tremendous Jordan.
What if the wild contentment were full
And there were nothing left in the world
But water and plains and sun
And space went on for ever to eternity, without a rim?
What if the wild contentment were full
With nothing else left, but only sun and sea?

What if liberty were multiplied
Around the rim of Indiana
And the Daughters of Louisville knew the poverty of St Clare?
Every drop of my Ohio is a million dollars
And the whole continent will feed me, if only I were poor!

iii

Down on the floodstreets of the West End, where the Sisters are,
The little houses sit upon dykes
And tuck their feet away from possible water:
There the secular follies, living behind onestoreyed eyebrows,
Watch the world for danger and the grim police
Where bricks are frying in the sun.

But the lean trees bend down to save my garden
And wash away Magdalen's fears with a little shadow
Where brambleblood has turned to rose.
The old buildings live like a village, behind their trees
Behind their polite stockade
And grand dogs lie by the borders of that home.

There in the Good Shepherd's vestibule
Where the Sisters came to meet us like blue and white yachts
The Mother General at once a child and a mother
A pupil and a teacher, an infant and a general
French and German nun and soldier
Young and old, an alien and a patriot in every country,
Speaks to our Vicar General in the accents of Loraine.

(Je ne vous aurais jamais reconnu en clergyman!)
The senator has gone to put away the car, with its locked instruments

And we bow to the veils and the fauteuils.
(*Et Schumann, est il tombé?*)
Then the formalities begin.
I take our own General's French
And transform it into little blue and yellow butterflies
And throw it like confetti to the American nuns.

iv

After that, there was silence.
We all moved slowly across the carpet.
They had promised us a flight down to the shore
In their mahogany elevator.

We came out on placid waters
Of what might have been a ballroom.
The wood winked like glass.
There was an altar bigger than a pagoda
Where I adored the captured Heart.
All you could hear was the sunlight
Humming on the houses and gardens
Trying to get through the trees and screens
To penetrate this room.
There they have kept His wings in a cage like a casino.
Breezes blow all around the chapel and His voice speaks to cool
        waters
Where they have surrounded His Life with virtues, like tender
        wires.

I found a place on the dancefloor of this harbor.
Lights fled like tropical fish where I cast anchor
And prayed (O Love!) but prayed (O Love!) to You
Although it was an afternoon at Deauville.

v

After that we spoke soberly.
Air and angels were in the room.
An efficient sister had charge of our hat.
Everything was calm.
They came with two glasses of ginger ale and cookies on a tray,
From a chamber where a dentist chair stayed in the corner
Like a bad-tempered relative.

The nuns followed us out under the iron porch,

And stood upon the cobbles
While great dogs guarded the buildings
And trees leaned down to brush the fears from the eyes of the
    Magdalen
We sank our oars into the waters of Louisville and slowly rowed
    away.

vi

The horns crowed
All the dogs came out to play.
The boats blew their ancient flutes.
Somewhere on the stone strand
The people in the beanery focused the lenses of a radio
And all the bromos in the south began to sing.
Five armies were locked in battle
On Fourth Street, by the big Hotel
And bands tuned up the trumpets of their dusk
While another August committed suicide.
Then the lights came on with a swagger of frauds
And savage ferns
The browneyed daughter of ravens
Bloomed in the doors.
Snipping the strings in their pale throats
They allowed their little birds to fly away
But the devil went up and down with a net
To capture their unconscious hymns.
Their night comes down their street like the millennium
Wrapping the shoals in feathers
Soothing the town with a dark sign
And the strong wings of sunstroke
Til the wind of the easy river
Brushes the flies off my Kentucky collarbone
And my broken bird is under the whole Church.
The claws of the renegade stars
Have ploughed all hopes without sorrow
Under the galleries and silent lifts.
With hinges and rocks, metal and cotton,
Steel and bone and hazel and cornflowers
I'll build the old Frenchlatin architecture of prayer
And there will be real fountains under the floor.

vii

Branches baptize our faces with silver
Where the sweet, silent moon escapes the smell of beatings
And frogs, at last, possess our empty land:
There, there, in the corn,
In parabolas of milk and iron,
The ghosts of the old generals dawn.
Seeds of sorrow and dust
Whose news weep in the fields like turpentine.
Here is where old Dom Edmond roared at the rocks
In the day of Pershing's war
And the signs cried: "Whiskey! Whiskey! Whiskey!"
With lighted arrows pecking at the door.
The flowering tobacco
Swims along forever under the moon
Like a sea of pachyderms
And the songs of death, water and panthers
Disturb the silver sawmills
And the red fortune of cedars.
The little cow is in the barn
The mules and the horses are gone
And the children are already sleeping
In the shadows of the convents and distilleries.
Therefore let us return where corn, tobacco and vine
Roaring in the wildwood, in a land of knobs,
Surround the drowning sons of Daniel Boone.

Interview with Lawrence Ferlinghetti

Conducted by Paul Wilkes[1] and edited by Gray Matthews

Lawrence Ferlinghetti: I read *Seven Storey Mountain* in the late 1940s. At the time I was reading a lot of Catholic literature; St. Augustine. . . . And I went to France, and just before I read *Seven Storey Mountain*, and then it meant a lot to me at that time. I can't . . . . now I couldn't put my finger on it. . . . He was probably the first modern Catholic writer that I had ever read. And inasmuch as I had gone to Columbia University also in 1946-47, I identified with him quite strongly. And then it was only in 1961 that at City Lights Books we published a *Journal for the Protection of All Beings*. This was issue number one. And the first thing in here is Merton's "Chant to Be Used in Processions around a Site with Furnaces." This *Journal for the Protection of All Beings* came into being because we asked a lot of non-political writers and thinkers and poets and artists to make a statement on the state of the world at that time. And . . . .

Paul Wilkes: How was Merton regarded in those circles . . . non-political or anti-war . . . ?

Ferlinghetti: Well, he was a poet. And that's the way the poets that we were publishing identified with him. We . . . this was the time of the early beat writing – 1950s and the early '60s. And I think most of the beat writers identified with Merton inasmuch as they read him at all. I don't know how much Merton they read, but . . . .

Wilkes: What does "beat writers" mean?

Ferlinghetti: Well, I was thinking of the main ones – Ginsberg and Gary Snyder and Gregory Corso, and Burroughs and Peter Orlovsky and . . . there were people associated with the group that also are in this issue. For instance, well, look on the back. Bertrand Russell – he wasn't exactly associated with the group. Gary Snyder. You see, it was a . . . we identified with a lot of people across . . . around the world. Albert Camus and . . . I see Norman Mailer is in here, Kenneth Patchen. Patchen certainly had . . . I don't know whether Patchen knew Merton or not. I sort of doubt it.

Wilkes: Let's go back to, to *The Seven Storey Mountain,* reading it. . . . Try to remember the quality. Was he a more serious or more acceptable religious writer – more intelligent or what?

Ferlinghetti: What do you mean?

Wilkes: Why would this be a book that you would remember or that you would . . .

Ferlinghetti: Well, because I was very involved in exploring Catholicism at that time. I remember when I was in France, just before that I had been down to Solesmes, which is a monastery in the south of France. And I was particularly interested in the Trappist discipline. But what made *Seven Storey Mountain* interesting to me was that here was this Columbia intellectual that was converted. Especially at a time when most poets were going the other way and becoming unconverted. I mean, Jack Kerouac went from Catholicism to Buddhism. It's not that he left Catholicism, but he became more and more of a Buddhist. It would be interesting to know whether Kerouac had read *Seven Storey Mountain* at Columbia or . . . shortly thereafter.

Wilkes: When you were at Columbia in '46-'47, did they know that Merton had been there?

Ferlinghetti: I wasn't conscious of that. I was in the English graduate school, whereas Ginsberg and Kerouac were in the undergraduate – in Columbia College, about the same time. But I didn't know them and I think in the English graduate school they weren't conscious of very much in the twentieth century at that time. I seemed to begin to get lost in the seventeenth century after I was there a few months. I escaped to France instead of going on for a Ph.D.

Wilkes: Merton's religious experience and going to join the Trappists – I mean a lot of people have religious experiences in their life but he's a guy who seemed to have held on to it. What do you think . . . did that mean something, that he had had . . . that he had stayed with it for so long – did it have any kind of validity in the outside world to people like yourself?

Ferlinghetti: That he had stayed with it for so long – when?

Wilkes: As a Trappist. That he had done that for 26 years, he had stayed in the trenches, I guess, really.

Ferlinghetti: Well, there must have been a conflict between the Trappist discipline of maintaining silence and his need to publish. And I think the Trappists probably welcomed his publication in the end because he certainly enriched their monastery. So that he evidently had a lenient Father Superior that allowed him to publish, which – it's debatable whether a Trappist should be allowed to publish at all.

Wilkes: Were you happy to have him in that particular issue?

Ferlinghetti: Oh, yes. We were very honored and delighted to get it. For one thing, we wrote many, many people, who never . . . famous people around the world who never. . . . We were very happy to have Merton in this particular issue of *Journal for the Protection of All Beings* because so many people of his stature didn't even answer when we asked them to sound off and take a position on the situation in the world at that time. We were hoping for political or trans-political statements from many people like Merton in various disciplines besides . . . I mean in religion and in painting and so forth. . . . Many never answered. I remember I had a marvelous letter from Alan Watts after this issue came out. He got a copy of it and he immediately wrote me a letter saying he was really sorry that he hadn't answered, because he would have been honored to be in here alongside of Merton and alongside of the other names in there. So . . . Alan Watts was in the San Francisco Bay area, so we were in contact with him but he just didn't have time to come up with it . . . and, yeah.

Wilkes: Tell me a little bit about your first meeting with Merton.

Ferlinghetti: The only time I met Merton . . . well, the only time I met Merton in person was when he came to San Francisco on the way to the Far East. And it was several years after we published his piece. And I don't think I had any correspondence with him.[2] I knew he was coming, we picked him up at the airport and then he stayed at the City Lights editorial apartment at 485 Filbert Street, in San Francisco – little, tiny two-room apartment. And then we went for a walk in the evening. Before we turned in we went to a coffeehouse – Malvina's Coffehouse on Grant and Union Street. And we sat at a table in the front window and he was quite interested in any beautiful woman that walked by, I remember. It was a natural Trappist interest – why not? So then, we took him to the . . . or I took him to the airport the next morning. And that was the last anyone saw of him. That was a great shock to hear that he'd died. And there seemed to be a great mystery around how he had died. I don't know whether you . . .

Wilkes: Well, what was your reaction when you heard that he had died?

Ferlinghetti: I thought that he had finally resolved the conflict about a Trappist remaining silent. It . . . there was very little to be found out about how he died, so . . . he just disappeared. He disappeared into silence.

Wilkes: Maybe we can have a little of that reading from that . . .

Ferlinghetti: This was the first issue of *Journal for the Protection of All Beings*. It was published in San Francisco by City Lights Books in 1961. The first piece in here is Merton's. It's a prose poem: "Chant to Be Used in Processions around a Site with Furnaces":[3]

How we made them sleep and purified them

How we perfectly cleaned up the people and worked a big heater

I was the commander I made improvements and installed a guaranteed system taking account of human weakness I purified and I remained decent

How I commanded

I made clean appointments and then I made the travellers sleep and after that I made soap

I was born into a Catholic family but as these people were not going to need a priest I did not become a priest I installed a perfectly good machine it gave satisfaction to many

When trains arrived the soiled passengers received appointments for fun in the bathroom they did not guess

It was a very big bathroom for two thousand people it awaited their arrival and they arrived safely

There would be an orchestra of merry widows not all the time much art

If they arrived at all they would be given a greeting card to

send home taken care of with good jobs wishing you would
come to our joke

Another improvement I made was I built the chambers for
two thousand invitations at a time the naked votaries were
disinfected with Zyklon B

Children of tender age were always invited by reason of
their youth they were unable to work they were marked out
for play

They were washed like the others and more than the others

Very frequently women would hide their children in the
piles of clothing but of course when we came to find them
we would send the children into the chamber to be bathed

How often I commanded and made improvements and
sealed the door on top there were flowers the men came with
crystals I guaranteed the crystal parlor

I guaranteed the chamber and it was sealed you could see
through portholes

They waited for the shower it was not hot water that came
through vents though efficient winds gave full satisfaction
portholes showed this

The satisfied all ran together to the doors awaiting arrival it
was guaranteed they made ends meet

How I could tell by their cries that love came to a full stop I
found the ones I had made clean after about a half hour

Jewish male inmates then worked up nice they had rubber
boots in return for adequate food I could not guess their appetite

Those at the door were taken apart out of a fully stopped
love by rubber made[4] inmates strategic hair and teeth being
used later for defense

Then the males took off[5] all clean love rings and made away
with happy gold

How I commanded and made soap 12 lbs fat 10 quarts water
eight oz to a lb of caustic soda but it was hard to find any fat

A big new firm promoted steel forks operating on a cylinder
they got the contract and with faultless workmanship delivered very fast goods

"For transporting the customers we suggest using light carts
on wheels a drawing is submitted"

"We acknowledge four steady furnaces and an emergency
guarantee"

"I am a big new commander operating on a cylinder I
elevate the purified materials boil for 2 to 3 hours and then
cool"

For putting them into a test fragrance I suggested an express
elevator operated by the latest cylinder it was guaranteed

Their love was fully stopped by our perfected ovens but the
love rings were salvaged

Thanks to the satisfaction of male inmates operating the
heaters without need of compensation our guests were
warmed

All the while I had obeyed perfectly

So I was hanged in a commanding position with a full view
of the site plant and grounds

You smile at my career but you would do as I did if you
knew yourself and dared

In my day we worked hard we saw what we did our self-
sacrifice was conscientious and complete our work was
faultless and detailed

Do not think yourself better because you burn up friends
and enemies with long-range missiles without ever seeing
what you have done

The rest is silence.

Wilkes: Thomas Merton as a poet.

Ferlinghetti: I don't know how I would classify him as a poet. He
was primarily a religious mystic who really couldn't escape the
real world and he wouldn't allow his conscience to escape the real
world. So it must have been a conflict all his life between retreat

and attack in the real world.

Wilkes: Was poetry more his . . . do you think it was a better form than prose for him?

Ferlinghetti: Well, I think *The Seven Storey Mountain* communicated with a much larger audience than any of his poetry ever did. I don't know . . . .

Endnotes

1. Editor's Note: this is the full transcript of the interview with poet Lawrence Ferlinghetti conducted by Paul Wilkes in preparation for his 1984 film, *Merton: A Film Biography;* an abbreviated version was published in Paul Wilkes, *Merton By Those Who Knew Him Best* (New York: Harper & Row, 1984) 28-31. Transcript edited by Gray Matthews.

2. Six letters from Merton to Ferlinghetti are included in Thomas Merton, *The Courage for Truth: Letters to Writers,* ed. Christine M. Bochen (New York: Farrar, Straus, Giroux, 1993) 267-73, four from 1961 dealing with the publication of Merton's prose poem, and two from 1968, the first concerning his upcoming visit, the second a note from Asia; the December 12, 1961 letter is also included in Thomas Merton, *Cold War Letters,* ed. William H. Shannon and Christine M. Bochen (Maryknoll, NY: Orbis, 2006) 19-21 [CWL 7]. There are also ten letters from Ferlinghetti to Merton in the archives of the Thomas Merton Center, Louisville, KY – eight from 1961 and two from 1968.

3. Thomas Merton, "Chant to Be Used in Processions around a Site with Furnaces," *Journal for the Protection of All Beings* 1 (1961) 5-7; Thomas Merton, *Emblems of a Season of Fury* (New York: New Directions, 1963) 43-47; Thomas Merton, *The Collected Poems of Thomas Merton* (New York: New Directions, 1977) 345-49.

4. While this is the reading of the published versions, the correct reading, found in an earlier ditto of the poem, is almost certainly "male".

5. In *Emblems* and *Collected Poems* the reading is "removed".

2008 Bibliographic Review

The Mystic's Hope: Thomas Merton's Contemplative Message to a Distracted World

Gray Matthews

In the concluding chapter of what many consider his most eloquent work, *New Seeds of Contemplation*, Thomas Merton raises again the choice of two identities: the external mask or the hidden, inner person. The choice is one of allegiance, affecting not only how others see us, but how we see the world. Merton is concerned with identity because of how much it plays in our awareness of "the General Dance," the unstoppable cosmic play of the Lord amidst His creation – "For the world and time are the dance of the Lord in emptiness" – a festival in which we, as participants, are "invited to forget ourselves on purpose, cast our awful solemnity to the winds and join in the general dance."[1] Too often, however, we are distracted by things that steal our attention away and block our ears from the music of the mystical festival. We begin to see things differently, on our own, for our own sakes, and "[t]he more we persist in misunderstanding the phenomena of life, the more we analyze them out into strange finalities and complex purposes of our own, the more we involve ourselves in sadness, absurdity and despair" (*NSC* 297). We turn away from the general dance to "the general distraction" of momentary amusements, which Merton described earlier in the work as a state of living "in the midst of others, sharing nothing with them but the common noise" which "isolates a man in the worst way, separates him from reality in a way that is almost painless" (*NSC* 55). The general distraction, in other words, can be so powerful as to divert our awareness from the very pain of our despair, distracting us from despair itself, distracting us from distractions.

According to the warnings of journalist Maggie Jackson, author of *Distracted* (2008), our culture is slipping more and more into a new dark age of distraction because "the way we live is eroding our capacity for deep, sustained, perceptive attention – the building block of intimacy, wisdom and cultural progress."[2] Cultural patterns of networked individualism, multi-tasking, perpetual mobility, work fragmentation, inattentional blindness, efficiency defined by acceleration and split-screen foci, are rendering the values of deep attention, open awareness, reflectiveness, pausing, trusting, wondering, nonfunctional if not irrelevant. "We risk losing our means and ability," she argues, "to go beneath the surface, to think deeply" (Jackson 155). There is no choice of identity for survival in a distracted world: "We're all air traffic controllers now" (Jackson 77). Like Merton, Jackson believes there is still time to realize we have a real choice to make: "We can create a culture of attention, recover the ability to pause, focus, connect, judge, and enter deeply into a relationship or idea, or we can slip into numb days of easy diffusion and detachment" (Jackson 266). But time is not on our side, or so it seems.

The sheer busyness of moving from one distraction to another, the automatism involved in constantly having to upgrade the technological equipment of our lives, the mass conformity to a postmodern lifestyle of fragmentation assuaged somewhat by the seductions of hyper-connectivity leaves us either open or closed to the contemplative message of Thomas Merton. Merton understood the dilemma of trying to deliver such a message in a culture of noise: "We must face the fact that the mere thought of contemplation is one which deeply troubles the modern person who takes it seriously. It is so contrary to the modern way of life, so apparently alien, so seemingly impossible, that the modern man who even considers it finds, at first, that his whole being rebels against it."[3] Hence we find no rest, no peace "except in a life filled up with movement and activity, with speech, news, communication, recreation, distraction" (*FV* 216).

The hope of Thomas Merton was the hope of a mystic, the hope of one who had contemplated and experienced the communion that unites all with God and the hope that others might come to know such deep relatedness. The recipe has always been simple to some, yet amazingly difficult for others: minimize your activity and maximize your receptivity. The year 2008 marks another year of increasing difficulty for contemplative communication in a world of noise and accelerated action, a world increasingly defined by activity for activity's sake.

This essay will survey a selection of works published in 2008 – the fortieth anniversary of Merton's death – that have sought to understand and promote the ongoing impact of Merton's contemplative message in this ever-distracted world we live in today. I could not possibly review all published works in this category, nor could I imagine a reader who would want to endure such a survey. Thus the thematic nature of this essay is reduced in scope to works selected for examination that help us see how Merton's ongoing contemplative message aids us in negotiating a world of distraction. I have divided this survey into three sections. The first section will focus on book-length works and conference proceedings, in which "mystical hope" serves as a unifying theme. The second section will focus on one particular author's set of essays in which Merton's contemplative message is lost from view and understanding, a matter that I will treat as an opportunity to delve further into the problem of distraction and some of its consequences. The third section, "contemplation regained," will cover a dozen individual articles from diverse publications, which taken together function as a resounding, positive response to the issues raised in the middle section and the overall cultural problem of distraction.

Jackson's work on distraction will serve mainly as a framing device, for there were, of course, other popular works published in 2008 that were critical of the cultural trends of diversion and division, an overall cultural pattern of adapting to a technology-driven world of constant shifts in focus and cognition (see, for example, the works of Bauerlien, Carr and Siegel[4]). The importance of culture or cultural setting is pertinent to Merton's own arguments about the prospects for the development of contemplative living in a world of hyperactivity. In *The Inner Experience*, Merton notes that "a certain cultural and spiritual atmosphere favors the secret and spontaneous development of the inner self" but "Unfortunately such a cultural setting no longer exists in the West or is no longer common property."[5] Merton knew well about the dangers of trying to thrust contemplation into a divided world "without warning upon the bewilderment and distraction of Western man" (*IE* 3). Thus the purpose of this bibliographic review is to discern how well we have learned from Merton, how well the authors, editors and conveyors of Merton's contemplative message fared in the midst of the fortieth clamorous year following his death.

I. Merton: The Mystic of Hope

The first and perhaps most major work to appear in 2008, *An Introduction to Christian Mysticism*, was Merton's own teaching notes for a series of conferences presented to monastic priests seeking an ascetical and mystical theological foundation for a ministry in the pastoral care and spiritual guidance of souls.[6] This work is the third volume in a series of Cistercian titles concerning "Initiation into the Monastic Tradition," all brilliantly edited thus far by Patrick O'Connell. This particular work is unique in the series because the primary audience of Merton's teaching is composed of priests in a monastic setting, not novices or students. I could not help but imagine, as I worked through the book, all that could possibly happen if priests outside a monastic setting absorbed such teachings, if Christian mysticism returned home like a prodigal son and was embraced by his brother.

The heritage of spiritual warfare in the Christian faith tradition is long, high and deep, beginning with Adam and Eve in Paradise, amplified during the early life of the Church, extended by saints throughout the centuries. We have learned from other, older faith traditions, that the battle for the soul is an ancient, primordial, perennial matter. To guide someone in the spiritual life, to provide needed wisdom and insight, requires more than a handbook outlining a set of practices, it requires a deeply transformed life. This is how Merton begins to frame the course, an undertaking he explains in which participants must live, not merely believe, their theology to understand it, emphasizing that one "must become *fully impregnated in our mystical tradition*" (ICM 35; Merton's emphasis).

Merton steps carefully around his subject at first, knowing that even though asceticism is a piece of cake in a monastery, mysticism is still – in the early 1960s – a sensitive matter due primarily to the lack of sufficient education on the subject and the stereotypical misunderstandings: a lingering prevalence of false mysticism as well as anti-mysticism since the rise of modernity. In this set of conferences, Merton seeks to restore the organic relationship of mysticism and asceticism as well as spirituality and theology. His intent is not so much to provide an historical survey of the development of Christian mystical thought as it is to set the subject in proper perspective as central to the heart of Christianity and to present mysticism as the foundation for the spiritual direction and guidance of contemplative monks.

Reading this work is, indeed, a course of study, though never dry and academic. What strikes me the most, in this sustained effort to eradicate what for too long had been a watered-down perspective of the mystical heart of Christianity, is how it alerts Merton readers to the fact that *this* is what he has been writing about so earnestly the whole time! Contemplation tended to be the term of choice, but Merton clearly viewed the two as interchangeable. Case in point: in the same year Merton taught this course, 1961, he published *New Seeds of Contemplation* and *The New Man*. Allow me to dwell only on *The New Man* for the sake of time and space to illustrate Merton's equivalence of contemplation and mysticism. "The mystic," Merton wrote, "that is to say the contemplative, not only sees and touches what is real, but beyond the surface of all that is actual, he attains to communion with the Freedom Who is the source of all actuality."[7] In the middle of *The New Man*, Merton exclaims: "The spiritual *anguish of man* has no cure but mysticism" (*NM* 114; Merton's emphasis). Later on, Merton declares "Christianity and Christian mysticism were, originally, one and the same thing" (*NM* 171). Mysticism was the basis of his ecumenism, the intersection where Merton was able to connect with so many other spiritual paths, as illustrated by the many interests charted in *Mystics and Zen Masters*, which culminated from a continual track of study as simply evidenced by the copyright dates for the material in *Mystics and Zen Masters*: 1961, 1962, 1964, 1965, 1966, 1967.[8] In his Preface to that work, Merton concluded that "All these studies are united by one central concern: to understand various ways in which men of different traditions have conceived the meaning and method of the 'way' which leads to the highest levels of religious or of metaphysical awareness" (*MZM* x).

Merton's introduction to Christian mysticism is the exact prescription we need in a culture filled with distractions that seemingly prevent the penetration of reality and communion with God Alone, especially as more and more lay people become interested in the ascetic disciplines of a monastic life that prepare the way for a mystical life.   Many people yearn to center themselves in prayer, realize the fruits of solitude, discover silence and stillness as life-giving virtues that practically save one from the false mysticism of a life propelled by distractions and diversions. In the Christian tradition, as early as the fourth century, we have Evagrius teaching monks why it is "a great thing indeed – to pray without distraction; a greater thing still – to sing psalms without distractions."[9] Merton ably shows how mystical awareness helps direct one's attention to God Alone, paradoxical as that may be. This paradox anchors *The Inner Experience*, in which he tries to explain mystical awareness and how one can be experientially aware of what one cannot experience on earth, to know "Him Who is beyond all knowledge" (*IE* 115). As O'Connell puts it so well in his Introduction to Merton's course on mysticism, "Mystical theology is not talk about God, it is encountering a God who cannot be conceptualized" (*ICM* xxviii).

The mystic's hope, therefore, is that others will come to such an experiential awareness, penetrate the superficial surface of a life of distracted activities, and plunge into an encounter that ultimately leads to eternal communion with God. But to understand Christian mysticism is to perceive the many false versions that divert us from what is real. As Merton has explained before, "It is precisely because the Christian view of history has lost too many of its contemplative and mystical elements that it has become something inert and passive, a mere reactionary obscurantism that tolerates injustice and abuse on earth for the sake of a compensation in the afterlife" (*IE* 150). Merton's *Introduction to Christian Mysticism* reveals his attempt to revive that lost history in 1961, and with its publication in 2008, we now have no excuse to lose it again.

Also working against that lost history was a significant conference in 2006 convened in the historic town of Avila, Spain – home of the cherished Christian mystic, St. Teresa of Avila – a meeting from which arose a bilingual collection of papers in 2008 entitled *Seeds of Hope: Thomas Merton's Contemplative Message*, edited by Fernando Beltrán Llavador and Paul M. Pearson.[10] *Seeds of Hope* contains nine essays by Merton scholars (which are reviewed in more depth later in this volume). The dominant hope in these papers is that more people will discover and read Merton's corpus and reap the rewards of real hope. Here, Merton is represented as a messenger to this era, a sower of seeds of hope, as someone wishing to help others celebrate "the Great Feast of Christian Hope" and provide hope in times of crisis. Merton's life is revisited as a life rooted in hope, a living expression of hope. His art, poetry, ecumenism, social conscience are all seen as integral to his call as a monk and to his development as a writer-messenger, prophet and spiritual master.

The opening essay of *Seeds of Hope*, by Fernando Beltrán Llavador, reminds us that Merton's understanding of hope came from the reality of his inner experiences and his experiences of the reality of the world we all live in. Christian hope for Merton is never blind optimism or a pious strategy of neglecting the uncomfortable, but rather, based on Christian love, having "nothing to do with the rejection of problems or an evasion of our deepest existential difficulties."[11] Genuine hope springs from awareness of the real.

In the article penned by Erlinda Paguio, a former President of the ITMS, we are led to reflect on Merton's view of hope in *The New Man*, in the same chapter where Merton equates mystics with contemplatives. The chapter focuses upon "the war within," how a terrible wrestling with a sense of being is mixed with a fear of nonexistence, an agonizing situation in which we find ourselves fighting for our lives and the very meaning of our lives. This agony is exacerbated by the countless distractions and diversions leveled at us as promises for salvation, as easements and stress reducers, replacement activities for living in reality that take our minds off our predicament, persuading us that we have the power to be whatever we want. "Yet hope in its full supernatural dimension is beyond our power," Merton assures us. "And when we try to keep ourselves in hope by sheer violent persistence in willing to live, we end if not in despair in what is worse – delusion" (*NM* 4). Paguio argues that when we are emptied of pipe dreams, when we lose our own strength and confidence, we are then enabled to realize that "Our hope lies in the communion and identification of our own suffering and anguish with the suffering and anguish of Christ."[12] This is the mystical death into life: the death of our false self, a fabricated being generated and sustained by delusions, and the rising to life of our true self in Christ.

Fr. James Conner puts the above understanding in other terms in describing the hope that continues to spring from Merton's life forty years after his death. Conner knew Merton personally and saw him as "a rare individual":

Certainly I can say that knowing him and living with him has been one of the great graces of my own life. The fact that he still speaks so eloquently to so many forty years after his death shows that he had truly lived that type of solitude of which he wrote – a solitude which led him not only into his own heart, but into the heart of every person with whom he is one in Christ.[13]

Perhaps it is our ability to enter our own hearts, to experience and learn from inner solitude, that a culture of myriad distractions most threatens. Such a situation is highly destructive for society if our underlying unity as persons is perpetually fragmented and divided, causing us to feel a constant need for connective devices, and therefore making solitude appear to be the enemy of communal life instead of its medicine. Part of Merton's contemplative message to us today, then, especially relayed by this conference in Spain, is our genuine need for solitude and the continual encouragement to enter our own hearts at least long enough to glimpse our unity with others in Christ.

One of the major problems that concerns Jackson in *Distracted* is the erosion of intimacy in human relationships, particularly how communication is reduced to information-gathering, trust is reduced to surveillance, and presence is reduced to messages. How we meet each other, fall in love, dwell in place, watch our children, work together and bury our loved ones are all experiences that have changed in line with cultural patterns of relating to each other. From her perspective, we have become "ghosts moving in and out of each other's consciousness" (Jackson 58). We live fluid, mobile lives in constant connection with others, never alone or lonely or still, as we buzz and beep our way past each other "often silently, but sometimes with a shriek and a howl" (Jackson 58).

In a distracted world, however, everyone is a stranger, a distraction, hence the timeliness of *The Voice of the Stranger*, three papers and a homily from the Seventh General Meeting and Conference of the Thomas Merton Society of Great Britain and Ireland.[14] The authors are Fr. Jim Conner, Bonnie Thurston and David Scott; Fr. Conner also presents the homily. With these papers we come closer to the gravity of our distraction-riddled situation: the possibility of *not* seeing or hearing God. For Merton, "God speaks, and God is to be heard, not only on Sinai, not only in my own heart, but in *the voice of the stranger. . . .* God must be allowed the right to speak unpredictably. . . . [I]f we cannot see him unexpectedly in the stranger and the alien, we will not understand him even in the Church."[15] In Merton's letter-essay, the context for the conference papers, the distracted person is likened unto a tourist "who wanders everywhere with his camera, his exposure-meter, his spectacles, his sun glasses, his binoculars, and though gazing around him in all directions never sees what is there. . . . Under no circumstances does it occur to him to become interested in what is actually there. . . . He does not know why he is traveling in the first place" (*ESF* 84; *CP* 386).

Fr. Jim Conner's article, "The Voice of the Stranger – A Manifesto for the 21st Century," focuses on the problems of unawareness and inattention that are rooted in human arrogance that disables people from realizing there is no monopoly on truth: "The great sin of today is for people to think that they have the truth and that others do not," which is why the tourist never sees the brother in the stranger (*Voice* 6). As in his contribution at the conference in Spain, Conner finds Merton's key to awareness to be in the mystery of true solitude where we find integration with the world. He is critical of "vain pretenses of solidarity" in which "much of what passes for 'community' or 'sharing' is actually mere diversion" (*Voice* 7).

Bonnie Thurston's essay, "Brothers in Prayer and Worship: The Merton/Aziz Correspondence, An Islamic-Christian Dialogue," highlights the rewards of seeing God in the stranger. Thurston relays a particularly enlightening quotation from one of Merton's letters to Aziz that underlines the importance of checking one's arrogance at the door:

> Personally, in matters where dogmatic beliefs differ, I think that controversy is of little value because it takes us away from the spiritual realities into the realm of words and ideas. In the realm of realities we may have a great deal in common, whereas in words there are apt to be infinite complexities and subtleties which are beyond resolution. . . . It is important . . . to try to understand the beliefs of other religions. But much more important is the sharing of the experience of divine light. (*Voice* 27-28)

In the spirit of learning, Thurston shows how Merton was eager to learn about the Moslem practice of retreat, especially the *Khalwa*, a forty-day solitary retreat. From that discussion the exchange between Merton and Aziz focused on the spiritual practices of prayer and meditation as their experience of an underlying unity grew.

David Scott's contribution centered on "The Poet as Stranger" and the seeming requirement of poets to see things strangely in order to challenge our blinding presuppositions and habits of inattentiveness. Scott emphasizes, too, that the poet must be a stranger to the prevailing culture as well. This seeming detachment, though, brings the strange into familiar relation. I was reminded of the etymology of the word "respect," which means to look again; to respect someone is to take another, deeper look beyond our initial judgments and certainties in order to really see someone. To respect a stranger, then, is to realize they are not so strange after all. Interestingly, Scott admits that Merton, himself, can "come to be a stranger to us," that Merton's poetry can be difficult for readers, but that this should not prevent further communication. Perhaps Merton's poetry allowed him a means to prevent being easily understood and categorized and hung up to dry; not intentionally opaque, but playfully alert to the truth behind all of us: we communicating beings whose messages can never exhaust their source. Hence the danger of cutting each other off as if we already have the message. As Merton put it in the "Letter to Cuadra": "If I insist on giving you my truth, and never stop to receive your truth in return, then there can be no truth between us" (*ESF* 81; *CP* 383).

Finally, Fr. Conner closes out this collection of papers with a "Eucharistic Homily." Jesus appeared as stranger on the road to Emmaus and the disciples' eyes were prevented from recognizing Him. Our problem today is that we still think

> we know one another and those we encounter in daily life. But we never truly get to know the heart of the other. We do not know their pain and anxiety. In fact, we do not allow ourselves to know their heart, because if we did, we would have to know our own heart. And that requires that we face our own pain and anxiety. Yet only then will our eyes be opened. (*Voice* 56)

Conner calls for the eyes to be opened as the bread is broken and we come to know that we are a part of everyone else in the world just as they are a part of us. Such awareness plants the seed of hope in a world of distraction where we are ceaselessly cajoled away from the heart of reality.

Letter-writing became an essential way for Merton to stay in personal contact with countless people whose relationship he valued. A careful reading of Merton's letters to someone over time provides more than enough evidence to prove that Merton took the time to co-respond with people. Far from a world of hasty emails, instant messaging and spur-of-the moment browsing for information, Merton developed relationships with people, often communicating from inner person to inner person. The time in between letter-writing was as important as the spaces between words on the page. Two collections of Merton's letters appeared in 2008 that help us continue to appreciate not only this important art form but Merton's value of time itself. One collection, edited by William H. Shannon and Christine M. Bochen, *Thomas Merton: A Life in Letters: The Essential Collection*, is the best overview of Merton's correspondence, gleaned from over 10,000 letters in the Merton Center archives at Bellarmine University.[16] The editors chose nine themes to organize the letters and each grouping is preceded by a helpful introduction to provide a context for understanding and appreciation. One may be struck by the boldness of Merton to initiate correspondence with a famous figure, but there seems to be a kind of innocence at work here too, innocence rather than audacity in approaching people high and low on the social status meter simply because he sensed an underlying communion with others so genuinely. Nevertheless, such an innocence never blinded Merton as to the varying ways he needed to approach making contact with someone for the first time. He was careful, wise, courteous and never demanding, cocky or hostile, even when writing to disagree with someone. As we have witnessed throughout Merton's vast writings, his letters reveal that mystical, ecumenical spirit that streamed throughout his life, moving him to seek correspondence above the level of words and ideas only in order to pave the way for a mutual sharing of the deeper realities of life.

In a more narrow collection of letters, *A Meeting of Angels*, edited by Paul Pearson, we are privileged to share the correspondence on both sides of a warm relationship between Merton and Edward Deming Andrews and, after his death, with his wife Faith Andrews.[17] Andrews and Merton shared a love of the Shakers; thus these letters provide even more insight into Merton's interest in Shaker culture that was roused by the publication in 2003 of Merton's *Seeking Paradise: The Spirit of the Shakers*, also edited by Paul Pearson.[18] After a brief background introduction by Pearson, we read the first letter by Andrews, who initiated the correspondence in 1960. Merton responds within two weeks with enthusiasm and three times the number of words! Andrews wants Merton to write an Introduction for a book on the Shakers, an idea on which Merton muses: "Certainly a Cistercian ought to be in a good position to understand the Shaker spirit, and I do hope that with leisure, study and meditation I will eventually be able to do something on this wonderful subject" (*MA* 19). Merton is not putting Andrews off, building an escape clause into the letter to allow himself the chance to worm his way out of a responsibility. To the contrary, Merton is letting Andrews know just how much Merton, himself, understands already; he is communicating a sincere willingness to help and a commitment to quality workmanship. In this same letter, he informs Andrews that he is working on a related project with Doña Luisa (Mrs. Ananda) Coomaraswamy. Andrews replies by sharing his own admiration for Ananda Coomaraswamy's work, particularly his knowledge of Shaker furniture (I'll return to Coomaraswamy in just a moment). As the correspondence continues over time, Merton feels free to admit that "In the contemplative life one imagines that one would spend all the time absorbed in contemplation, but alas this is not the case. There are always innumerable things to be done and obstacles to getting them done, and large and small troubles" (*MA* 51).

I highlight this last excerpt to recall the thematic problem of distraction, and to reiterate how and why the contemplative message of a monk can be so helpful to those of us who literally bounce to and fro among innumerable things. Merton's exchange with Andrews reminds us of our need for discipline in finding the leisure to study and meditate on what we most need to attend to. Mysticism, for Merton, is never speculative but always deals in the concrete, a thought that brings me back to Coomarawamy, whose published review of Andrews' book on Shaker furniture is appended at the end of *Meeting of Angels*, in which he raises a question full of hope that the answer be realized sooner than later: "Is not the 'mystic,' after all, the only really 'practical' man?" (*MA* 117).

Speaking of being practical, Patricia Burton's *More Than Silence: A Bibliography of Thomas Merton* is the most practical resource available to students and scholars of Merton.[19] To just begin to appreciate the magnitude and complexity of the work Burton has accomplished here, I would ask you to conduct a simple timed exercise. Start your timer and proceed to a grocery and buy fifty canned vegetables. Once home, list all the vegetables in alphabetical order, followed by a list of brand names in alphabetical order. Next, list the content weight of each can in order from lightest to heaviest, followed by a list of prices for each can, beginning with the cheapest to the most costly. Cross-check your list with other groceries in your area. Return to the grocery and find all canned vegetables not included in the first sampling. Revise your lists. Return to the market and buy fresh vegetables, fruits, breads, etc. You will start to have a feel for the complexity of the task before Burton, which she has patiently and masterfully accomplished. All of Merton's writings, revisions, translations into other languages, printed in different editions, appearing under different titles, and so on are included. Opening the book at any page, one is struck by the sheer work involved in finding, ordering and presenting the work on that page for others' ease in research. Clearly, such a work is essential for anyone in the world doing research on Merton, or who simply wants to dig deeper into the treasure trove of his writings. But Burton provides another reason for owning this work: it helps one better appreciate the life work and impact of Merton. As Burton puts it,

> Merton brought the idea of contemplation within the ambit of ordinary non-monastic people, and he did it almost entirely with writing. This bibliography demonstrates not only the vast reach which the mass-market paperbacks implied, but a durability that is astonishing in an era where gurus come and go: splashy promotions one minute and the remainder pile the next. (Burton xiii)

Burton is concerned not only with Merton's impact during his lifetime, but his continual impact through his writings today. It is not an easy task keeping up with all of Merton's writings and all the new venues and contexts in which they appear; thus Burton admits as a bibliographer, "Merton will always be a moving target" (Burton xiv). She adds, this bibliography, therefore, "is not an obituary for a long-mummified literary figure: it is a report from the front" (Burton xiv). Burton's hard, invaluable work should help all of us appreciate how much Merton's contemplative message continues to thrive.

II. The Contemplative Message: Lost in Distraction

In this section I will examine a series of three articles about Merton published by a single author for whom Merton's contemplative message is unfortunately lost from view and understanding. The articles share many problems that deserve fuller analysis and critique, but I would like to take the opportunity that an initial review provides to consider the set as an example of distraction-at-work in the scholarly realm, which will allow me to explore the problem of distraction in more depth. Even though these articles were published a few months before the year presently under review, a critique is nevertheless warranted here, I think, because of the responsibility that Merton scholars shoulder in studying, representing and sharing Merton's contemplative message. There must be care in communicating a contemplative message as well as care in its reception; Merton's life taught that lesson if none other. Unfortunately, it is quite easy to be distracted away from contemplation. The problem of distraction in relation to contemplation, however, is not merely that there is a shift in attention, for we can regain attention; yet, left unchecked, distraction erodes leisure, erodes the time needed for deep study, erodes the practice of meditation, all of which are consequences resulting from a mindset of distraction. Sustained distractedness, furthermore, impedes communication, fragments relationships, reduces knowledge to infotainment, distorts truth, misleads and closes minds.

The three articles I wish to spotlight were authored by Joseph M. Kramp and were published 2007 in three successive issues (January, March and May) of the academic journal *Pastoral Psychology*.[20] The three articles appear to be extracted from he author's Master's thesis, "The Lives of Thomas Merton: A Study in Psychoanalysis, History, and Identity" upon graduation from Princeton Theological Seminary and before moving on to become a doctoral candidate in the Religion and Society program at Drew University in Madison, New Jersey. The articles explore what Kramp refers to as "Merton's melancholia," a condition that is argued to have resulted after the loss of Merton's mother, which later compelled him to enter the Catholic Church, become a monk, engage in a shameful affair and eventually commit suicide. Kramp argues that understanding Merton from a psychoanalytic perspective is necessary for a full appreciation of his life and work given the fact that he is such an important religious figure. I have no doubt that most Merton scholars and students of Merton would find Kramp's thesis ludicrous, but such gross misinterpretations of Merton's writings require a degree of patient attention to discern the problematic causes of an errant process of reasoning.

Kramp is working from a Freudian perspective as filtered through the theoretical work of Donald Capps, a leader in pastoral psychology and Kramp's mentor at Princeton (Capps retired in 2007 and is now professor emeritus). Kramp's theoretical starting point, borrowed from Capps, is that Merton's inability to mourn his mother's death led to a condition of melancholia, which developed more fully over time, influencing Merton's life in crucial ways. For Capps, melancholia is often the reason why males enter religious life.[21] Kramp also borrows a set of theoretical terms from Capps that serve as an interpretive lens through which he analyzes Merton's writings and life, terms associated with three alleged stages in the melancholic life of religious men: religion of honor, religion of hope, religion of humor. Kramp asserts that each of these phases or stages helps explain Merton's psychological condition, despite Kramp's lack of a clear explanation of the terms and general thesis.

As best as I could gather, the terms are used in reference to Merton in the following way: (1) *religion of honor* refers to asceticism and a felt need to work for one's salvation; (2) *religion of hope* refers to a period of growth in the religious male, but allegedly in the case of Merton, his only hope was to leave the monastery and Catholicism, which he was unable to do – hence his melancholia grew into despair; (3) *religion of humor* refers to the sign of maturity in which one develops the ability to laugh at one's religion and assert one's individuality, which Merton was unable to do because he took religious life too seriously – hence his unhappiness led to the tragic decision to commit suicide.

This set of articles deserves a more thorough critique than I can provide here. There are many serious problems with this project, some of which must be mentioned before I move to discuss Kramp's perspective in relation to the problem of distraction. In terms of critical objections to the articles as scholarship, let me state at least six general but grave concerns.

First, the author is working from a prejudiced ignorance of both Catholicism and monasticism; no effort is made to identify anything remotely positive or healthy about these two institutions and traditions. Kramp even goes so far as to intimate that Merton was anti-Protestant, supposedly being evidence of his presumed identity conflict, a claim that in and of itself demonstrates unfamiliarity with Thomas Merton. Second, this first problem seems to have caused a very jaundiced perspective of "contemplative prayer" in particular; although Kramp never explains precisely what he thinks is wrong with such prayer, he gives several reasons why he thinks Merton's use of it was highly problematic. Somehow Kramp thinks he has provided a reasonable basis to claim that "Merton used contemplative prayer to justify his own suffering," and thus while having "cloaked this issue in heady language," contemplative prayer becomes "one of the vehicles for Merton's own evasion from the responsibility of mature adult personhood" (Kramp, "Suicide" 624, 625).[22] Third, Kramp claims to be "a student of Merton" but his convoluted narrative of Merton's life, continual misinterpretations of Merton's writing and gross neglect of existing Merton scholarship prove otherwise (Kramp, "Melancholia [2]" 444). For example, he does not make use of any authoritative or respected scholarship on Merton, and builds his case on his own assumptions and less than a handful of isolated, minor conjectures by others; he tortures Merton's words to force countless false confessions until he breaks their meanings and contexts entirely. Fourth, Kramp makes it a habit to equate his own assumptions as logical premises for argument that almost immediately become conclusions. As a glaring example, his rationale for claiming Merton committed suicide is cavalierly presented to be justified by two reasons, both of which Kramp invented himself in the first two articles of the series. Fifth, Kramp appears completely unaware of the spirituality of the interior, of the inner life and the reality of spiritual warfare; the war between soul and flesh (choose your terms here) seems reduced to mental contradictions and a weak sense of identity. Thus Kramp is unable to read Merton very deeply at all and is left to a shallow analysis of words on a page instead of a legitimate psychoanalysis of a dynamic person. Even so, Kramp wildly deems his own analysis, in fact, to be an extension of Merton's work and desire:

> I do not pretend to offer the final definitive interpretation of Merton's sexual life and his relationship with his mother, nor do I pretend to assert that Merton's humanity (which is so obvious in this paper) is a reason to disregard salient contributions he has made. Still I believe this paper to be an essential contribution to the literature already written on Merton since it is, from my viewpoint, the fruit of his own labor. Merton struggled repeatedly to make sense of his conflicts, and pointed shyly and yet courageously to psychoanalysis in his journals and latter works on monastic reform for help. This is what Merton himself desired to be done and I have chosen to respond with vigor. (Kramp, "Melancholia [2]" 444)

A sixth problem with Kramp's work is that it is an example of cookie-cutter criticism, a critique that is more concerned with consistency in use of terminology and framework than any consistency in facts regarding the subject itself; that is to say, Kramp appears more concerned to showcase his admiration for his mentor's work than he is about his distortion of his object of study, Merton.

In short, we learn more about Kramp's respect for the work of Donald Capps than we learn anything about Merton because of the unhesitant forcing of Merton's life into an inappropriate framework. In the end, we do not have simply an alternative interpretation of Merton's life, but rather a display of crude negligence in conducting an intellectual inquiry.

But, how is this a problem of distraction? My objective is not to force Kramp's work into a theoretical framework and repeat the error I just criticized; rather, my intention is to use my critique of Kramp's articles as an opportunity to further illumine the relationship between distraction and attention and its relevance to Merton's contemplative message. I will come back to Kramp in a moment, but first I want to introduce some ideas from Joseph Urgo's study, *In the Age of Distraction* (2000), that I hope will extend our appreciation for the range of the problem of distraction as well as the value of Merton's contemplative message in such an era.[23] This will, in turn, prepare the way, I hope, for greater appreciation of the many good works of Merton scholarship that appeared in 2008 that will be spotlighted in a moment.

Urgo, an English professor, has long been concerned about the disappearing role of imagination in building the interior life of his students, a capacity he argues is increasingly eroded by a culture of distraction. Sounding a bit like Evagrius, Urgo argues that "to gain access to this interior realm, one must exert control over what is ingested intellectually. Simply stated, one must control the distractions" (Urgo 7). For Urgo, distraction is paradoxical in that it involves the absence of attention while simultaneously functioning as a form of attention. "Distraction is," he writes, "simply, attention to something other" (Urgo 8). He explains that "distraction is attention to something other than that which, at the moment, is not attended to"; thus distraction "depends on absence for its existence" (Urgo 8). We develop habits of attention that are learned through cultural and social conditioning; for example, the concept of "attention complicity" has arisen in reference to a perceived process of socialization that trains one to focus attention on some things instead of others, resulting in an attention deficit by approval or a reduced capacity for awareness that conforms to social pressures.

What is worrisome here are the consequences of distraction, the results of inattention and neglected attention. For example, the constancy and ceaselessness of information all around us can condition us to pay attention only to what attracts us or relates to us, insuring that we will not likely attend to other things, even matters that might be of greater importance. Information, in other words, is most likely attended to if it satisfies egocentric concerns. Here, Urgo argues that information too easily becomes infotainment, reduced to something that is "consumed for diversion rather than for consequential purposes" (Urgo 35). One serious result of this situation is that "the world represented by infotainment appears eternally on the brink of disaster, with little time available for contemplation or the cultivation of real, consequential knowledge" (Urgo 43). We seize an idea or judgment, feel comfortable with it, and then rush to enshrine it as knowledge. He further argues that infotainment (information that entertains the mind instead of nourishing or challenging it) distracts the mind by consuming time and leads to a "kind of passivity that flows from satisfaction, coupled with an arrogance that is produced by a continuous, structured reinforcement that one is in the know" (Urgo 55). Urgo contrasts infotainment with "consequential knowledge" which transforms the knower from one intellectual state to another and expands one's

> sense of now so that time is among the least of one's anxieties. Such knowledge does not satisfy, it agitates, so that the mind is enlivened with a sense of renewal and purpose . . . as one discovers not information but the depths of what one does not know and the expanse of what can be explored, absent the interference of consumption. (Urgo 56)

Two kinds of attention, then, are described here: one is arrogant, the other is humble. Arrogant attentiveness leads one to a willingness to be distracted from what one does not know in order to focus on what one claims to know. Humble attentiveness seeks to attend to what one does not know, and thus is open to change. The disquieting question of distraction is not "what are you attending to now?" but rather "what are you not attending to and why?"

For Maggie Jackson, a distraction is an interruption that diverts our attention; this is not problematic in and of itself because we can choose to return our attention to its original focus – we can regain focus. Multi-tasking, however, is more problematic in that it is essentially "the juggling of interruptions, the moment when we choose to or are driven to switch from one task to another" (Jackson 84). (Imagine the destruction of silence, simplicity and solitude in a hermitage by trying to juggle one's attention among various tasks). Ultimately, the concern about distraction and attention involves the larger function of awareness itself. Arrogant attentiveness closes the range of awareness and is less alert to other demands on understanding, whereas a more humble form of attention can withstand distractions because it remains open to the larger and dynamic circumference of awareness.

We can understand Merton's contemplative life and message, in part, as a plea for humble attentiveness, a rallying cry for greater awareness and openness for the sake of attending to the most consequential knowing, the mystical unknowing, of God Alone, for here we find our true selves and our communion with all of creation. "We cannot see things in perspective," Merton wrote, "until we cease to hug them to our own bosom."[24] In other words greater awareness should dictate our attention, not distractions that divert and drain our attentiveness while reducing our capacity for awareness. A culture that caters to a short attention span dulls our awareness even while it supplies a million objects for attention. A lifestyle of distractedness, therefore, may involve the twin dangers of eroding our awareness of what transcends us as well as what is deepest within. Seemingly, we are always distracted to something, and away from an awareness of emptiness, of what we cannot fathom. Merton explains in *The Inner Experience* that a genuine sacred attitude never recoils from emptiness; in fact

> This is a most important discovery in the interior life. For the external self *fears* and recoils from what is beyond it and above it. It dreads the seeming emptiness and darkness of the interior self. The whole tragedy of "diversion" is precisely that it is a flight from all that is most real and immediate and genuine in ourselves. It is a flight from life and from experience – an attempt to put a veil of objects between the mind and its experience of itself. (*IE* 53)

Unfortunately, for Kramp's misguided psychoanalysis of Merton, his attention is diverted ironically away from Merton's interior life in order to focus attention on a theoretical explanation of the possible connections between external events in Merton's life. Distraction recoils from the emptiness it is, by nature, disposed to avoid.

Kramp's forced analysis of Merton reveals a choice of attention, and Kramp chose to attend to his mentor's theories rather than to the subject of his proposed analysis. One consequence of this distraction is poor scholarship, but another consequence is the likelihood that his articles may mislead and therefore divert the attention of possible readers from Merton's life and writings. If these three articles were extracted from his master's thesis, then there is a graduate team of professors who were complicit in Kramp's distractedness. Distraction is at work in others, too, in that such errant scholarship was allowed to pass the peer review process of an established academic journal. We are all, of course, subject to and seduced by distractions. Distraction is a cultural and social problem, but it must be understood chiefly as a spiritual problem. Merton's contemplative message, in all its myriad forms, provides wisdom in dealing with our distracted culture and lives. Unfortunately for readers of Kramp's perspective of Merton, that contemplative message is completely lost.

In closing this section, I cannot help but be struck by the contrast between Kramp's self-proclaimed contribution to pastoral psychology today and what we find in Merton's own contribution concerning spiritual guidance in his *Introduction to Christian Mysticism.* But what is most distressing of all, to me, is Kramp's bypassing of the spiritual, his collapse of Merton's deep spiritual life into an elementary grid of psychological terms and concepts, followed by an apparent satisfaction with the distraction he has now projected for others' diversion. Kramp tries to empathize with Merton. He notices that "Merton himself was very good at self-effacing, but how about a joke to ease the psychic pain he experienced every morning in this recurring battle with melancholia?" (Kramp, "Suicide" 622). Kramp then confesses that "it is painful to study and write about this myself without considering humorous possibilities to ease the severity of the pain I vicariously feel as I study Merton's identity conflicts" (Kramp, "Suicide" 622). In the end, Kramp cannot recognize the brother in the stranger, and seems to fit rather well the description Merton gave of the "tourist" in his "Letter to Pablo Antonio Cuadra." Under a forced psychoanalysis, Merton becomes a stranger to Kramp, a stranger who "becomes part of his own screen of fantasies" (*ESF* 83; *CP* 385), and "For all practical purposes, the stranger no longer exists. He is not even seen. He is replaced by a fantastic image. What is seen and approved, in a vague, superficial way, is the stereotype that has been created by the travel agency" (*ESF* 84; *CP* 386).

III. Merton's Contemplative Message: Regained

I would now like to direct the reader's attention to a dozen individual articles published mostly in 2008 that were clearly more successful in examining Merton's contemplative message in a distracted world.

Interestingly, another article on Merton appeared in the same journal that Kramp's work was presented, *Pastoral Psychology* –

same volume, different issue – but this time the scholarship is more accurate, well-reasoned and helpful. The essay is by Paul M. Kline and concerns "Merton's 'True Self': A Resource for Survivors of Sexual Abuse by Priests."[25] Kline argues that Merton's writings on the true self can potentially help victims of sexual abuse by priests in providing a means to conceive of themselves as not fated to live with an identity tied their body and what affects it, to conceive of themselves as more than a victim, and to realize that there is an essence to their personhood that is untouchable by man because it is rooted in God. How stark the contrast between Kline's healthy portrayal of Merton and Kramp's tragic projection. Kline does not make the mistake of trying to set Merton on a pedestal as a model of the true self; rather he places attention on the fact that Merton's strong, positive reputation within the Catholic Church, particularly, along with his teaching about the true self, is a solid resource for children grappling with identity conflicts due to abuse by priests. "Alienated from their sacred identity," Kline explains, "trauma especially in childhood, assaults victims with experiences which may contradict and overpower the developing awareness of the true self" (Kline 737).

Turning now to someone who knows Merton, monasticism and psychology quite well, we must consider Fr. John Eudes Bamberger's contribution to *Cistercian Studies Quarterly*'s commemoration issue of the fortieth anniversary of Merton's death with an essay on "Thomas Merton: Monk and Contemplative."[26] Bamberger claims contemplation was the dominant focus and concern throughout Merton's life, but "[h]owever important contemplative prayer was to Merton, he well understood that such experience was in the service of union with God, not an end in itself" (Bamberger 393). In direct contrast to Kramp's thesis of despair, Bamberger writes that Merton spoke of being transformed and that "the transformation he has in mind is a life-long process that culminates in the formation of a person so constituted that he is capable of participating happily in the very life of God himself" (Bamberger 401). In his capacity as editor of this issue, Bamberger asserts:

There is every reason to believe that in the coming years there will continue to be many lay persons, as well as nuns and monks seeking a deeper spiritual life and ways of expressing their Christian faith, people who find inspiration in the life and writings of Thomas Merton. This publication, which he helped to found in 1966, intends to make available the future studies and insights that his life and work continue to stimulate.[27]

The significance and contemplative message of Merton is certainly safe with Bamberger as he sees Merton's influence continuing to help others find a deeper spiritual life in the midst of a world full of competing distractions.

A third article examines Merton's contemplative message as expressed through his poetry as Patrick O'Connell makes a solid case in "'The Surest Home is Pointless': A Pathless Path though Thomas Merton's Poetic Corpus" for the necessity to understand Merton's poetry as integral to his spiritual and social vision and our appreciation of him as a writer.[28] O'Connell's argument is also good advice not only for understanding Merton's contemplative message, but for countering misreadings and misconceptions of Merton's life and work, as well. O'Connell notes that even in Merton's poems of "sacramental awareness, there is often a direct or implicit contrast with the perspective of those who fail to perceive the truth because they try to force reality to conform to their own expectations" (O'Connell 525). In surveying the entirety of Merton's poetry, O'Connell recommends that readers approach the poetry as a whole, in which case it exists as an integral part of the whole of Merton's writings in general, and that they be particularly attentive to the patterns and themes that weave throughout Merton's poetry across the decades, as opposed to being distracted by this or that poem as if they represented the corpus. O'Connell understands that the seeming contradictions in Merton's writing are most often paradoxes, that "getting nowhere," "pathless paths" and "pointless points" are not tantamount to despair but express openness and spiritual maturity. The interior and exterior of our lives are not contradictory but are correlative dimensions of the whole person. Anyone seeking to understand the sapiential and sacramental awareness with which Merton wrote and saw our world would find much to learn in this substantial essay.

Merton's contemplative message of awareness is still infective in 2008 in light of the numbers of people influenced by his writings and continuing to express a desire to see reality as Merton saw it. Gerald Twomey published a two-part series of articles highlighting Merton's influence on Henri Nouwen that provides a significant case in point: "'Tools in the Hand of God': Thomas Merton's Influence on Henri J. M. Nouwen."[29] Nouwen (1932-1996), of course, has himself influenced countless individuals and readers since he was ordained a priest in 1957, shortly after beginning work as a pastoral psychologist. Nouwen played an important role in spreading Merton's contemplative message to his native country of Holland despite only having met Merton once, personally, in 1967. Twomey uses three headings – solitude, compassion and community – to focus his exploration of Merton's influence on three areas of spiritual life that were of most importance to Nouwen. As Twomey explores the parallel thought of Merton and Nouwen, he lends insight into the nature of conflict in each person. "Merton's foibles and weaknesses often manifested themselves, but as he readily confessed, 'We are not meant to resolve all contradictions, but to live with them and to rise above them'" (Twomey [2] 17). It was Merton's healthy and mature spirituality that provided so much encouragement to Nouwen, which he in turn relayed to all his contacts and communities.

Richard Hauser, SJ, begins his essay casting a wider view of Merton's influence in "Thomas Merton's Legacy: A Personal Reflection," arguing that Merton's influence stretched beyond individuals such as Henri Nouwen and Thomas Keating to affect an entire generation, altering many people's approach to spirituality.[30] Hauser then begins to recount that influence on his own life as a member of a generation affected by Merton. Hauser selects five thematic areas for focused attention: (1) models of spirituality, (2) personal prayer, (3) the sacred and the secular, (4) nonviolence, and (5) interreligious understanding. Reflecting upon Merton's influence forty years after his death, Hauser does not consider "it an exaggeration to say that Merton was a prophet heralding a new age of spirituality" (Hauser 355). Hauser credits Merton, too, with helping him better understand and appreciate his own Ignatian roots as a Jesuit, particularly in helping him overcome a false self identity that had distracted him from attending to his vocation.

Thus far we have examined five articles that provide an alternative to Joseph Kramp's thesis and inability to appreciate Merton's contemplative message, especially given a world filled with identity struggles, inner conflicts, contradictions and distractions. I am led to wonder how Kramp could possibly resolve a central contradiction in his own writings about Merton; he is able to acknowledge Merton's significant influence on others, but tries to maintain the claim that Merton sacrificed his own true self to project a highly inspiring false impression. It is possible for me to imagine the possibility, for a micro-moment, that Kramp is right, that Merton lived in futility, shame and despair to the tragic point of committing suicide in order to sacrifice his life for the purpose of showing people how *not* to live (do as I say, not as I do). But how can a negative example influence so many people to live so radically differently and continue to inspire them to thank Merton for affecting them so positively? Let us return to more sensible perspectives.

David King, an Associate Professor of English and Film Studies at Kennesaw State University in Atlanta, Georgia, published a wonderful essay for educators entitled "'Fine and Dangerous: Teaching Merton," arguing very effectively for why the contemplative message of Merton should become a more consistent subject matter in higher education.[31] This is a delight to read, filled with encouraging ideas and arguments if you are a college teacher. King does not propose teaching Merton strictly as a historical or literary figure so much as teaching Merton's contemplative message, his method, his way of awareness, his perspective. King is well aware of arguments from colleagues against trying to teach Merton at the higher levels of education, but King is just as easily able to dispense with them. It is through his teaching experience that King is convinced Merton will be well-received by post-9/11 college students, especially because of Merton's example of openness, willingness to learn and transcend prejudices, his honesty and candor, his appreciation for paradox. The author has taught Merton in a variety of contexts but mantains that "Merton is best taught in a course that is dedicated solely to him and his primary works" (King 81). King teaches Merton under "the twofold assumption that what Merton has to say is beautiful, and that it is said beautifully" (King 81). He recommends using books and films as well as heeding two principles in teaching Merton: allow for silence in the classroom and know that everything cannot be learned in one course. I am aware of an ITMS committee that is overseeing the tracking of this important goal of teaching Merton's contemplative message at the university level. May King's article inspire more work in this area.

How do you teach Merton in a postmodern culture is one question, but another is what Merton would think about postmodernity. What would Merton read and who would he seek correspondence with in these times? Such questions are raised by Melvyn Matthews in "Thomas Merton: Postmodernist *Avant La Lettre*?"[32] Matthews wonders about what Merton would think regarding postmodern thought and theology and feels confident in asserting that Merton would agree with the postmodern dethronement of the self and reject the modernist enshrinement of reason, or at least he would be fascinated with the issues. "Yes, Merton would have been interested in the postmodernists," he writes, and "he would have agreed with them about the need to dethrone the ego and the centrality of reason. But, I thought, they would have had a thing or two to teach him as well. He never went far enough. Because he was so hung up on ontological thinking he could still not dissolve the ego sufficiently" (Mathews 29). I see his point but am not sure if I completely agree with it. For one reason, I do not think Merton scholars have given enough serious and sustained attention to the mystical vision of Merton. Matthews provides more food for thought on the question: "Devotionally he was there, but philosophically speaking he was not" (Matthews 29). But what about mystically-thinking? Matthews drops the names of religious intellectuals he suggests we should all be reading along with Merton if he were here, for example, Jean-Luc Marion, Emmanuel Levinas, René Girard. If anyone is looking for a good doctoral dissertation idea, here is something to chew on. As needed as such speculative studies are, I am leery of endorsing contemporary thought as the most proper position from which to judge and measure past thought. I recall the motto of Bernard McGinn: "We can turn to the past not only to mine it for our own purposes, but also to be undermined."[33] We must surely try to put Merton into conversation with postmodern thinkers, but more importantly we should be pulling our own weight in the conversation, not speaking for Merton, but speaking from our own contemplative experience. Merton is certainly a splendid role model to learn from as we move to dialogue with our contemporaries and deepen our own experiences of reality.

Raising different questions is Philip Sheldrake in "Contemplation and Social Transformation: The Example of Thomas Merton," who prods us to consider mysticism and action in contrast to misinterpretations of interiority in Christian thought.[34] Sheldrake focuses upon Merton's notions of the interior true self and contemplation as providing the basis for what theologian David Tracy calls "a mystico-prophetic model" (Sheldrake 184). In regard to interiority, Sheldrake tries to show that its meaning for Augustine and other classical teachers is not the meaning we generally attribute to it today, that is, a private, internal world all our own. In turn, the outer world, as it is conventionally understood, is not merely a public world in which one can reject one's role or obligation. In short, Sheldrake is opposing a privatized spirituality, opposing a "dichotomy between inner contemplation and outer life" (Sheldrake 187). Merton understood this well, and so helps us realize that the contemplative "has a strange and paradoxical power to confront a world infected by false consciousness" (Sheldrake 188). Sheldrake appreciates Merton's contribution to our thought on social transformation from a contemplative perspective but, rightly, does not see him as unique for the reason that he is actually a contemporary representative of a long-standing tradition of Western mysticism. Referring to John Ruusbroec and Evelyn Underhill as examples, Sheldrake argues that the "one defining characteristic of Christian mysticism is that union with God impels a person towards an active, outward, rather than purely passive, inward life" (Sheldrake 189). He concludes by discussing recent theologies and theologians such as the work of Gustavo Gutiérrez, Dorothee Sölle and Rowan Williams, as reflecting this view, realizing that the mystical self can only act in the world out of its center in God, enabling social transformation. Sheldrake gives us one more significant reason for appreciating Merton as a mystic of hope.

Kathleen Deignan provides more food for our thoughts regarding Merton's contemplative message of transformation in connection to the ecology of our world in "'Love for the Paradise Mystery': Thomas Merton, Contemplative Ecologist."[35] Deignan declares Merton's love for the paradise mystery was a dominant motif through all his writings and that "Merton spent his whole monastic life teaching ways to awaken the paradise mind by the practice of contemplation" (Deignan 546). Deignan spends time informing the reader of Merton's naturalist sensibilities and how Merton, a "paradise mystic," learned "that the quest for paradise was an explicitly Cistercian habit of heart" (Deignan 551). She concludes that Merton's legacy is "not simply a rapturous poetics about creation but also a disturbing challenge to humankind's unconscionable irresponsibility regarding our stewardship" of earth (Deignan 554-55). Deignan explores the *Rule of Benedict* for additional assistance in linking an eco-monastic perspective with an eco-spirituality perspective. As Deignan argues, "The wisdom of Benedictine teaching and practice in our time of planetary crisis may be evolving into its most mature and necessary expression, and

Merton remains its most prophetic interpreter" (Deignan 559). She concludes by building on Merton's hope for lay contemplatives in the world to realize their identity as contemplative change agents in helping humanity rediscover its lost true self as an integral part of the cosmos.

The final three articles to be considered are by authors who have devoted much time and energy to ecumenism, each inspired by Merton in some way. The first, by John Wu, Jr., is entitled "Thomas Merton's Inclusivity and Ecumenism: Silencing the Gongs and Cymbals."[36] Wu describes Merton as "unwittingly committed . . . to the search for truth in a life of dialogue," whose "secret" lay in the fact that "he did not regard other traditions as alien but integral to what he recognized as a unified human legacy that we all – without exception – rightfully share" (Wu 28). Wu wonders if there has ever been a writer who has taken the oneness of humanity as seriously as Merton. Merton accomplished this, Wu argues, by paradoxically taking his own faith exclusively seriously, which naturally thrust him into "the waiting arms of other traditions" (Wu 29). Merton valued and emphasized experience as being just as important as theology, and believed "that no matter what differences lay between traditions, there are universal links that will make dialogue not only possible but necessary and inevitable" (Wu 31). Wu compares Merton to "the ancients" who perceived the necessity of "uniting action with what is deepest in each of us, a contemplative vision based on love and compassion" (Wu 33). Merton's appeal, writes Wu, is that he challenged others to see things through a universal prism, to adopt a universal consciousness. Ecumenism for Merton is argued to have been an ongoing process of learning how to live. Looking to Merton, Wu ponders: "the fundamental question that haunts us is: What exactly constitutes wisdom in an age of unprecedented technological innovations and fashion that find their demise the moment they hit the market?" (Wu 43). The lesson Wu says we need to learn from Merton concerns our own radical reeducation to regain an understanding of the roots of life. Wu concludes beautifully: "How wondrous in such an ordinary day, he shows – *without showing* – how to live close to the flesh, to bridge that wounded brokenness that separates us from ourselves and the rest of creation in a niche – his hermitage, the only earthly home he could claim his own – which, because given by the Creator, has a manifestly universal *feel* to it" (Wu 46).

Archbishop Rembert G. Weakland, OSB takes us back to Merton's involvement in an ecumenical conference in Bangkok on the last day of his life in a Fortieth Anniversary Memorial essay for *Buddhist-Christian Studies*, entitled "Thomas Merton's Bangkok Lecture of December 1968."[37] Weakland, who attended Merton's final lecture and was a member of the planning committee for the conference itself, shares his memories of the context and events of this significant occasion. He goes into detail concerning the confusion, and resistance, that many felt in attending a conference on ecumenism. The Archbishop's stated intention in recalling these factors "is to point out that perhaps we were expecting too much of Merton's talk in opening up the question and clarifying it for this diverse crowd" (Weakland 94). Weakland helps the reader appreciate the context of Merton's presentation by providing information about other talks and lectures and how they were received by the audience. One feels, however, the drama nearing climax as the audience anticipates Merton's address. Curiously though, immediately after Merton's presentation, the planners reacted negatively to the talk on Marxism, feeling as if Merton had "hijacked" the conference, for he did not touch on the conference theme at all or follow through in meeting expectations. Furthermore, Merton did not seem to be reading from his notes, but rather delivering an off-the-cuff speech that confused the confused even more. Weakland later speculates that Dom Jean Leclercq, also present and who had addressed the conferees earlier, may have slightly misled Merton through correspondence as to what Merton's subject area should be, which had not been within the planners' original scope. Weakland does not go into any depth about Merton's death, preferring to focus on the immediate confusion surrounding Merton's address, but he is quite clear that "what had been a conference begun on a theoretical level turned into a shared experience" (Weakland 96). Prayers and silent vigils became the focus of the gathering after Merton's death "as the group coalesced as never before and the death of Merton gave new meaning to their reflections, certainly the result of a common human and spiritual bond that his death had created among the participants" (Weakland 96). His death somehow communicated what the conference had actually been about: communion. And in hindsight, that's what Merton was talking about.

Someone who knows a great deal about ecumenism, particularly between Catholics and Orthodox in Poland, is Waclaw Hryniewicz. In the final article under a review here, a chapter from his book *The Challenge of Our Hope: Christian Faith in Dialogue,* he discusses Merton in favorable comparison to Julian of Norwich in writing about the links between mystics, hope and universal salvation.[38] One can find in this beautiful essay one of the most accurate and eloquent descriptions in modern times of what being a mystic entails. Because Hryniewicz's essay connects so many of the above articles as well as major themes of this bibliographic essay, I feel compelled to allow him to speak at length from the beginning of his chapter on Merton and Julian:

> Great spiritual culture is shaped by people who are open, capable of understanding and compassionate of others. Mystics belong to this category. They can cross over religious and confessional divisions. A mystic is far from being a bitter recluse, devoid of any sense of human solidarity. Quite the opposite, his spiritual experience allows him to find the deepest bonds between people. He is able to discover that beauty, which is a herald of their ultimate rescue and transformation. Those who read thoroughly the witness of the mystics will find in it a rejection of all fundamentalisms or narrowness of spirit. They will discover mercy and compassion encompassing all people and all creatures. In this witness there is a great wisdom of the view of the world and the human lot, wisdom releasing from exclusivism and overconfidence in oneself. This wisdom is born out of a deep experience of community among people. (Hryniewicz 91)

Hryniewicz begins with a study of Julian of Norwich and then turns his attention to Merton, identifying three phases in Merton's thought and writings that are very typical of mystics: "The untouched and 'virginal point' of humanity becomes a 'point of nothingness' and a symbol of extreme poverty in comparison to the Creator of all" (Hryniewicz 102). The article concludes with a treatment of a dominant theme in Hryniewicz's life's work, universal salvation, as he argues that Julian and Merton, in their own lives and words as mystics, hoped for universal salvation, too. Opposing universal salvation, according to Hryniewicz, is "an exclusiveness in understanding salvation and the authenticity of one's own religion" which he believes is "one of the motives leading to [a] most obstinate persistence in narrow and closed religious identity. It is also one of the main sources of the historical phenomenon of intolerance and modern fundamentalism" (Hryniewicz 106). The thrust of the article is that the mystic's hope lay in the eventual universal receptiveness of the contemplative's message of union with God. Any distraction from this hope leads to the narrowing of attention, identity and mercy.

Conclusion

In closing, all the works examined above (except one) embrace Merton's contemplative message and continue to honor his legacy by approaching his writings as a resource for those who suffer and as a model of education in a distracted and fragmented world. Merton is regarded as a monk, poet and mystic who steadfastly continues to influence countless others in regard to our needs to transform culture, commune with each other as human persons, and heal our relations with this earth. Far from being misperceived as a tragic figure of despair, Merton remains appreciated as model of openness, wholeness, compassion and hope.

Social critic Mark Slouka has warned us about the "ever diminishing role played by the natural world in our lives" that parallels the "gradual erosion of the soul's habit" or what could be referred to as "the terrain of the spirit – by which I mean the domain of silence, of solitude, of unmediated contemplation – is everywhere under siege, threatened by a polymorphous flood of verbal and visual signals (electronically generated, predominantly corporate), that together comprise what we might call the culture of distraction."[39] Given our daily experience in a culture of distraction, it is good to know that the vibrant contemplative message of Thomas Merton is as strong as ever forty years after his death. But what seems most pressing to me is our own need to learn from Merton how we ourselves should live contemplatively in dialogue with the world today as authentic mystics of hope.

Endnotes

1. Thomas Merton, *New Seeds of Contemplation* (New York: New Directions, 1961) 297; subsequent references will be cited as "*NSC*" parenthetically in the text.

2. Maggie Jackson, *Distracted: The Erosion of Attention and the Coming Dark Age* (Amherst, NY: Prometheus Books, 2008) 13; subsequent references will be cited as "Jackson" parenthetically in the text.

3. Thomas Merton, "The Contemplative Life in the Modern World," *Faith and Violence: Christian Teaching and Christian Practice* (Notre Dame, IN: University of Notre Dame Press, 1968) 216; subsequent references

will be cited as "*FV*" parenthetically in the text.

4. Among works published in 2008 that, along with Jackson's *Distracted*, present popular social commentary on the changing cultural world in which action trumps contemplation, see: Mark Bauerlein, *The Dumbest Generation* (New York: Tarcher/Penguin, 2008); Nicholas Carr, *The Big Switch* (New York: W. W. Norton, 2008); Lee Siegel, *Against the Machine* (New York: Spiegel and Grau, 2008).

5. Thomas Merton, *The Inner Experience: Notes on Contemplation*, ed. William H. Shannon (San Francisco: HarperCollins, 2003) 7; subsequent references will be cited as "*IE*" parenthetically in the text.

6. Thomas Merton, *An Introduction to Christian Mysticism: Initiation into the Monastic Tradition* 3, ed. Patrick F. O'Connell (Kalamazoo, MI: Cistercian Publications, 2008); subsequent references will be cited as "*ICM*" parenthetically in the text.

7. Thomas Merton, *The New Man* (New York: Farrar, Straus and Cudahy, 1961) 15; subsequent references will be cited as "*NM*" parenthetically in the text.

8. Thomas Merton, *Mystics and Zen Masters* (New York: Farrar, Straus and Giroux, 1967) iv; subsequent references will be cited as "*MZM*" parenthetically in the text.

9. Evagrius Ponticus, *The Praktikos and Chapters on Prayer*, tr. John Eudes Bamberger, OCSO (Kalamazoo, MI: Cistercian Publications, 1981) 35.

10. Fernando Beltrán Llavador and Paul M. Pearson, eds., *Seeds of Hope: Thomas Merton's Contemplative Message / Semillas de Esperanza: El Mensaje Contemplativo de Thomas Merton* (Cobreces: Cistercium-Ciem, 2008); subsequent references will be cited as "*Seeds of Hope*" parenthetically in the text.

11. Fernando Beltrán Llavador, "Thomas Merton and 'the Great Feast of Christian Hope,'" (*Seeds of Hope* 11).

12. Erlinda Paguio, "Hope as an Unexpected, Incomprehensible and Total Gift: Reflections on Merton's Life and Writings" (*Seeds of Hope* 128).

13. James Conner, OCSO, "A Monk of Compassion, A Man of Paradox" (*Seeds of Hope* 154).

14. Jim Conner, Bonnie Thurston and David Scott, *The Voice of the Stranger* (Somerset, UK: Thomas Merton Society of Great Britain and Ireland, 2008); subsequent references will be cited as "*Voice*" parenthetically in the text.

15. Thomas Merton, "A Letter to Pablo Antonio Cuadra Concerning Giants," *Emblems of a Season of Fury* (New York: New Directions, 1963) 82 (subsequent references will be cited as "*ESF*" parenthetically in the text); see also Thomas Merton, *The Collected Poems of Thomas Merton* (New York: New Directions, 1977) 384; subsequent references will be cited as "*CP*"

parenthetically in the text.

16. Thomas Merton, *A Life in Letters: The Essential Collection*, ed. William H. Shannon and Christine M. Bochen (San Francisco: Harper One, 2008).

17. Thomas Merton and Edward Deming Andrews, *A Meeting of Angels: The Correspondence of Thomas Merton with Edward Deming & Faith Andrews*, ed. Paul M. Pearson (Frankfort, KY: Broadstone Books, 2008); subsequent references will be cited as *"MA"* parenthetically in the text.

18. Thomas Merton, *Seeking Paradise: The Spirit of the Shakers*, ed. Paul M. Pearson (Maryknoll, NY: Orbis, 2003).

19. Patricia A. Burton, with Albert Romkema, *More Than Silence: A Bibliography of Thomas Merton* (Lanham, MD: Scarecrow Press, 2008); subsequent references will be cited as "Burton" parenthetically in the text.

20. Joseph M. Kramp, "Merton's Melancholia: Mother, Monasticism, Contemplative Prayer, and the Religion of Honor," *Pastoral Psychology* 55 (January 2007) 307-19; "Merton's Melancholia: Margie, Monasticism and the Religion of Hope," *Pastoral Psychology* 55 (March 2007) 441-58 (subsequent references will be cited as "Kramp, 'Melancholia [2]'" parenthetically in the text); "The Suicide of Thomas Merton: Moral Narcissism, Contemplative Prayer, and the Religion of Humor," *Pastoral Psychology* 55 (May 2007): 619-35 (subsequent references will be cited as "Kramp, 'Suicide'" parenthetically in the text).

21. Donald Capps, *Men and Their Religion: Honor, Hope, and Humor* (Harrisburg, PA: Trinity Press, 2002); see also Donald Capps, *Men, Religion, and Melancholia: James, Otto, Jung, and Erikson* (New Haven, CT: Yale University Press, 1997). In 2008, Capps published *Jesus the Village Psychiatrist* (Louisville, KY: Westminster John Knox Press, 2008).

22. Kramp does admit that contemplative prayer allowed Merton to make contributions to the general well-being of others, but at the cost of his life. Try as I did, I was never able to discern Kramp's understanding of contemplative prayer, but it, as well as Merton's life as a contemplative monk, were deemed negative factors in Merton's tragic life, according to Kramp.

23. Joseph Urgo, *In the Age of Distraction* (Jackson, MS: University Press of Mississippi, 2000); subsequent references will be cited as "Urgo" parenthetically in the text.

24. Thomas Merton, *Thoughts in Solitude* (New York: Farrar, Straus and Cudahy, 1958) 18.

25. Paul Kline, "Merton's 'True Self': A Resource for Survivors of Sexual Abuse by Priests," *Pastoral Psychology* 55 (July 2007) 731-39; subsequent references will be cited as "Kline" parenthetically in the text.

26. John Eudes Bamberger, OCSO, "Thomas Merton: Monk and Contemplative," *Cistercian Studies Quarterly* 43.4 (Winter 2008) 391-408;

subsequent references will be cited as "Bamberger" parenthetically in the text.

27. John Eudes Bamberger, OCSO, "Editor's Note," *Cistercian Studies Quarterly* 43.4 (Winter 2008) 378.

28. Patrick F. O'Connell, "'The Surest Home is Pointless': A Pathless Path through Thomas Merton's Poetic Corpus," *Cross Currents* 58.4 (December 2008) 522-44; subsequent references will be cited as "O'Connell" parenthetically in the text.

29. Gerald Twomey, "'Tools in the Hand of God': Thomas Merton's Influence on Henri J. M. Nouwen," *Cistercian Studies Quarterly* 43.4 (Winter 2008) 409-26; "'Tools in the Hand of God': Thomas Merton's Influence on Henri J. M. Nouwen (part two)," *Cistercian Studies Quarterly* 44.1 (Spring 2009) 1-20 (subsequent references will be cited as "Twomey [2]" parenthetically in the text). I should note in passing that Victor Kramer, former editor of *The Merton Annual*, also had an article in the same issue in which Twomey's and Bamberger's appear, but it is not reviewed in this bibliographic essay essentially because Kramer's essay is a review of two books already reviewed in *The Merton Annual*: Merton's *Pre-Benedictine Monasticism* (Kalamazoo, MI: Cistercian Publications, 2006) and *Introduction to Christian Mysticism* (both edited by Patrick O'Connell).

30. Richard J. Hauser, SJ, "Thomas Merton's Legacy: A Personal Reflection," *Review for Religious* 67.4 (2008) 342-57; subsequent references will be cited as "Hauser" parenthetically in the text.

31. David A. King, "'Fine and Dangerous': Teaching Merton," *Cross Currents* 59.1 (March 2009) 69-87; subsequent references will be cited as "King" parenthetically in the text.

32. Melvyn Matthews, "Thomas Merton: Postmodernist *Avant La Lettre?*" *The Merton Journal* 15.2 (Advent 2008) 25-30; subsequent references will be cited as "Matthews" parenthetically in the text.

33. Bernard McGinn, "Introduction," *Isaac of Stella: Sermons on the Christian Year*, Volume I (Kalamazoo, MI: Cistercian Publications, 1979) x.

34. Philip Sheldrake, "Contemplation and Social Transformation: The Example of Thomas Merton," *Acta Theologica Supplementum* 11 (2008) 181-207; subsequent references will be cited as "Sheldrake" parenthetically in the text.

35. Kathleen Deignan, "'Love for the Paradise Mystery': Thomas Merton, Contemplative Ecologist," *Cross Currents* 58.4 (December 2008) 545-69; subsequent references will be cited as "Deignan" parenthetically in the text.

36. John Wu, Jr., "Thomas Merton's Inclusivity and Ecumenism: Silencing the Gongs and Cymbals," *Cross Currents* 59.1 (March 2009) 28-48; subsequent references will be cited as "Wu" parenthetically in the text.

37. Rembert G. Weakland, OSB, "Thomas Merton's Bangkok Lecture

of December 1968," *Buddhist-Christian Studies* 28 (2008) 91-99; subsequent references will be cited as "Weakland" parenthetically in the text.

38. Waclaw Hryniewicz, "Western Mystics and the Hope of Universal Salvation: Julian of Norwich and Thomas Merton," *The Challenge of Our Hope: Christian Faith in Dialogue* (Washington, DC: The Council for Research in Values and Philosophy, 2007) 91-109; subsequent references will be cited as "Hryniewicz" parenthetically in the text.

39. Mark Slouka, "In Praise of Silence and Slow Time: Nature and Mind in a Derivative Age," *Tolstoy's Dictaphone: Technology and the Muse*, ed. Sven Birkerts (Saint Paul, MN: Graywolf Press, 1996) 148.

Reviews

MERTON, Thomas, *An Introduction to Christian Mysticism: Initiation into the Monastic Tradition* 3, edited with an Introduction by Patrick F. O'Connell, Preface by Lawrence S. Cunningham, Monastic Wisdom Series 13 (Kalamazoo, MI: Cistercian Publications, 2008), pp. lviii + 416. ISBN 978-0-87907-013-7 (paper) $39.95.

The third and much-awaited volume of Thomas Merton's conference notebooks, an introductory survey of Christian mysticism, has been worth waiting for. Unlike the preceding two works in this series, we are privileged this time to step into the teaching mind of Merton as he prepares a course of study for monastic priests, not novices. The course was intended for priests interested in pastoral theology, particularly a foundation in ascetical and mystical theology fitting for superiors responsible for spiritual direction. Merton's notebook for the course is basically entitled: "Ascetical and Mystical Theology." The course began on March 1, 1961 and semi-ended on May 19, 1961, the original projected end of the course as planned. Twenty-two lectures in eleven weeks was the plan. Merton, however, extended the course into the summer, prolonged and justified by popular demand.

In his Foreword to the work, Merton admits his notes are imperfect, incomplete and possibly erroneous in places as he sought to adopt a broad, historical perspective of mystical theology in a monastic context. The work is, indeed, sketchy in places; for example, left out of the survey are sustained treatments of various key mystics and much of the Orthodox or Byzantine mystical tradition. Merton simply realized the impossibility of commenting on everyone and everything under the mystical sun. His aim was not to inspect every flower, but to glimpse the whole field itself. "The main task," he writes, "will be to *situate* the subject properly in our life" as a perspective radiating from the center of one's being (15). Thus this work is not a survey of individual mystics nor an outline of theological lineage, but rather an exploration of the history of Christian mysticism as it has informed spiritual counsel and direction. There is great value in adopting and learning such a perspective, thus this work has tremendous relevance today and offers many benefits to readers, mystics and spiritual guides in the twenty-first century.

Merton made a concerted effort to be systematic in a subject area where too few had worked. Between two other landmark systematic presentations in the twentieth century—Evelyn Underhill near the beginning and Bernard McGinn near the end—stands Merton's 1961 effort to ignite a living, mystical fire for living a deeper life. In fact, Merton uses the words of Underhill as the "guiding principle" of his own course: "The essence of mysticism being not a doctrine but a way of life, its interests require {the existence of} groups of persons who put its principles into effect" (3). Merton's emphasis throughout this work, therefore, is focused on a tradition that must be lived to be understood, not merely talked about. Although the work is thick, ordered, structured and systematic, it is never dryly academic or abstract. The intellect is guarded by the heart here.

The guiding assumption behind the work is that the mystical tradition is not, and cannot be, separated from the dogmatic and moral dimensions of Christian theology. One can sense the excitement that the priests taking this course under Merton must have felt when, in light of his stressing the fundamental mystical dimension of theology, they realized Merton's genuine desire was "to help us to do what we must really do: live our *theology*. Some think it is sufficient to come to the monastery to live the *Rule*. More is required—we must live our theology, fully, deeply, in its totality. Without this, there is no sanctity. The separation of theology from 'spirituality' is a disaster" (16).

Merton recognized that the subject of asceticism in a monastery was not likely to be resisted or misunderstood; here, he knew, we are on familiar and common ground. Mysticism, however, is a different matter, even in a monastery, for as Merton acknowledges early on: "Here we are on more difficult ground. Nowhere is it more important to define your terms and show where you really stand" (23). Merton provides a sampling of historic and then-current approaches to the study of mysticism, noting the growth of intellectual interest by religious and nonreligious thinkers, rich and varied literature on the subject. Merton argues that it is an unfortunate modern misunderstanding and error to separate asceticism from mysticism, but that there have been many hearty efforts of late to realize their interconnections and value for spiritual rebirth and revival, "not the spurious and superficial supposed 'religious revival' that has driven people to church since the atomic bomb, but the deeper revival, the awakening of the basic need of man for God" (35).

The deeper revival. This is what Merton was always working on, and it is clearly the basis for these conferences on ascetical and mystical theology that also reject any division between theology and spirituality. Thus Merton strongly affirms early on in the text that

> this study we are about to undertake is absolutely *vital to our vocation*. In a sense we will be trying to face "THE"questions which are at the very heart of our spiritual life. We are here looking at a spiritual movement of which we form a part, and not a negligible part. However, it is not merely a matter of study and reading. We must become *fully impregnated in our mystical tradition*. (35)

He goes on to emphasize that "[t]his tradition *forms and affects the whole man*: intellect, memory, will, emotions, body, skills (arts)—all must be under the sway of the Holy Spirit" (35-36). I have spent time highlighting Merton's initial framing of the course because I think his rationale permeates the entire text and illuminates a characteristic of Merton that makes him so readable, so influential and relevant still to this day: his burning desire to cut through all that is superficial to get to what is most vital, most alive, most real. Much like St. Paul, Merton is always emphatic in his encouragement to his listeners and readers to press on to what is higher and deeper. What perhaps makes this book extraordinarily valuable is that he is prodding spiritual guides to do the same for others; the priests must be spiritually alive to enliven those seeking living counsel. For Merton, this is the defining mark of a real theologian.

After Merton's introductory framing and rationale for the course, he begins the actual survey with a brief reminder of the scriptural basis for Christian mysticism, focusing on St. John's Gospel, Paul's epistles and the Book of Acts. He then moves to discuss the martyrs and Gnostics in relations to emerging explanations of the mystical life. This is followed by a more substantial section under the heading "Divinization and Mysticism" in which Merton discusses *theosis, theoria mystike*, the Cappadocian Fathers, and the spiritual senses. Gregory of Nyssa is especially featured here. Next, Merton spends considerable time on Evagrius Ponticus, the problems, the life and the teachings of a rediscovered and very important Christian mystic. (In terms of individual mystics figuring prominently in this course, Evagrius is first; others to receive individualized attention are Augustine, Dionysius, Eckhart and Teresa of Avila).

After the section on Evagrius, Merton turns to contemplation and the cosmos, *theoria physike*. He then moves to treat Dionysius and the Dionysian tradition before backing up to survey the Augustinian tradition under the heading of "Western Mysticism." In presenting both traditions, Merton covers various questions, figures and syntheses between the fourth and twelfth centuries that shed light on the maturing relationship between asceticism and mystical theology especially as it affects the monastic life.

The fourteenth century stands out in history for Merton as a golden age. We know that on a number of other occasions in his writings, Merton has declared himself to be a fourteenth-century man, and we see clearly in this text a special focus on the fourteenth-century thought of lay spiritual movements and Rhineland mystics as it strengthened and developed conceptions of the mystical core of a life of faith. This section is followed by a presentation on "Spanish Mysticism" dominated by St. Teresa. The emphasis here, as throughout the book, is on how mysticism informs spiritual guidance. One might be surprised that John of the Cross is not featured heavily here, but Merton returns to conclude the course by drawing from his writings and example in particular.

After Teresa, Merton delves into the heart of the course in the final two sections: "Spiritual Direction of Contemplatives" and "Direction and Therapy." The relationship between mysticism and spiritual guidance has woven Merton's various historical forays thematically, but here in the final 100 pages Merton hits the target right in the middle. He answers questions concerning the nature and necessity of spiritual direction; the authority, functions and characteristics of a good director; the distinction between spiritual direction and counseling, psychoanalysis, as well as the distinction between spiritual and vocational crises. Merton concludes by extracting the wisdom of St. John of the Cross on the dark night of the soul as exemplary of what one needs to know as a spiritual director. Finally, Merton recommends, in an appendix, Guigo the Carthusian's *Ladder for Monks* as "a first-class example of the medieval approach to *lectio, meditatio, oratio, contemplatio*" (332).

This series of Merton's teaching notebooks is the most exciting and significant collection to appear since the publication of

Merton's personal journals. Merton was a teacher's teacher, and reading the volumes in this series is a real education. We can be especially grateful that the series is edited by Pat O'Connell, an editor's editor. O'Connell's editing of Merton's manuscripts is expert, pristine, professional; his notes on the text and various explanations are extremely helpful to any reader desiring more information. O'Connell senses the reader's questions before they are raised. His own introduction to each work in the series is substantial, eloquent, insightful and especially helpful in placing Merton's work in various contexts for better understanding and appreciation. We can be grateful that O'Connell has more work to do, that there are more teaching notebooks by Merton to appear, a veritable curriculum forthcoming!

My final thought in review of this book is that it convinces me that a fervent desire for the mystical dimension of reality, the mystical core of a life of faith, the heart of Christianity itself, is not misplaced, that mysticism itself should no longer be banished to the margins but should be seen as the foundation it is. Merton's life and writings have done so much to resurrect the meaning of contemplation. May this book further the rescue of the language and meaning of Christian mysticism and contribute to an undaunted, unblushing intellectual-spiritual basis for declaring: "Yes, I am a mystic."

Gray Matthews

BURTON, Patricia A., *More Than Silence: A Bibliography of Thomas Merton*, ATLA Series No. 55 (Lanham, MD; Toronto; Plymouth, UK and American Theological Library Association: The Scarecrow Press, 2008), pp. xxiv + 210. ISBN 0810860953 (cloth) $66.00.

The year 2008 finally saw the publication of a new major bibliography about the writings of Thomas Merton. Patricia Burton continues her diligent work of documenting the legacy of Merton. She has provided several earlier works (*Index to the Published Letters of Thomas Merton, Merton Vade Mecum* (two editions) and *'About Merton': Secondary Sources*) that catalog various important aspects of the Merton canon. The series editor, R. Justin Harkins, clearly characterizes the author when he notes in his Foreword, "Burton's enthusiasm for this subject – coupled with the depth of the bibliography itself – makes this an indispensable resource for scholars interested in Merton."

This form of bibliographic work has been long needed for those who work in the Mertonian world of both academic adventures and individual, personal reading. The very best aspect of this volume for me is the fact that it is in print and widely available at a reasonable price. Given the state of publishing associated with the life and works of Thomas Merton, a real problem exists in having available a resource that is *current* for students of Merton who wish to include the most recent reflections on Merton's work or recently published work that Merton wrote more than forty years ago but are just now being published for the general readers. For example, Merton compiled more than twenty volumes of teaching notes that are just now beginning to be published (the *Initiation into Monastic Wisdom* series by Cistercian Publications). Indeed, the author herself notes "This is not an obituary for a long-mummified literary figure: it is a report from the front. There will always be more to find" (xiv).

So, please remember, the strongest point of reference for this volume is the fact that it is the most current attempt to provide solid, bibliographic content on the writings of Thomas Merton. Ms. Burton also has attempted to provide some visualization clues (strength number two) with many of her citations which definitely indicates actually holding the books in your hands as you describe the characteristics. This was one of the great hallmarks of Frank Dell'Isola's classic bibliography (*Thomas Merton: A Bibliography*: Kent State University Press, 1975) which has been long out of press and also lacks more than thirty years of publications. Dell'Isola handled each book and thoroughly described each book so that distinctions could readily be made. For most readers of Merton, the idea of having complete descriptions is not really very important since they are more interested in the genuine content of Merton's writing and thought processes rather than the fact that the smaller-in-size edition indicates a "first-edition characteristic" while the larger size indicates a later edition with small editing corrections. For the book collector who is genuinely interested in building a collection of true first editions, however, these nuances are very important and can make a very large difference in how much a book costs (indeed, how much is it really worth). Ms. Burton, on page 32, provides a special box to indicate the characteristics of a first edition of *The Seven Storey Mountain*. She notes a very small difference in size of a "pirated edition" as well as the "unnaturally bright paper" of the dust jacket. That pirated edition (which if genuine could sell for as much as $2,000) also lacks the $3.00 price on the dust jacket and has the later caption "Trappists at work in the fields (author on the left)." Folks who use this bibliography will not be cheated out of a lot of money if they would look the book up before spending their money on a fake (many book dealers have been stuck with pirated copies). There are also two other clues that the book is pirated; one version has a white paper cover in place of the original white cloth; another common version has simple, white cotten cloth as the cover in place of the original "linen-like" cloth used for the original run.

The entry for *Seven Storey Mountain* exemplifies another strength (number three) of this volume. Ms. Burton has gathered extensive identification data on all the out-of-print and in-print versions of the book including timelines on publications and versions that have been translated into languages other than English, with special notes on versions that are "abridged" as well as versions that have added elements such as a Czech version that includes seven of Merton's letters written beween 1960 and 1963. Ms. Burton also notes that our idea of edition or printing may not have the same meaning in non-English-speaking countries.

A fourth strength that is regularly found throughout the volume is the listing of forewords, prefaces, introductions and tables of contents. This allows the researcher to locate topical content much more easily instead of locating a book only to discover that anticipated content is in another volume. She has also clearly identified authors of introductions, forewords and prefaces written by friends. While only a few of the books published by Merton before his death have such essays, those are important since they indicate something of Merton's relation to that author. Merton's writings published after his death have many more such essays and the writers were chosen for their appreciation of Thomas Merton.

Personally, I think another strength (number five) is Ms. Burton's use of little notes (in distinct font) in many citations that indicate some special context for the given book. Sometimes she links one book to another, such as the note for *The Behavior of Titans* (3) which explains Merton's thinking that led to that book's content being used as a building block for a future paperback – *Raids on the Unspeakable*.

The series editor, ATLA's R. Justin Harkins, cites a special feature, "Title Finder" as potentially another strength (number six). It allows the searcher to locate shorter materials that have not been widely published to be found.

Ms. Burton provides a serious Introduction (strength seven) that explicates the rationale for the volume as well as the nuances that set this work apart from other bibliographies. It presents her model for formatting the volume and cites some of the limitations which form the boundaries of the work.

Indeed, Ms. Burton notes one of the common weaknesses of any bibliography when she states in the Introduction (xv) that this volume includes "all the information that could be found." She notes that more information is being revealed every day. Indeed, "pockets" of Merton letters continue to be made available to the reader/researcher as they come into research collections. One example is the privately published collection of letters exchanged between Mimi Gaither and Thomas Merton (1956-1968). Mimi's son, John Gaither, photo-copied the letters and bound them as a gift to his mother on her eightieth birthday. The originals now are part of the Merton Collection at Bellarmine but were "lost" for almost forty years.

Since there is not one "complete" Merton collection, Ms. Burton could not be expected to have "found" every existing significant volume or every version of known works. One example is her listing for the early work –*Thirty Poems* (49). Only the hardcover edition is cited. There is also a paperback first edition and this volume was sold individually and was also specially packaged with other 1944 "Poets of the Year" volumes in a slip-case edition and singly in a special "mailer" version. Similarly, her citation for *The Tears of the Blind Lions* does not note that it was also issued as a paperback at the same time as the hardback version (cited on page 49). Another example is the citation for *Ishi Means Man: Essays on Native Americans* (61). This citation, while noting the two paperback editions, does not tell the researcher that there are at least four different covers for the paperback editions. This is reasonable since maybe only one or two collections have all four versions.

One other example where material has only recently been added to the canon of known works is in reference to the little booklet – *Cistercian Life* (86). Since 2004, Albert Romkema has discovered two more variations published by otherwise unknown monasteries. This brings to 15, not 13, the known versions of Merton's little publication.

Thus, most bibliographies suffer from this problem, that of only being able to review what is available to the bibliographer.

For the casual reader, the use of special typographical devices to indicate special treatment of information is probably more a distraction than an assistance. Ms. Burton carefully explains the use of such devices in her Introduction but that may well be lost on the non-academic reader.

In some citations, *Bread in the Wilderness* for example (3), Ms. Burton notes that there are "errata" in certain versions but only refers the reader to another bibliography rather than simply adding an explanation of what the "errata" says that is later corrected. Indeed, in the case of this book, the "errata" is one characteristic of a first edition. The identification of significant errata, mostly typos, is mostly an academic concern and the "reader" of Merton would only be interested if the error changed the meaning of the writing.

Omissions, then, are not uncommon to any bibliography. One that occurs in the section "Contributions to other Books" is the Prologue to *Monastery* by Fr. Basil Pennington. Pennington has taken part of a Merton letter and "constructed" a prologue. Since it was not intended as a prologue, Ms. Burton may have excluded it as "unauthentic" for this section. In fact she notes that Merton introductory essays on occasion are called "preface" in one version and "foreword" or "introduction" in another: cf. the citation for *To Live is to Love* (79).

One conclusion asserted by Ms. Burton is that the Daggy/ Breit Bibliography is "the rarest of rare Merton books" (xiv). At least one other book(let) might well have that title: *Devotions in Honor of Saint John of the Cross* has only one copy (at the University of Texas Library) in a known collection. Besides this, there are several volumes that were released in very limited editions, some with less than fifty copies. While the Daggy/Breit volume is very hard to obtain for a personal collection, it is readily found through major libraries.

All in all, Ms. Burton certainly has done a great service to the field of Merton studies. For a relatively small sum, the average reader can have a wonderful reference volume in their personal collection. We all can hope that timely revisions that update the Merton canon are forthcoming. The ability to keep up with new volumes as well as new finds of old material is essential to the field remaining credible to the critical analysis of the works of Thomas Merton.

John King

BELTRÁN LLAVADOR, Fernando and Paul M. Pearson, Eds., *Seeds of Hope: Thomas Merton's Contemplative Message / Semillas de Esperanza: El Mensaje Contemplativo de Thomas Merton* (Cobreces: Cistercium-Ciem, 2008), pp. x + 158 / x + 171. ISBN 978-84-612-4211-5 (paper) $25.00.

The seeds of Merton's thought have been scattered throughout the world. Seeds grow where nourished. Like the shoots on Mencius' Ox Mountain, we are reminded that trees of contemplation used to fill the land. Thus with *Seeds of Hope: Thomas Merton's Contemplative Message*, a collection of papers from a historic meeting in Spain in 2006, we learn that the message of contemplation continues to grow. Books themselves, like seeds, can be symbols as well as expressions of hope that the life they contain will mature and flourish. What one finds in this collection of papers is the germination of a living conference, a packet of seeds from what has been planted in Spain. This bilingual book continues the relay of Merton's contemplative message to the world, and I think it is best approached as a set of highlights from what must have been a significant, joyful and beautiful conversation in Spain.

This book has roots. The first seeds were planted in 1993 when a proposal was made to pursue a working relationship between the Merton Center at Bellarmine University and the International Center for Mystical Studies in Ávila. The agreement was formalized in 2004 at the Fifth Meeting of the Thomas Merton Society of Great Britain and Ireland, which led to the planning of the conference in Spain in October of 2006. The conference was attended by 350 participants from 19 countries.

Seeds of Hope is composed of nine articles, with most of the authors being very familiar to readers of Merton in America. Hope is the theme of the book but not necessarily the literal focus of each and every essay; hope comes through every page, however, as in the hope that the reader will heed Merton's contemplative message no matter what the subject matter might be. What stands out the most in these articles is the portrait of Merton, a kind of celebration of his life as a contemplative message to all of us. For many readers of Merton, this book will not provide much in the way of new information, but that is not where its value lies; rather, its value lies in giving voice to a more international and multicultural appreciation for Merton's life and writings. All the essays are presented in both English and in Spanish, for good reasons.

May the seeds of this book grow.

The opening essay, "Thomas Merton and 'the Great Feast of Christian Hope'" (1-16) is by Fernando Beltrán Llavador, a long-time International Advisor to the ITMS, who presents Merton as "a peace-bearer and a source of hope for our critical times" (1). Beltrán is concerned about the ethics of love in an unjust world and finds Merton exemplary for our times because of his constant interconnections of contemplation, action and compassion.

Paul Pearson's presentation, "Emblems for a Season of Fury: The Art of Thomas Merton" (17-31) appears next as Pearson continues Beltrán's appreciation for Merton's concern for the world we live in by showing how his contemplative message was communicated through his art in parallel with his spiritual journey. Pearson expertly conveys Merton's "turn to the world" as evidenced in his poetry, experimental work with Zen calligraphies, graffiti, ink-blots, as well as his friendship with Ad Reinhardt, someone who was also influenced by the apophatic mystical tradition – a point of particular interest at this meeting in Teresa of Ávila's hometown.

The third entry is written by a Cistercian monk at the Abbey of Viaceli in Cantabria, Francisco R. de Pascual, OCSO, intriguingly titled "The Secret Hope and the Hoped for Secret: Keys for Life" (33-45). For Pascual, "The end is not the person of Merton, but rather to gather the seeds of contemplation in hope that he scattered them in the furrows of the world" (35). To remember the message is essential because "there is no hope when memory of the past has been lost, when personal or collective continuity with all that has gone before us has been broken: we are the fruit of seeds planted long ago" (35).

Jim Forest reminds us of the hope presented by "Thomas Merton as a Living Bridge Linking Christians East and West" (47-59). Forest expounds on the ways in which Merton drew from the wells of the Orthodox tradition, his indebtedness to and insights into icons, and his dedication to promoting the wisdom of the Desert Fathers.

Sonia Petisco Martinez, a former recipient of a Daggy Youth Scholarship and a Shannon Fellowship offered by the ITMS, is an associate professor at University of Las Palmas de Gran Canaria. Her essay (61-79) relates her reflections on a set of Merton's poems that she had translated into Spanish. The poems are quoted in full in the essay and include the following: "Macarius the Younger," "Hymn of Not Much Praise for New York City," "A Letter to My

Friends," "The Communion," "The Poet, to His Book," "The Sting of Conscience," "Whether There is Enjoyment in Bitterness" and finally "Night-Flowering Cactus." She finds his contemplative message through poetry to "constitute an authentic source of strength, inspiration, and joy" (61).

Familiar to many ITMS conference goers is the enthusiastic face and voice of Cristóbal Serrán-Pagán y Fuentes who supplies the next essay on "Seeds of Hope in Times of Crisis: Saint John of the Cross and Thomas Merton" (81-100). After briefly surveying the life and writings of both men, he concludes that the crises of our lives are "sometimes a necessary part of our own growth" (97) and that we should be encouraged by the realization that both Merton and John "found hope even in the most desperate situations" (98), and that the contemplative message is a prophetic message.

Islam has a strong presence in Spain; thus Bonnie Thurston's thoughtful essay, "'A Realm of White-Hot Faith:' Thomas Merton on Islam in Spain" (101-21) is particularly fitting in this volume for the hope that it brings to the conversation. Thurston notes that both Spain and Islam influenced the thought of Merton. She teases out, in particular, Islamic threads in a variety of Merton's writings. In concluding, Thurston alerts us to two "white-hot" contemporary issues that Merton's universal contemplative message of hope can help us with: (1) the war between intellect and experience in religious life, and (2) the still-stubborn tendency to regard the "other" as evil.

The eighth essay, "Hope as an Unexpected, Incomprehensible and Total Gift: Reflections on Merton's Life and Writings" (123-40) by Erlinda Paguio explores Merton's message of hope as the fruit of a deep prayer life. Merton's hope in Christ, his acknowledgement of Mary as the model of hope and his hope for a deeper prayer life fed his own hopes to live out his vocation as a hermit. From his deep solitary prayer life sprung his contemplative message for the world.

The final chapter follows Paguio's return to Merton's home at Gethsemani in tracing the roots of his message of hope: "Thomas Merton: A Monk of Compassion, A Man of Paradox" (141-54) in which Fr. James Conner, OCSO, shares his personal reflections of the man behind this contemplative message. Conner discusses Merton's impact on the novices and students under his care. Conner reviews the life of Merton at Gethsemani and argues for the continued relevance of his message for today, correcting misperceptions that some may have, and reassuring us that "Merton's love for solitude was not an evasion from conflicts in community" (148). Merton faced the world and he faced himself, which enabled him to find real hope for unity with all in the solitude of the heart.

After you read this book, which can be ordered through the Merton Center (www.merton.org/seeds), share your own seeds of hope with others.

Gray Matthews

FOREST, Jim, *Living with Wisdom: A Life of Thomas Merton*, Revised Edition (Maryknoll, NY: Orbis Books, 2008), pp. xxvi + 262. ISBN 978-1-57075-754-9 (paper) $22.00.

Those of us who study the life and work of Thomas Merton are often asked, in one form or another, the same question from a myriad of well-wishing people who may have just heard of Merton for the first time and want to learn more. Whether in the basement hall of some parish, at a dessert reception after a Merton lecture or on a plane ride home from the International Thomas Merton Society conference, inevitably those at first unfamiliar with our beloved Fr. Louis and now intrigued by our enthusiasm for this figure will ask: "What books would you recommend for me to learn more about Thomas Merton?"

I have found myself in this situation enough times now to have a quick list ready to give at a moment's notice. It usually follows this sequence: *The Seven Storey Mountain, New Seeds of Contemplation* and *Conjectures of a Guilty Bystander* for the "must read" primary source texts from each major Mertonian era. Then comes the recommendation for which of the many biographies I would endorse. My choice has always been Jim Forest's *Living with Wisdom*.

At this point Forest's book has been around for quite some time, if in a variety of forms. In 1979 Forest published *Thomas Merton: A Pictorial Biography* (Paulist), the first incarnation of what would eventually become *Living with Wisdom* (Orbis, 1991) and now the revised edition under review here. The first book, as Forest recalls in the acknowledgments of the revised edition, was much smaller yet featured an element that would remain a distinguishing staple of Forest's biography for decades to come – lots of photographs. When invited by Orbis Press to expand the text twelve years later, Forest returned to the manuscript to enlarge what had been primarily a pictorial collection. It is this 1991 text that has been an accessible volume and a helpful introduction to the life of Merton for nearly two decades. This revised edition stands in the shadow of that first version and it is in that context that we look at its new manifestation.

There are a few things that *Living with Wisdom* is not. It is not an academic text. For a scholarly biography, Michael Mott's *The Seven Mountains of Thomas Merton* remains the flagship resource. Forest's book is also not a monograph dedicated to a particular period or influence in Merton's life. There are plenty of other volumes to consult for that sort of study. It is instead a general introduction to his life and work. Forest explains his intention well when in his preface he writes, "Nothing will please me more than to know that this book helped open the door to Merton's own writing and to some of the other books about him" (xvi). This is a text that serves as a general orientation guidebook or something of a "Merton's Life 101" course. It is precisely for this reason that it is so highly recommended to those who are getting to know Merton for the first time.

There are some significant and helpful changes to the revised edition. Perhaps most noticeably, the size and cover design are different. There are about forty additional pages in the revised edition that can be accounted for in added content, additional images and the inclusion of several resources not found in the earlier version. For example, in the front of the book one will find a seven-page chronology of Merton's life. This is a wonderful asset for it chronicles not only the major liminal experiences throughout his life, but lists his major publications alongside these biographical details. It is a nice "at a glance" reference tool. Forest includes an afterword to this edition that is insightful and reflective, marking recent developments in the world of Merton scholarship as well as tracing future trajectories of interest in and study of Merton's work.

Also new to this edition is a one-page list of Internet resources, something that would not have been conceivable in 1991 when the earlier version was published. Additionally, if one compares the chapter endnotes from each edition, a major difference between the two is noticed. The 1991 edition was printed four years before the first volume of Merton's journals was published. All references to the journals in the earlier edition contain only the dated entry, whereas the new edition includes cross-references to the page location of each entry in the seven-volume collection of his journals.

This is a helpful improvement on the earlier text. Perhaps most helpful, though, is the addition of a reasonably comprehensive index. For a book this size, the number of index entries is pleasantly surprising.

Forest organizes his presentation of Merton's life in twenty-eight chapters. Although the number remains the same as the earlier edition, five of the chapters have been re-titled ("The Court of the Queen of Heaven" in place of "Gethsemani and Harlem," "Father Louis" in place of "Vows," "Abbey Forester" in place of "In the Belly of a Whale," "Containing the Divided Worlds" in place of "The Hermit of Times Square," and "A Hermitage on Mount Olivet" in place of "Blessings"). Although the chapter headings have dramatically changed, little difference exists in the content of each section except for a few additional journal entries and other minor modifications.

Forest, having known Merton personally, writes in a way that reveals a comfort with and connection to his subject that few other Merton biographers have successfully accomplished. The book is written in a popular style and in accessible language that invites the reader into the life and experiences of Merton through the lens of the author. The book continues to live up to its subtitle, namely "a life" of Thomas Merton. Whereas some other biographers have made claims that imply their work is the definitive, authentic or most honest depiction of Merton's life to date, Forest's book is more humble and forthright about the scope and breadth of its project. As such, the particular moments of Merton's life – from the disappointment of not becoming a Franciscan friar to the frustration of censorship from the Cistercian Order to the experience of falling in love with M. – are generally presented without gloss or hyperbole. As best an author can, Forest allows the sequence of events in Merton's life to stand on their own and reveal something of a glimpse into the complex and multifaceted person that this modern monk was.

The choice to include as many quotes from Merton's own texts as Forest has suggests the author's willingness to step aside so that Merton might introduce himself. In so doing, the reader is invited to continue learning about Merton by setting *Living with Wisdom* down in order to pick up one of Merton's own books. In addition to the inclusion of the recently published journals, Forest does a fine job of referencing several texts by and about Merton that were published since the earlier edition of *Living with Wisdom*. Among these additions are Merton's own *Peace in the Post-Christian Era* (Orbis, 2004), *Cassian and the Fathers: Initiation into the Monastic Tradition* (Cistercian Publications, 2005) and *In the Dark before Dawn: New Selected Poems of Thomas Merton* (New Directions, 2005).

This book is without a doubt a necessary addition to anyone's Merton library. Unlike some revised texts that offer only aesthetic and minor changes, thereby rendering the new book's purchase unnecessary, owners of the 1991 edition of this book will find "up-grading" to the revised edition an investment well worth making. Forest's revised *Living with Wisdom* will continue to be a reliable introduction to Merton's life even as additional biographies and studies are published. While this book is perfect for those just getting acquainted with the monk from Gethsemani, it is also a refreshing "biographical booster shot" for those of us deeply en-meshed in the particularities of Merton scholarship.

Daniel P. Horan, OFM

HARMLESS, William, SJ, *Mystics* (New York: Oxford University Press, 2008), pp. xvii + 350. ISBN 978-0-19-530038-3 (cloth) $125.00; 978-0-19-530039-0 (paper) $18.95.

Unlike his previous book, the splendid *Desert Christians*, an inten-sive examination of the entire body of fourth- and fifth-century desert father literature, *Mystics*, the most recent work of William Harmless, ranges widely but selectively over the whole course of the Christian era, but has in common with its predecessor a depth of insight and clarity of presentation that make it a superb introduc-tion to the varieties of mystical experience and expression within and even beyond the Christian tradition.

After an introductory chapter providing a preliminary orien-tation to the meaning and significance of mysticism, the author examines eight particular figures whom he considers representative mystics, six Christians, a Muslim and a Buddhist, and concludes with an extensive summary chapter that draws together into a more systematic exposition the insights provided by the lives and writings of his chosen examples. Thus the major focus, as the title indicates, is on mystics rather than mysticism, on specific persons rather than on abstract theory, but in his final synthesis Fr. Harmless does provide a clear and balanced evaluation of various recent approaches to mysticism, and a satisfying and convincing discussion of its essential elements.

The rather brief opening chapter, "A Theology Called Mystical" (3-18), first distinguishes authentic mysticism from various forms of the paranormal or occult popularly labeled "mystical," then considers two influential theoreticians of mysticism, the early fifteenth-century theologian Jean Gerson and the early twentieth-century psychologist and philosopher William James. Both authors emphasize experience, but Harmless shows how the traditional perspective of Gerson, which regards the mystic's experience of the Divine as an integral dimension of a broader religious life as a member of a believing community, provides a necessary check on James' highly individualistic conception of mysticism, detached from corporate worship and theological content and tending to claim that all mystics' experience, as distinguished from its articulation, is identical.

The body of the book then features "case studies" of the author's eight representative mystics, evidently drawn from the much larger group that are included in the classes on the mystics that Harmless regularly teaches at Creighton University (xi). In each instance he first situates the person's teaching in the context of his or her life and of the specific period and location in which that life took place, then provides a detailed reading of a significant work or works typifying the characteristic approach of the figure being examined. It is initially somewhat disconcerting, but pedagogically effective, that the chapters move backward from the contemporary period to the middle ages to the patristic era, before moving beyond the boundaries of Christianity.

Thus the author's first example, the "Mystic as Fire Watcher" (19-40), is none other than Thomas Merton, who Harmless states "had a knack for getting the mystical to speak to the modern" (19). Harmless visits familiar ground here, stopping at Fourth and Walnut and Polonnarua, quoting from *New Seeds of Contemplation*, the passage from *Conjectures of a Guilty Bystander* about "contain[ing] all divided worlds in ourselves" (25), *Day of a Stranger*, the famous letter to Abdul Aziz that is the most revealing description of Merton's own practice of prayer, and the conclusion to *The Sign of Jonas* that provides the chapter's title. But the discussion is not merely warmed-over material: it might seem quite unlikely that at this point anyone could provide new insights on Merton's "Louisville epiphany," but Harmless makes the suggestive observation (32-33) that a comparison of the original journal passage from March 1958 with the final version in *Conjectures* provides evidence of a

deepening over time of Merton's own understanding of the significance of this experience, a process he likens to that of Julian
of Norwich (an aspect of Julian's teaching that Merton himself
notes [see *Conjectures*, 191-92], though Harmless makes no explicit
reference to this). Some attention could have been given to the
profoundly paschal orientation of Merton's approach to mysticism
as a participation in Christ's death, resurrection and return to the
Father, but otherwise this is a sensitive, perceptive introduction to
Merton's "mystical spirituality" (30).

The four medieval figures Harmless discusses (in proper chronological order) are evidently chosen to provide a broad spectrum of
approaches to mystical experience: the affective, cataphatic interpreter of scripture Bernard of Clairvaux ("Mystic as Experienced
Exegete": 41-58); Hildegard of Bingen the visionary, polymath
and prophetic reformer ("Mystic as Multimedia Artist": 59-78);
Bonaventure, the highly organized systematic theologian and
profoundly Christocentric follower of St. Francis ("Mystic as Car-
tographer": 79-105); and Meister Eckhart, the apophatic preacher
creating a language of paradox that reveals the limits of language
to describe union with the infinite Ground of all reality ("Mystic as
Mystagogue": 107-34). (In the process he manages to include both
a Cistercian and a Benedictine, both a Franciscan and a Dominican!)
Harmless then moves back to the fourth-century Egyptian desert,
his area of particular expertise, to consider Evagrius Ponticus,
"The Mystic as Desert Calligrapher" (135-57), the highly influential "psychologist of the spirit" (136) and analyst of the stages
of spiritual development whose contributions were obscured for
centuries because of his controversial Origenist theology. The two
final figures Harmless examines represent non-Christian religious
traditions: Rumi, the thirteenth-century Persian Sufi whose mystical poetry has become remarkably popular in the West in recent
decades (159-88), and his contemporary, Eihei Dōgen, the founder
of the Soto school of Zen Buddhism in Japan (189-223). In these
chapters, the author provides not only a thorough discussion of
the life and work of the two individuals, but a brief yet incisive
introduction to the religious tradition each represents.

This eclectic group of spiritual adepts and teachers may seem
to constitute a rather arbitrary selection, and it is certainly true,
as the author himself acknowledges (xi), that the figures are not
evenly distributed across time and space. There are no mystics considered between the early fourteenth and the twentieth centuries,

not even the great sixteenth-century Carmelites, Teresa of Avila and John of the Cross, who are deliberately passed over because of the common tendency to use them as the standard against which other figures are measured (xi); and while there are four medieval mystics studied, only a single representative of the patristic period is included; only a single woman appears in the group; and of course no Jewish or Hindu or Taoist mystic is considered along with the Muslim Rumi and the Buddhist Dōgen. The discussions of the figures that are included are so uniformly excellent that one would have liked to see, had space permitted, additional chapters on Teresa or Julian or Gregory of Nyssa or Ramakrishna or one of the great Hasidic masters.

But it is important to note that the author has not merely made his selection at random, or simply for the sake of the very real intrinsic interest each of his figures possesses. Each of the central chapters can stand on its own as a penetrating analysis of a particular mystic, but they also serve to provide empirical evidence for the synthesis Harmless undertakes in his final chapter, "Reading Mystics: Text, Community, Experience" (225-69), in which he endeavors "to bring readers to the doorway of a many-sided, long-standing, and ongoing scholarly conversation on the nature of mysticism" (225) by developing a three-fold frame of reference. In considering the variety of genres in mystical writing, the normative role of the scriptures, the tension between articulation and the ineffable mystery of encounter with the Divine, Harmless highlights the importance of mystical texts. In pointing out the importance of the transmission of spiritual insight from master to disciple, as well as the relationship of personal contemplative prayer to public worship and corporate life, he emphasizes the context of community as central to mystical realization. In presenting the heights of mystical experience as continuous with the entire journey of the spiritual life he warns against isolating mysticism from the rest of human existence. By situating mystical experience in this three-fold framework Harmless counters the tendency represented by William James and other modern psychologically-oriented theorists to consider mysticism largely or exclusively as a subjective state of an individual essentially removed from his or her own time, place, religious tradition and ordinary experience. He rejects the idea that all mysticisms are basically identical, and that differences in description are merely due to different intellectual and doctrinal frameworks, while at the same time refusing to go to the opposite extreme of recognizing little or no common elements across times and religious traditions. Thus the variety of individual lives and testimonies that Harmless provides for his readers in the central chapters of his book are indeed "case studies" that support his contention that both within and beyond specific religious traditions, "points of convergence are real; so too are the points of divergence; both are illuminating, but should not be overdrawn" (264).

The book is finally not just a collection of separate essays on remarkable individuals, but a process of exploration that leads to an understanding of mysticism as "a domain of religion that deals with the search for and the attainment of a profound experiential knowledge of God or of ultimate reality [which] takes its literary form in mystical texts, its organizational form in mystical communities, and its practical form in the remarkable experiences and the broader lives of individual mystics" (263). The book as a whole provides concrete evidence that "mystics matter" because, in Karl Rahner's formulation, their experiences of the transcendent "are not discontinuous from our own" (268) but constitute a heightened realization of the human capacity for the divine present in all. "They are pioneers who explore the frontiers and limits of being human" (268), a description that echoes, not by chance, Thomas Merton, whose image as the fire watcher, "stand[ing] vigil at night in a lonely belfry" (268), aware both of the darkness of human personal and social sin and of the luminous darkness of divine love, provides a final paradigm of the "night vision" of the mystics, who "have learned to peer into the divine darkness long and hard enough to see a God-drenched world" and who "remind us that we too have eyes to see those fragile ephemeral beauties where drops of dew glisten like sapphires for a few fleeting moments in an inbreaking dawnlight through which most of us routinely sleep" (269). This very fine book is itself a wake-up call that encourages us to see and shows us where to look.

Patrick F. O'Connell

THURSTON, Bonnie B., *The Spiritual Landscape of Mark* (Collegeville, MN: Liturgical Press, 2008), pp. 84. ISBN 978-0-8146-1864-6 (paper) $12.95.

Can you remember your experience of an excellent retreat? Did the retreat experience have a transforming effect on your life? Would you like to rekindle this spirit? Thurston's book, based on her retreat notes given to a group of contemplative, monastic nuns in Wales, has produced such a retreat experience. This is a captivating commentary on the Good News, stories of suffering and triumph told from the background of geographical and symbolic Palestinian scenes and landmarks. The work is complemented with an abundance of fitting contemplative prayers, reflections, sources as well as personal accounts and instructive confessions. The themes of place and spiritual landscape served as the focus of the 2003 ITMS conference in Vancouver, British Columbia, with many papers from that conference featured in volume 17 of *The Merton Annual*. Those who attended that conference or read the essays would undoubtedly appreciate *The Spiritual Landscape of Mark*.

A prayer of gratitude and a more intense desire to know and experience the divine mystery came to the reviewer during the reading. An entry to this mystery is presented through a deeper communion with Mark's Jesus. The spiritual retreat guide for this journey, Bonnie Thurston, is gifted, personable, and gracious in inviting the reader to take an eighty-some mile walk with her from the region of Galilee to the city of Jerusalem using the Gospel of Mark as the compass. Jesus says, "Come, follow me". Mark's compass needle points to the Suffering Jesus. Why the Suffering Servant? The author reminds us that the first readers of Mark's Gospel knew severe religious threats and persecution, personal and communal suffering, and daily fears. Mark's story was meant for these ordinary, everyday people. And, Thurston wonders, is it not meant for us today as well? (31)

Thurston is a Markan scholar. She has published several works on Mark's writings and she confesses, he "speaks deeply to me" (35). She delights in exploring and meditating on Mark's Gospel. There is an ease in her conversational style. Her spiritual commitment and longing is contagious. Thurston is eager to share how Mark purposefully mixes common regional landscape markers of desert, wilderness, valley, mountains, river, hills, sea, villages, gardens, and lake to reveal Jesus' journey and salvation mystery. We learn how Jesus deliberately makes use of these central geographical locations to reveal God's plan. They are sacred places for His teaching, healing, and spiritual journey. This journey is more than a walk. Thurston describes it in multiple ways as a living spiritual ecosystem of mind, heart, spirit in space and time. This pilgrimage is historical and it is present. It is a spiritual commitment to join the Suffering Jesus in His Passion, Death, and Resurrection. These landscape landmarks are physically identifiable, but they also are spiritually present, hidden in the human heart. Thurston reminds us that our spiritual journey changes like the landscape, like the very scenery around us responding to varying rays of light. We look with anticipation and also with fear. Jesus is on this journey with us each moment, in each step.

Thurston draws on contemplative and scriptural scholarship to highlight these sacred landmarks. Early in the work she recalls how Thomas Merton quietly reflected on how vital his monastic home landscapes were to his own tranquility and contemplation (ix). Merton is referenced several times. She uses her own and others' poetry, hymns, commentaries, Greek root words and a map to add color and texture to her fabric. She begins each chapter with a personal contemplative prayer. Her introduction opens with a poignant, promising thought from Meister Eckhart. The entire book is vibrant, rich, solid with character, and meditative in tone. Spontaneous pausing for reflection and meditation on Mark's Gospel or from the text is expected.

Locations and places are used by Jesus to teach his disciples. Thurston wonders whether Jesus may have had a house, a home base, as written by Mark (2:1; 15:3, 19). This house was a stable place to rest and teach the disciples (16). Mark uses landmarks and ordinary places as doorways to union with God. He speaks about Jesus' power over the forces of nature. Jesus calms winds and waters, He transcends mountains, He gives sight to the physically blind, He exercises power over life and death; and after His own death, He arises from the ground through God's power. What is to be feared by His followers? Jesus prepares His disciples. He encourages the fearful as He pushes toward Jerusalem. Jesus is resolute. He teaches us what to expect as disciples. He is the Living Word. Are we not living this mystery of suffering and dying, says Thurston (31). Are we not on this journey? This is more than a walk; it is more than a retreat. This is the life of discipleship. We are walking toward our Jerusalem, our last supper, our suffering and death and resurrection with our Teacher.

About mid-point in the journey the author provides an "Excursus," a digression up the mountain for a brief respite, an unexpected rest from the long walk. But instead of restful leisure, we encounter a glorious manifestation of the divine mystery; we witness with Peter, James, and John the Transfiguration of Elijah, Jesus, and Moses. The author suggests that Mark's Gospel rests on the pillars of three theophanies or divine manifestations: Jesus' baptism, the Transfiguration, and the cross/resurrection (44). She beautifully describes the deep spiritual value of the Transfiguration from the point of view of the Eastern Orthodox tradition. For this mystical tradition the Transfiguration is one of the most complete symbols of God's manifestation (48). On the front cover of the book is a beautiful iconic depiction of the Transfiguration by the remarkable medieval Eastern Orthodox artist, Theophanes the Greek.

This experience of revelation, of seeing God's veiled presence, strengthens us for the final few miles. We are renewed in a spiritual sense. But there are more hills yet to climb including the Mount of Olives to the Garden of Gethsemane and Calvary. Mark spends five full chapters on the Passion. Jesus urges the disciples on; He encourages and leads us. "We must finish the journey, travel up Mount Zion, enter the city of Jerusalem and face all that transpires there" (43). Mark stays at length with the suffering and crucifixion. God suffers alone and He suffers with us. God does not abandon us. His suffering is completely solitary and radical solidarity with all human suffering (64). Mark teaches us that this is our suffering as well. We learn to know God best through our "woundedness" (66).

Out of suffering comes the mystery of triumph. From the grave comes resurrection. The gravesite's heavenly messenger tells us that we are not to be afraid, but that He goes before us and is with us in our immediate uncertainties and future unknowns. Suffering will not end; but it has been divinized. We join Thurston and wonder, where do we choose to go from here? A new beginning awakens.

Patrick Minderman

Contributors

David Belcastro is Professor of Religious Studies and Chair of the College Faculty at Capital University and adjunct Professor at Ohio Dominican University, Columbus, Ohio. A long-time contributor to ITMS conferences and publications, he currently serves as co-editor of *The Merton Annual*. He presently serves on the Board of ITMS.

Jeffrey Bilbro is a Ph.D. student at Baylor University. His research focuses on Thomas Merton, Gary Snyder and other American writers who grapple with issues of faith and nature in an effort to construct environmental ethics from various religious perspectives. His essays on Wendell Berry are forthcoming in *Mississippi Quarterly* and *The Southern Literary Journal*.

Lawrence Ferlinghetti is an American poet, novelist, painter and activist who co-founded City Lights Booksellers & Publishers in 1953, which served as a kind of headquarters for Beat writers during the fifties and sixties. He is perhaps best known for promoting the literary career of Allen Ginsburg, as well as his own 1958 collection of poetry, *A Coney Island of the Mind*, of which a fiftieth-anniversary edition was published in 2008 by New Directions along with a CD of the author reading his work. Thomas Merton stayed with Ferlinghetti, who had published some of Merton's work, prior to his journey to Asia.

Michael Higgins, past President of St. Jerome's University in Waterloo, Ontario and of St. Thomas University in Fredericton, New Brunswick, is currently Visiting Senior Executive-in-Residence at Sacred Heart University in Fairfield, Connecticut. Author of scores of scholarly and general interest articles and columns, he is also the author or co-author of eleven books, including *Heretic Blood: The Spiritual Geography of Thomas Merton* and *Stalking the Holy: In Pursuit of Saint-Making*. He has recently been appointed the authorized biographer of Henri Nouwen.

Daniel P. Horan, OFM is a Franciscan friar of Holy Name Province (NY) and a graduate student at Washington Theological Union (DC). A member of the ITMS and a former Daggy Scholar, he has published a number of articles and delivered papers on Franciscan theology and spirituality, the Millennial generation, and Thomas Merton. His work has appeared in or is forthcoming in several journals including *America, The Heythrop Journal, Spiritual Life, Review for Religious, The Merton Journal* and *The Merton Annual,* among others. More information is available on his work at: www. danhoran.com.

Deborah Kehoe teaches English at Northeast Mississippi Community College and Professional Writing at the University of Mississippi. She earned a Ph.D. in English from the University of Mississippi. Deborah is a frequent participant in ITMS meetings. In addition to her involvement in Merton studies and her professional duties of teaching composition, developmental reading, and world literature, her other commitments include advocating the physical, environmental, and spiritual benefits of a compassionate diet and lifestyle.

John E. King is a retired Professor of Social Work at the University of Arkansas. A licensed, certified social worker, he continues to conduct workshops for practicing social workers. He has published and presented articles on Thomas Merton, leads the Merton Study Group of Northwest Arkansas and conducts retreats and days of recollection based on the writings of Thomas Merton.

Ross Labrie, Professor Emeritus of the University of British Columbia in Vancouver, is the author of a number of books and articles on American literature. These include *The Catholic Imagination in American Literature* (1997) and two books on Thomas Merton, *The Art of Thomas Merton* (1979) and *Thomas Merton and the Inclusive Imagination* (2001). He has served as an international advisor to the International Thomas Merton Society and is currently the President of the Thomas Merton Society of Canada.

Gray Matthews is an Assistant Professor of Communication at the University of Memphis. He has served the ITMS as a member of the Board and of the membership committee, site coordinator for the 2007 General Meeting, and coordinator for the Memphis ITMS chapter since 2001; he has contributed essays to *The Merton Annual* and currently serves as its co-editor. He also teaches courses on Merton, mysticism and contemplative spirituality for the Catholic Diocese of West Tennessee and the Memphis Theological Seminary.

Patrick Minderman is an Academic Advisor at the University of Memphis and a licensed mental health professional counselor. He is an active Lay Cistercian of Gethsemani Abbey (LCG), a member of the International Thomas Merton Society, and a regular participant in the ITMS Memphis, TN Chapter activities.

Susan McCaslin, Ph.D., is a poet, educator, scholar, and author of twelve volumes of poetry, including her most recent, *Lifting the Stone* (Seraphim Editions, 2007). She has edited two anthologies of sacred poetry (*Poetry and Spiritual Practice* and *A Matter of Spirit*), is on the editorial board of *Event: the Douglas College Review*, and is an editorial consultant for *The Journal of Feminist Studies in Religion* (Harvard Divinity School). Her work has appeared in literary journals across Canada and the United States. After twenty-three years as a professor of English and Creative Writing at Douglas College in New Westminster, British Columbia, Susan is now a full-time writer, giving poetry workshops and readings. She has recently completed a new poetry cycle called *Demeter Goes Skydiving*, to be published by the University of Alberta Press.

Patrick O'Connell, Professor of English and Theology at Gannon University in Erie, PA, is a founding member and former president of the International Thomas Merton Society and editor of *The Merton Seasonal*. He is co-author (with William H. Shannon and Christine M. Bochen) of *The Thomas Merton Encyclopedia* (2002), and has edited four volumes of Merton's monastic conferences, most recently *The Rule of St. Benedict* (2009).

Malgorzata Poks holds a doctorate in American literature from the University of Lublin, Poland. Her main interests concern spirituality and modern American poetry. She teaches courses and seminars in American Literature and Culture. A Shannon Fellow in 2001/2, she has contributed articles to scholarship journals and publications, including *The Merton Annual*. In 2009 her book *Thomas Merton and Latin America: A Consonance of Voices* received the "Louie" award from ITMS.

Lynn Szabo is Associate Professor and Chair of the English Department at Trinity Western University in Vancouver, BC, Canada, where she teaches American Literature and Creative Writing. Her research interests are focused on the relationship between literature and mysticism, particularly in the poetry of Thomas Merton. She is the editor of *In the Dark Before Dawn; New Selected Poems of*

Thomas Merton.

Bonnie Thurston, a native of West Virginia, currently lives in solitude near Wheeling, WV, having resigned the William F. Orr Professorship in New Testament at Pittsburgh Theological Seminary in 2002. She wrote her doctoral dissertation on Thomas Merton and is particularly interested in his poetry and inter-religious thought. She was a founding member of the International Thomas Merton Society and served as its third president. She has written more than twenty scholarly articles on Merton and given retreats and lectured on Merton widely in the United States, Canada, the United Kingdom and Europe. She is editor of *Thomas Merton and Buddhism* and of *Hidden in the Same Mystery: Thomas Merton and Loretto.*

Paul Wilkes is an American writer and filmmaker best known for his work on Roman Catholicism and the monastic tradition, particularly the highly acclaimed *Merton: A Film Biography,* a 1984 Public Broadcasting Service documentary. He began his career as a writer for newspapers and later taught writing at Brooklyn College, the University of Pittsburgh, Boston University, College of the Holy Cross, Clark University and the University of North Carolina at Wilmington. His most recent work is the publication of his memoir, *In Due Season: A Catholic Life* (San Francisco: Jossey-Bass, 2009).

Index